THE
WAGNER COMPANION

Other books by
RAYMOND MANDER & JOE MITCHENSON

HAMLET THROUGH THE AGES
(Rockliff, 1952)
(Second revised edition 1955)

THEATRICAL COMPANION TO SHAW
(Rockliff, 1954)

THEATRICAL COMPANION TO MAUGHAM
(Rockliff, 1955)

THEATRICAL COMPANION TO COWARD
(Rockcliff, 1957)

THE ARTIST AND THE THEATRE
(Heinemann, 1955)
(The Story of the W. Somerset Maugham Theatrical Pictures)

A PICTURE HISTORY OF BRITISH THEATRE
(Hulton, 1957)

A PICTURE HISTORY OF OPERA
(Hulton, 1959)
In collaboration with Philip Hope-Wallace

THE GAY TWENTIES
(Macdonald, 1958)
In collaboration with J. C. Trewin

THE TURBULENT THIRTIES
(Macdonald, 1960)
In collaboration with J. C. Trewin

THE THEATRES OF LONDON
(Hart-Davis, 1961)
(Second revised edition Harvest Books, 1963)
(Third revised edition New English Library, 1975)

A PICTURE HISTORY OF GILBERT & SULLIVAN
(Vista, 1962)

BRITISH MUSIC HALL: A Story in Pictures
(Studio Vista, 1965)
(New edition revised and enlarged Gentry Books, 1974)

THE LOST THEATRES OF LONDON
(Hart-Davis, 1968)
(New revised edition New English Library, 1976)

MUSICAL COMEDY: A Story in Pictures
(Peter Davies, 1969)

REVUE: A Story in Pictures
(Peter Davies, 1971)

PANTOMIME: A Story in Pictures
(Peter Davies, 1973)

THE
WAGNER COMPANION

by
Raymond Mander and Joe Mitchenson

With a musical appreciation and an essay on the
Bayreuth Festival Centenary Celebrations
by Barry Millington

W. H. Allen · London
A Howard & Wyndham Company
1977

Printed and bound in Great Britain
by Butler & Tanner Ltd., Frome and London,
for the publishers,
W. H. Allen & Co. Ltd.,
44, Hill Street, London, W1X 8LB

ISBN 0 491 01856 8

For

FRANCES FLEETWOOD

who knows only two tunes:
one is
GOD SAVE THE KING
and the other isn't.
With love and thanks
over the years.

CONTENTS

PREFACE

We have tried in this volume to apply to Wagner's operas the same principles we used in our approach to the plays of Shaw, Maugham and Coward, bringing to the reader details of original casts, production data, plots, background and criticism. These details are otherwise not easily available. The search for casts has been of far greater difficulty in the field of opera than that of the theatre. Opera has always lacked documentation, performances being of a less permanent nature. Libretti and scores, unlike plays, from the earliest times, mostly lack information on original casts. The opera programme of one particular night is of necessity rarer than that of a theatrical production.

We have included first performance criticisms from England, with slight editorial compressions, and have mainly chosen to include, for London, those from *The Era*. The files of this theatrical weekly present a middle view of contemporary reaction and have, so far, not been made generally available; we have only edited these to omit description of the plot. The rest of the notes speak for themselves. They have been kept to a minimum to carry on the sequence of events in Wagner's life. The definitive work of Ernest Newman in the field of biography is easily available for further expansion. We have also left matters of musical criticism, other than in the reviews, to Barry Millington, to whom our thanks.

For the initial data of first performances we have drawn on Dr. Alfred Loewenberg's monumental *Annals of Opera* (in its Second Edition) and it says much for his pioneer work that only in two cases have we to contradict a date recorded by him (the 'Paris' version of *Tannhäuser* was first given at Covent Garden on July 15, 1895, not May 27, 1896; this is proved by a programme in our Collection). It was sung in French, though Harold Rosenthal in *Two Centuries of Opera at Covent Garden* states it was being sung only in Italian even in 1896; and the first production of *Siegfried* in English was in 1897 (at Manchester) not London 1901.

As usual we have to thank Miss Frances Fleetwood for her detailed synopses of the plots, re-told from the original German, correcting small misinterpretations which have grown into some versions.

We would like to place on record our gratitude to the following for many services, advice and encouragement:

The Enthoven Collection (now the Theatre Museum) at the Victoria and Albert Museum, The B.B.C. Reference and Music Library, The British Council, The Libraries of Liverpool, Manchester, Birmingham, Boston and Cincinnati, the collections of Harvard University, The New York Public Library, the Archives of the Paris Opera, The Clara Ziegler Museum, Munich, The Seattle Opera, U.S.A., and the Metropolitan Opera Archives, New York, The Central Opera Service, Lincoln Center, New York. We have also had the fullest co-operation from the Librarian and Press Officer of Bayreuth throughout our work.

We want also to thank our friends, Dr. Wolfgang Sauer, Raymond Howarth and Colin Mabberley for their assistance, also Valerie Emery for many kindnesses in our search for information. Mary Quinnell has, as always, coped with our almost illegible manuscript and our Editor, Robert Dirskovski, patiently kept the book on the right lines.

For the pictorial side of the book we wish to thank:

The Bayreuth Archives, the modern photographers (as credited), as well as the libraries and collections noted. Other pictures are from our own files. The dedication page is from the cover by Henry Holiday for the Queen's Hall Wagner Festival 1896.

We are also pleased to acknowledge permission to reprint notices from *Punch*, *The Daily Telegraph*, the *Financial Times*, and The Society of Authors for allowing us to use Shaw's *Wagner in Bayreuth*.

Raymond Mander and Joe Mitchenson
June 1977.

THE OPERAS
of
RICHARD WAGNER

In Order of Composition

	Composed	Produced
1. DIE HOCHZEIT (The Wedding) a Fragment	1832–1833	—
2. DIE FEEN (The Fairies)	1832–1834	Munich 1888
3. DAS LIEBESVERBOT ODER DIE NOVIZE VON PALERMO (Forbidden Love or the Novice of Palermo)	1834–1836	Magdeburg 1836
4. RIENZI DER LETZTE DER TRIBUNEN (Rienzi the Last of the Tribunes)	1837–1840	Dresden 1842
5. DER FLIEGENDE HOLLÄNDER (The Flying Dutchman)	1840–1841	Dresden 1843
6. TANNHÄUSER UND DER SÄNGERKRIEG AUF WARTBURG (Tannhäuser and the Song Contest at Wartburg)	1842–1845	Dresden 1845
7. LOHENGRIN	1845–1848	Weimar 1850
8. DER RING DES NIBELUNGEN (The Ring of the Nibelung)		
I. DAS RHEINGOLD (The Rheingold)	1851–1854	Munich 1869
II. DIE WALKÜRE (The Valkyrie)	1851–1856	Munich 1870
III. SIEGFRIED	1851–1871	Bayreuth 1876
IV. GÖTTERDÄMMERUNG (The Twilight of the Gods)	1848–1874	Bayreuth 1876
9. TRISTAN UND ISOLDE (Tristan and Isolde)	1854–1859	Munich 1865
10. DIE MEISTERSINGER VON NÜRNBERG (The Mastersingers of Nuremberg)	1845–1867	Munich 1868
11. PARSIFAL	1845–1882	Bayreuth 1882

WAGNER'S OPERAS

In Order of First Production in England and America

England		America	
Der fliegende Holländer	1870	Tannhäuser	1859
Lohengrin	1875	Lohengrin	1871
Tannhäuser	1876	Der fliegende Holländer	1877
Rienzi	1879	Die Walküre	1877
⎡ Das Rheingold	1882	Rienzi	1878
⎢ Die Walküre	1882	Die Meistersinger	1886
⎨ Siegfried	1882	Tristan und Isolde	1886
⎢ Götterdämmerung (The complete Cycle)	1882	Siegfried	1887
⎣		Götterdämmerung	1888
Die Meistersinger	1882	Das Rheingold (In the first complete Cycle)	1889
Tristan und Isolde	1882		
Parsifal	1914	Parsifal	1903
Das Liebesverbot	1965		
Die Feen	1969		

RICHARD WAGNER

A musical appreciation by Barry Millington

Wilhelm Richard Wagner was born on May 22, 1813. It remains to be proved conclusively whether he was the son of Friedrich and Johanna Wagner, or whether his father was in fact Ludwig Geyer, the Jewish painter and actor whom Johanna married in 1814, nine months after Friedrich's death. What is certain is that from his early years he was attracted, even allowing for parental bias, to the atmosphere of the theatre; but an enthusiasm for music was not fostered and his decision to study it seriously in 1828 was also a gesture of independence. If the idea of becoming a composer was conceived and acted upon with remarkable suddenness, it was backed by a self-confidence and determination to succeed that were to characterise his whole career.

His family having resigned themselves, Wagner entered the University of Leipzig and studied briefly with Weinlig, the Kantor of the Thomaskirche, producing for him a handful of works. A Symphony in C, composed shortly after, made a greater impact. In 1832, he wrote a drama *Die Hochzeit* but never completed the music, after his sister Rosalie objected to the gruesome nature of the story. This was followed by *Die Feen*, which unashamedly adhered to the German Romantic opera tradition of Weber and Marschner in both its fairytale subject-matter and its musical language. However, a certain individuality and technical fluency were developed in *Das Liebesverbot*, freely based on Shakespeare's *Measure for Measure* (Wagner again writing his own libretto as he was to do throughout his life). A succession of conductorships in the 1830s, at Würzburg, Magdeburg, Königsberg and Riga, was largely responsible for an increasing professional awareness in these works and also for the abandoning, in *Das Liebesverbot*, of the German style, in favour of the lighter French–Italian style of composition.

An essay on Bellini, published in 1837, elevates the 'stable' forms of Italian opera in which passions might be communicated un-equivocally by a single, clear *bel canto* line, over the fussy, intellec-tualised German style with its obsessive disorder of forms, periods and modulations. This of course is a direct antithesis to the ideas of

the mature Wagner, though there are also indications of a dis-
satisfaction with the self-contained recitative–aria units of traditional
opera. As yet it is merely a perception that contemporary opera is
lacking psychological insight; there is no remedy proposed, nor was
Wagner's compositional technique sufficiently advanced to enable
him to grapple with such innovations.

It was during his tenure as conductor with the Magdeburg theatre
company that Wagner met and was instantly captivated by Minna
Planer, the leading actress. It was not his first affair, nor hers, but
her enforced absence from Magdeburg (she had accepted an offer
to appear at the Königstadt Theatre in Berlin) blinded them to their
temperamental and cultural differences. He first proposed to her in
one of his frenzied love-letters and they married on November 24,
1836. By the following summer, Minna had left him twice and Wagner
drowned his sorrows by plunging into Bulwer-Lytton's novel
Rienzi. This subject seemed to lend itself to a grand opera in the
style of Meyerbeer and the entire libretto plus two acts of the music
had been written by the spring of 1839. Minna had rejoined him and
was more sympathetic to the struggling artist than were his creditors,
who had followed him from Magdeburg and Königsberg to Riga.
Wagner looked to Paris, where Meyerbeer and grand opera reigned
supreme, and imagined at once a haven free of creditors and an
audience for his music. His departure from Riga with Minna and
their Newfoundland dog, Robber, was not only undignified but also
dangerous, as, his passport having been impounded, it was necessary
either to bribe or to dodge the sentries that guarded the frontier.
They set sail in a small vessel and were driven by fierce gales to take
refuge in a Norwegian harbour called Sandvika. After a brief visit
to London, they boarded a steamer for Boulogne, where Wagner
stayed for four weeks, making the acquaintance of Meyerbeer.

The reception was cordial but Wagner was soon disenchanted by
the atmosphere of the Paris Opéra and its clientèle. They hankered
after mock-seriousness and spectacle of a kind that the rising
Teutonic idealist, even in his dire pecuniary straits, would not stoop
to. Consequently the completed score of *Rienzi* was sent, not to the
Opéra, but to the royal court at Dresden. Already in the last three
acts of *Rienzi* we can glimpse the style towards which Wagner was
working, though undeniably it is the idiom of grand opera that
dominates the work. There has been a revival of interest recently in
the three earlier works; our generation appears to be more indulgent

towards juvenilia, not only for the light they throw on established masterpieces but also as works valid in their own right. With growing self-assurance he turned to Heine's story of the Flying Dutchman, by which he had been haunted for some time, and in a mere seven weeks had fashioned the first masterpiece of his maturity.

Der fliegende Holländer is the earliest work to have entered the Bayreuth canon and is of particular interest for two reasons: in the first place it exemplifies the element of autobiography, which was to become so important in the later works. The story tells of a lonely seafarer, condemned to wander the oceans until redeemed by the selfless love of a woman. The Dutchman is driven by storms to a Norwegian harbour and is eventually rescued from his plight by Senta, who, in pity, forgoes her own lover. Wagner identified himself closely with all this: persecuted, uprooted, harassed from all sides, unfulfilled in love, even down to the storm at sea and the Norwegian harbour. In the second place, as well as illustrating the link between life and music, *Holländer* also shows the one between Wagner's theory and music. During these early Paris years (1839–42), he produced a number of essays in a vivid, racy style, the ideas of which reflect his development as a composer at this time. There are indications of the technique of leitmotif (short musical phrases capable of symphonic development and usually associated with a specific idea or mood), and suggestions as to how the overture should be made relevant to the succeeding work by exposing melodic or rhythmic features which later assume importance in the dramatic action.

Both of these principles are present, if only in embryo, in *Der fliegende Holländer*, but are only part of a tendency towards greater unity in opera that was to be fully expounded in Wagner's epoch-making essay *Opera and Drama* (1850–51). From this point of view, one of the most instructive, as well as entertaining, of the writings from Paris is *A Pilgrimage to Beethoven*. In this imaginary meeting with his hero, the young composer is vouchsafed the information that Beethoven could never compose another *Fidelio* with all its arias, duets, terzettos and what have you; what he is looking for is an organic synthesis of instruments and voices. 'Of course', says Beethoven, 'voices must have words, and where is poetry to be found worthy of such a union?'

Wagner saw the answer to this problem in providing his own

librettos. This was not only because he was convinced that he was a great poet and therefore the best person for the job, but also because he realised that this would allow him to conceive his music and drama simultaneously, or, more accurately, to set down his poem with the musical composition already taking shape in his mind. Meanwhile, *Rienzi* had been accepted for performance at Dresden. After a series of frustrating delays it was eventually produced there on October 20, 1842 and was a huge success. The following January it was the turn of *Der fliegende Holländer* but this new, forbidding music took people by surprise and the work had to be taken off after four nights. Wagner was, however, offered the post of *Kapellmeister* at the Dresden court and the next few years were spent in the composition of music for ceremonial occasions and of *Tannhäuser* and *Lohengrin*.

The legend of *Tannhäuser* had caught Wagner's imagination in the last Paris winter of 1841–2 and text and music were completed in April 1845. In *Holländer* the protagonist had been under a curse, albeit a self-inflicted one; here the curse is internalised and Tannhäuser is tortured by his craving for the two worlds represented by Elisabeth and Venus. Still discernible is the style of grand opera, particularly in the Act II duet between Tannhäuser and Elisabeth, but there is also a significant shift towards the true music-drama synthesis in the amount of declamatory recitative. One extended passage, Tannhäuser's narration of his journey to Rome, in Act III, is considerably more developed in this respect: the musical phrases arise spontaneously from the poetry, having no preconceived melodic shape; accents fall according to the demands of the metre; and the actual character of the melodic lines is governed by the changing moods of the narration as it passes from the journey, to Elisabeth, to the pilgrims and so forth. The orchestra assumes an important role here too, both recalling and anticipating, assisting in pictorialisation, and reinforcing changes of mood.

The principles behind Tannhäuser's Narration are extended over a much larger area in *Lohengrin* (1845–8). The style is altogether more fluid; recitative and aria are virtually indistinguishable – indeed, Wagner told Liszt, who conducted the first performance, that the singers were not to know that there were recitatives in it. A new, continuous, arioso-like texture was created and the number of set pieces, the very backbone of conventional opera, drastically reduced. Paradoxically the chorus has more to do than in *Tannhäuser*, but it is also more skilfully integrated into the musical texture; nor do crowd scenes or stage action occur unless they arise out of the musical drama. Finally, the overture, which Wagner and others had striven to make more relevant to the succeeding drama, becomes in *Lohengrin* a prelude, important both symbolically – it may be said to represent the descent of the Grail and the ascent to heaven – and as an exposition of (musical) elements.

Wagner wrote no more music for six years after *Lohengrin*. Not only was he dimly aware that he was on the threshold of his *magnum opus*, but there were also ideas within him seeking non-musical expression before this could take place. He had long since been advocating reforms of various kinds in theatre and court (and not confined to music); when revolution broke out in 1848 Wagner embraced it as a response to his own challenge. He became seriously involved in the struggle, manning barricades and assisting such popular figures as Bakunin and Röckel. It was these activities that forced him in 1849 into exile in Zurich, which remained his primary home until he was granted a pardon in 1860. He immediately began to formulate his revolutionary artistic theories, producing a series of essays including: *Art and Revolution* (1849), *The Art-Work of the Future* (1849), *Opera and Drama* (1850–51) and *A Communication to my Friends* (1851).

Treated with caution, these works provide valuable insights into Wagner's compositional processes. The verbose, turgid style adopted for these technical essays in contrast to the lighter touch of the Paris writings, has all too often caused them to be dismissed as the rantings of a megalomaniac who frequently contradicts his own theory in his practice. This is actually not far from the truth, but it is as well to remember two things: first, that the artist's intuition often enables him to work instinctively in his own best interests, even though rationally he may seem to have erred; and second, without unburdening himself in this thoroughly characteristic manner, Wagner could never have achieved the concentration of purpose necessary to initiate and carry through such an immense undertaking as the *Ring*.

In the first important essay, *Art and Revolution*, he equated the materialistic world of the capitalists with a decaying culture, and the intended social reconstruction with a new form of art. Culture, he said, had declined since the era of the Greeks; they had regarded art as the celebration of the community spirit, of life itself, and to this end all the various elements of art had been brought together in one ideal – the Greek drama. Now all the rabble clamoured for was a new opera, with tuneful arias and duets, bravura passages for the singers and a sumptuous display on stage (Wagner's memory of Paris was clearly less than nostalgic).

The concept of a unified art-form was elaborated in *The Art-Work of the Future*: the individual arts could only regain their stature in combination with each other, and drama was only to discover its meaning by its relevance to 'the folk' – their common interests and aspirations. As Wagner was to point out, such a synthesis had actually been approached by Beethoven: he had constantly burst through his medium, and the last movement of the Ninth Symphony, for all its imperfections, had fulfilled the unassuageable need for a more articulate form of expression by breaking into song. It is noteworthy that at this point Wagner's theoretical ideal drama elevates speech – or at least poetry – to a dominant role; in none of the major works, however, does the word attain this distinction.

This brings us to the most important of Wagner's essays, indeed, a landmark in the history of dramatic music: *Opera and Drama*. The essay is remarkable as a blueprint for the new 'music drama' – Wagner's creation that was to compel reappraisal of the roles of music and drama by a synthesis of their elements. But it was not to be a mere setting of the words to more appropriate music; rather, a fusion of poetic verse with a melodic line that followed its actual configuration – 'die Versmelodie', as Wagner termed it. The kind of verse that he was evolving for the purpose was to be highly alliterative (the likeness of sound could in itself link contrasting ideas), condensed (inexpressive conjunctions and prepositions largely eliminated to yield a higher proportion of root syllables) and in free rhythm (able to accommodate the natural accentuation of words instead of being forced into one of the conventional metres).

Wagner contended that the 'tone-speech' of primal man, based on vowel sounds, had become, in the course of civilisation, suffocated by consonants in the interests of communication. So the new poetry was not only to add another dimension to consonantal sounds, but to redeem the vowel from the 'word-speech' into which it had sunk. This was all to be combined with an elaborate orchestral tissue in which the drama itself was to be enacted. Such a tissue would be able to modulate freely as required by the sense of the words and the whole would be unified by a motivic device of presentiments and reminiscences; these 'leitmotifs', as they are now called, were originally to arise directly from the poetic-musical verse. Finally, there were to be no set-pieces in the new music drama: no ensembles, no duet-singing and none of the divisions of conventional opera. (Wagner left himself with some room for manœuvre here with a parenthetical rider that ensemble singing might on occasions just be allowed, and, as we shall see, the principle was not rigidly enforced.)

Having taken this brief look at Wagner's theory, we can now consider how these principles were applied in subsequent compositions. The congeniality of Switzerland, where he had settled after his hasty departure from Dresden, was tempered by his distance from Minna – an increasingly emotional as well as physical distance. They were briefly reunited in September 1849 but when he returned the following year to France, seeking in desperation a way to pursue his career, he met and fell in love with a recent benefactress – Jessie Laussot. Herself unhappily married, Jessie listened sympathetically to Wagner's grievances; he almost persuaded her to elope to the Middle East, but Jessie retracted and went back to her husband, leaving Wagner and Minna to retrieve what they could from their marriage.

Back in the autumn of 1848, when he was still officially attached to the Dresden court, Wagner had started work on an epic drama called *Siegfrieds Tod*. In 1851 he was commissioned by Liszt, now a close friend, to compose it for performance at Weimar. Instead Wagner produced a prelude to it, *Der junge Siegfried*, and themes began to appear. It became evident to Wagner that the narratives which had originally been compressed into *Siegfrieds Tod* needed to be expanded yet further, and *Der junge Siegfried* was prefaced by *Die Walküre*, the whole trilogy being preceded by a fourth, introductory, drama – *Das Rheingold*. *Der junge Siegfried* and *Siegfrieds Tod* were recast and eventually became *Siegfried* and *Götterdämmerung*. The whole cycle had outgrown Weimar; Wagner repaid Liszt the money he had been given for the original commission and turned to the music, trusting that the Revolution would provide the means for such a worthy enterprise. He considered that he would need at least three years for *Der Ring des Nibelungen* if it were not to endanger his health. The inspiration for the Prelude of *Rheingold* came in September 1853; the scoring of *Götterdämmerung* was completed in November 1874, twenty-one years later.

As will be apparent, the conception of the *Ring* occurred before the corpus of theoretical writings of the revolutionary years. Most of the poem, however, took shape in 1851-2 and this chronology throws interesting light on the relationship, previously mentioned, between Wagner's theory and his works. It would be reasonable to assume that the already completed text of *Siegfrieds Tod* guided him to some extent in the formulation of his principles in *Opera and Drama*; but these principles went further than *Siegfrieds Tod*, and when the latter was revised into *Götterdämmerung*, it was in accordance with the theory laid down in *Opera and Drama*.

So the years after the completion of *Lohengrin* were far from fallow: a subtle interchange of theory and practice was taking place, and the colossal *Ring* cycle was gestating. The theoretical writings, then, provide a point of reference, from which the works, including those before, during and after the *Ring*, might be studied. The *Ring* itself cannot be considered as a single entity because between 1857 and 1869 Wagner laid it aside to compose *Tristan und Isolde* and *Die Meistersinger von Nürnberg*; most of the resulting stylistic differences can be attributed to a shift in emphasis in the relationship between words and music.

Even in the works written before 1857 – *Das Rheingold, Die Walküre* and *Siegfried* (as far as Act II) – the music can be seen to adopt a more prominent role, the correspondingly greater weight being borne by the orchestra. Large portions of the drama in *Das Rheingold* are projected in a rather functional, recitative-like manner and although there is considerable use of alliteration, it is frequently used not to illuminate inner meanings, as Wagner intended, but merely as a poetic device. Some of the finest pages of the score are purely orchestral, notably the Prelude and the interludes before and after the Nibelheim scene. *Die Walküre*, however, at times represents the perfection of the *Opera and Drama* synthesis. Line after line of *Versmelodie*, blending ideally the poetic and melodic elements, creates a web of glowing orchestral polyphony. If the orchestration has not yet the virtuosity of *Tristan* or *Götterdämmerung*, there is nevertheless a considerable advance over *Das Rheingold* in this respect.

An analysis of Wagner's use of leitmotif throughout the *Ring* shows quite clearly his increasing preoccupation with the musical aspect. Although the principle had been laid down in *Opera and Drama* that motifs of reminiscence and presentiment would result from the poetic-musical verse, in practice, many were either purely orchestral in origin, or arose from less specific contexts. This tendency increases as the *Ring* progresses. Thus *Das Rheingold* exposes a large number of motifs, of which that of the curse is typical: engendered by Alberich's fury of frustration, it returns as Fafner kills Fasolt and the curse begins to take effect. The first act of *Die Walküre* contains no textual reference to the events of *Das Rheingold*, but 'motifs of reminiscence' help to achieve unity. A striking example occurs when Sieglinde is relating to Siegmund the history of the sword: a stranger appeared at her wedding and put it in the tree; the Valhalla motif sounded quietly on the brass identifies the stranger for us. Later in the *Ring*, however, we see motifs used rather differently. Siegfried's Rhine Journey in the prologue of *Götterdämmerung* is a free symphonic treatment of motifs connected with Siegfried and the Rhine, and the prelude to Act III of *Siegfried* is an even finer, more concise example of symphonic development, using nine motifs appropriate to the Wanderer's urgent summoning of Erda.

That Wagner began to think more symphonically should not surprise us: the composition of *Tristan* and *Die Meistersinger* had brought his technique to a peak and effected the complete abolition of operatic set-pieces in favour of a closely-woven orchestral fabric. Moreover, the origins of the leitmotifs themselves might be considered indicative of their future development. They each have a memorable characteristic – melodic, harmonic or rhythmic – and yet they grow out of one another; ultimately, every motif in the tetralogy is retraceable to the primary arpeggio at the beginning of *Das Rheingold*.[1] Sometimes the connections only become apparent in retrospect, but it is the symphonist's art to integrate large-scale structures, linking backward and forward to create a continuous texture, rich in associative ideas.

A further change in Wagner's approach can be seen in the progressive – some would say regressive – use of ensemble singing. *Das Rheingold* adheres rigidly to the principles of *Opera and Drama* in that, with the exception of that of the Rhinemaidens, who are treated almost as a single entity, there is no music for concerted forces. In *Die Walküre*, with a similar proviso for the Valkyries, the same applies, even in the rapturous Act I love-duet of Siegmund and Sieglinde.

1. This is demonstrated lucidly by Robert Donington in *Wagner's 'Ring' and its Symbols: the Music and the Myth* (London, 1963, 3/1974) [appendix of musical examples].

When we reach Act III of *Siegfried*, however, the duet is another matter; it is, in many ways, a duet of the conventional type that Wagner had so vehemently renounced. But that is not all. In *Götterdämmerung*, there is a chorus for the vassals, a conspirators' trio and an oath-swearing duet that is positively Verdian. Needless to say, such ensembles are by now thoroughly integrated, arising directly out of the drama; even so, they proved too much for Bernard Shaw, who denounced *Götterdämmerung* as a sell-out to traditional opera.

A work such as the *Ring* could not materialise without a considerable expansion of existing procedures, and two important aspects not yet discussed are Wagner's orchestration and his use of tonality. In music of the Classical period, the scoring, though frequently masterly in its imaginative deployment of instruments, is limited by the smaller resources available. The nineteenth and twentieth centuries have seen a gradual democratisation of the orchestra, as composers have drawn more specifically on tone-colour to articulate the language of emotion. Wagner participated in this process by exploiting timbres of instruments, both in families and individually. To some of the less familiar instruments – the bass clarinet and bass tuba, for example – he gave a respectability that has remained with them ever since. He even invented, for the *Ring*, an instrument to bridge the gap in tonal colour between the horns and trombones. The 'Wagner tuba' is played by each of four extra horn players who alternate between the two instruments, and gives a sombre dignity to such passages as the announcement of the Valhalla motif. So Wagner's contribution to the development of the orchestra was not simply to increase its size – though he did that as well – but also its range of tone-colour.

If the larger forces employed in the *Ring* denoted a laying of foundations for the vastly expanded emotional content of the cycle, Wagner's use of tonality is both a means toward and a product of this intensification. The harmonic language of the *Ring* is a continual jostling of chromatic and diatonic elements. There are of course passages of pure diatonicism – the opening of *Rheingold* has 136 bars of unadulterated E flat major – and the music associated with Loge, the elusive trickster (*Rheingold*), or that of the Magic Sleep (*Walküre*), is largely chromatic, but such passages are atypical and generally for pictorial or symbolic reasons. Normally even predominantly diatonic passages are affected by enharmonic modulations and chromatic inflections and the result is a homogeneous continuum capable of infinite nuance.

Wagner's persistent, almost obsessive, chromaticism contributed in large measure to the eventual disintegration of tonality, which reached its crisis in the first decades of the twentieth century and led to the evolution of serial methods of composition. Other important features of Wagner's harmonic vocabulary which aided this process include his use of $^6_4$s (second inversions), diminished 7ths and mediant relationships. The $^6_4$ being a tonic chord sounded over a dominant bass contains a fundamental ambiguity that undermines the tonic–dominant polarity of the tonal system, a possibility previously realised by Beethoven and Schubert and further exploited by the later Romantics. The diminished 7th is ubiquitous in Romantic music and used with tremolando was the stock-in-trade for nineteenth-century melodrama; tonally it is also an ambiguous chord and Wagner uses it frequently.

Another procedure initiated by Beethoven and Schubert is the use of the mediant (or its inversion the submediant) in place of the Classical dominant. Where the latter represents logical development and progression, the mediant generally suggests passive acceptance, indulgence and transformation. It would be impossible to pinpoint precisely the extent to which each composer of the nineteenth century was responsible for the breaking down of the Classical tonal system: they all used devices of the kind described to varying degrees and for their own purposes. Wagner reached his own zenith in *Tristan und Isolde* and it is universally agreed that this is one of the key works of the century.

We have to return to the years 1853 and 1854 to see the origin of some of the impulses that generated *Tristan*. This was a time of some material success; having already conducted a number of concerts in Zurich, Wagner also had a festival organised there in his honour. Yet he was troubled by his own ill-health and even more by that of Minna, which compelled him to spend some time with her at Seelisberg. He came under the influence of Schopenhauer, whose *Die Welt als Wille und Vorstellung* seemed to be a formulation of Wagner's own pessimistic outlook at this time, and of Mathilde Wesendonck, who was in turn overawed by his genius and whose husband Otto had assisted with the finances of the 1853 festival. For Mathilde, Wagner had written a little piano sonata that year and the autograph of *Die Walküre* bears cryptic endearments to her.

The completion of that score was delayed by first a visit to London in 1855 to conduct a season of the London Philharmonic Society's concerts, during which he defied the united opposition of the Press and was partially successful in winning over the public, and second by a recurrence of an old nervous condition – erysipelas. He finished *Die Walküre* at last in March 1856 and turned to *Siegfried*. This was interrupted at first in October by a visit from Liszt, and again the following year, but for a rather longer period – some twelve years – when the desire to compose *Tristan* became overwhelming. Shortly before, he had occupied a cottage called the 'Asyl' adjoining the Wesendoncks' estate in the Enge, just outside Zurich, and the prospect of closer contact with Mathilde no doubt spurred him on. The hope of a production of the entire *Ring* could still only be entertained by one as convinced of its necessity as Wagner, and he announced that with *Tristan* he would provide a 'thoroughly practicable' opera.

To get *Tristan* produced was no straightforward matter, and part of the reason was another major shift of emphasis in words and music. In *Tristan*, Wagner's aim was the ultimate Romantic ideal of a unification of the arts. Schopenhauer's importance for Wagner was that he exalted music to a position of superiority over all the other arts, believing that it was an objectification not of the 'eternal ideas' (as were other arts), but of the metaphysical will itself. But while he concluded that a complete synthesis of the arts was not possible, Wagner, stimulated by this elevation of music, began to attempt just such a synthesis. In fact he seems to have convinced himself (and many others) that *Tristan* was a perfect *Gesamtkunstwerk*.[2] A more objective analysis shows that this is not the case but that he was nearer the mark when he said that *Tristan* was 'more thoroughly musical than anything I have done up to now'. The supreme importance of music in *Tristan* represents a considerable departure from the principles of *Opera and Drama*, a fact which until recently has been generally overlooked.[3] There are, for example, many instances of vowel extension and phrase repetition, where the intelligibility of the words is sacrificed in the interests of dramatic effect or musical design. Again, where in *Opera and Drama* Wagner had scorned the

2. Literally 'total art-work'.
3. The issue has been clarified by Jack Stein in his invaluable *Richard Wagner and the Synthesis of the Arts* (Detroit, 1960), to which my analysis is indebted.

contrivance of rhyme by which words at the end of lines had become unduly prominent, in *Tristan* there is a considerable use of rhyming words, justified by the fact that they are almost invariably the salient words of a phrase, and by their highlighting of vowel sounds.

Perhaps the most important divergence in *Tristan* from *Opera and Drama* is in the use of concerted singing. By the time of *Die Walküre* all the patterns of conventional opera – the self-contained overture, the recitative/aria divisions, the duets, trios and choruses – had been transformed into the continuous flow of music drama; now in *Tristan* there is a partial retraction as Tristan and Isolde indulge in a duet which lasts them most of the second act, involves much simultaneous singing and even a passage, at 'O sink' hernieder', which appears to pay allegiance to traditional opera. That this was a turning-point in Wagner's development is proved by the fact that all the music dramas composed after *Tristan* (*Die Meistersinger*, *Götterdämmerung* and *Parsifal*) contain concerted singing of the type previously disallowed.

The subservience of drama to music in *Tristan* affects the continuity of the work in an interesting way. The *Ring*, following more closely as it does the principles of the *Gesamtkunstwerk*, has a system of dramatic unification which corresponds to and complements the musical one. There is one central character, Wotan, and all the others represent aspects or projections of his psyche; the E flat arpeggio which opens the tetralogy, its *ur-motif*, stands not for Wotan or even more generally the psyche itself, but for the Rhine, the symbol of undifferentiated Nature, and the starting-point of both external and internal (i.e. psychological) drama.[4] However, the dominating psyche of *Tristan* is Wagner himself – so close is the correlation between the drama and the composer's private life. Isolde and King Marke are the dramatic counterparts of Mathilde and Otto Wesendonck, and as the progression of the drama effects a gradual concentration of interest on Tristan/Wagner, so Isolde and Marke lose some of their definition as the positive and negative aspects of the central psyche, Isolde becoming, in the *Liebestod*, pure anima.

It is therefore to be expected that the thematic motives of *Tristan* differ from those of the *Ring*. They are varied in character but not readily identified with a particular idea or emotion, even less specific

4. See Donington: ibid.

objects or people (cf the 'sword' or 'Wanderer' motive in the *Ring*). Exceptions are the hunting-horn motive and that associated with Marke (first heard on the bass clarinet in his Act II monologue). Although the motives of *Tristan* can all be traced to a common origin, and are therefore likely to be interrelated, they do not dispose themselves in groups like those of the *Ring*. So the unity achieved in *Tristan* is primarily a musical one, a result of the fundamental subservience of drama to music.

Dramatic action in *Tristan* is kept to a minimum. In Act II, for example, there are only three major dramatic events: the entrance of Tristan, that of Marke and Melot, and the fight. But the drama is a psychological one and the absence of external activity allows greater concentration on symbolic gestures (such as the extinguishing of the torch) and the philosophical issues generally, the day/night, life/death dualisms in particular. The basic harmonic language of *Tristan* consists of an unending succession of high-powered chords that never resolve, but sometimes the bouts of activity are emphasised by a change in the nature of the musical language. Whereas chromaticism is equated throughout the work with yearning and the impossibility of passion's fulfilment in this life, diatonicism is generally used to depict either temporary alleviation of suffering or the temporal values of society represented by Marke, Melot, Brangäne and Kurwenal. The merest mention of honour, loyalty, or feudal rights provokes a spate of common triads; Marke's monologue is predominantly diatonic; and the triadic calls of the hunting-horns again represent the social *milieu* of the king and courtiers.

By an unusual arrangement, Wagner sent *Tristan und Isolde* to the publisher act by act as each was completed. In April 1858, having dispatched Act I, Wagner made a gift to Mathilde Wesendonck of his sketch for the prelude. The scroll, which also contained a love-letter, was intercepted by Minna; this proved the final breach in a marriage which had now become impossible. After a 'rest-cure', Minna left for Dresden; Wagner for Venice, where the affair apparently provided the right stimulus for the composition of the white-hot second act. There were hopes of *Tristan* being performed, first in Karlsruhe, where Wagner's old friend Eduard Devrient was director of the Opera, and later, when several other projected venues proved impossible, in Vienna. But one catastrophe followed another: a production of *Tannhäuser* in Paris had to be taken off after three nights because the aristocrats of the Jockey Club were denied their second-act ballet; the death of their dog Fips deprived Wagner and Minna of one of their few remaining links; and Aloys Ander, the proposed Tristan, lost his voice, causing both further delays and jibes about the unsingability of the new work. A brief visit to the Wesendoncks in Venice convinced him that his longing for Mathilde was hopeless; she was reconciled with her husband and the latter felt sufficiently secure to continue his financial assistance of Wagner. But the visit was responsible for him taking up again the scenario of *Die Meistersinger* which he had sketched at Marienbad in 1845.

In March 1862, Minna, pleading ill-health, at last won permission for Wagner to re-enter Saxony. But a short visit to her in Dresden that November was to be the last: he had determined to break the lingering ties of this miserable relationship. Meanwhile, he consoled himself with the company of Friederike Meyer, the sister of the intended Isolde in Vienna, Louise Dustmann-Meyer, and with the young Mathilde Maier, who declined to marry him fearing an hereditary deafness. At this time Wagner also made the acquaintance of the tenor who was eventually to create the part of Tristan – Ludwig Schnorr von Carolsfeld. But Wagner's material fortunes had reached their nadir, and it seemed that only a miraculous event could save him from utter ruin. A miracle did occur: the good fairy was the eighteen-year-old Ludwig II who succeeded to the throne of Bavaria. Passionately fond of Wagner and his music, Ludwig was to fulfil the dream of a theatre built for the sole purpose of his music drama. In return, Wagner produced a few pieces for special royal occasions.

Tristan und Isolde was scheduled for performance in Munich in May 1865 with Ludwig Schnorr and his wife Malvina in the title roles. The day arrived but was again fraught with disaster: creditors had to be fobbed off by the King; the imminent death of Minna was announced – it did not actually occur until the following January; and, worst of all, Malvina Schnorr fell ill. This 'practicable' work had to be postponed yet again; it was performed at last on June 10, 13 and 19 with Hans von Bülow conducting and a fourth performance followed by royal command on July 1. The death of the inestimable Ludwig Schnorr three weeks later was a severe blow.

The unpleasant aspects of royal patronage – Ludwig, fearing for Wagner's safety, begged him to leave Munich temporarily – were offset by his intimacy at this time with his friend von Bülow's wife, Cosima. She was continually by his side, ostensibly as his secretary, though the child born to her on April 10, 1865 (Isolde) was the daughter of Wagner. At the request of Ludwig, Wagner began to dictate to Cosima his autobiography; first printed privately in four parts, *Mein Leben* presents a colourful and sometimes idealised account of his career. Cosima's fourth and fifth children, Eva and Siegfried, were also fathered by Wagner, and von Bülow's patience reached its limit soon after; he obtained a divorce on July 18, 1870, the marriage of Cosima and Wagner taking place on August 25. By then it was too late to return to Munich, but Ludwig, though disappointed at his hero's behaviour, continued to support him. *Die Meistersinger von Nürnberg*, meanwhile completed, was performed in June 1868 and *Das Rheingold* and *Die Walküre* in 1869 and 1870 respectively, also at Munich.

Die Meistersinger is sometimes cited as evidence that there can be no direct connection between the events of a composer's life and the character of the music he produces at any point in it. Certainly this work is the most radiant and life-affirming that Wagner wrote and it was at least begun at a time of great hardship and depression. But this takes into account neither the fact that the bulk of *Die Meistersinger* was composed after Wagner's fortunes had started to turn, nor a possible compensatory mechanism that sublimates earthbound frustrations into timeless art. In any case it is a work of paradoxes and in many ways atypical of the composer. To begin with, it is the only one of the mature operas to deal with a real world peopled by real human beings; here the contrast is greatest with its immediate predecessor *Tristan*, which inhabits almost entirely the private world of the lovers. *Die Meistersinger* is set in sixteenth-century Nuremberg and has, at the centre of the drama, a cobbler, who plies his trade on stage and in view of the audience.

The realism of the setting is reflected in the nature of the music, which is predominantly diatonic and square in rhythm. Moreover, even though the work is basically through-composed, in Wagner's later manner, it makes abundant use of traditional forms – fugue, chorale, German song – and there is even a set-piece at the focal point of the drama. The Prize-song is the means by which the young knight, Walther von Stolzing, both wins his bride, and finds the ideal balance between unfettered spontaneity and the inhibiting rules of convention. In the first act he learns the rules, and in the third he conceives his song and makes his bid, at the climax of a song-contest, for the approval of both the masters and the 'folk'. Perhaps only a Wagner could set himself the task of writing such a song, by which the whole music drama must either stand or fall; the important point, however, is not so much that he had the self-confidence to accomplish it, and with irrefutable success, but that he thereby exalted a traditional set-piece to the highest pinnacle of his composition.

Die Meistersinger proved an artistic triumph in Munich but the united opposition of rival factions exhausted Wagner. He left Munich, determined to sever his connections there, and in fact was not to see Ludwig again for eight years. The impossibility of producing the *Ring* in Munich rekindled the desire to have built a theatre where his works could be adequately and, of course, exclusively presented. The place Wagner now had his eye on was Bayreuth and in 1871 he finally managed to obtain the consent of the town authorities. Thus he entered the last stage of his life's major enterprise. The cycle was complete with the composition of *Götterdämmerung* by 1874, but there were two more years of frenzied fund-raising (including more help from Ludwig) before the first festival could take place. The final rehearsals began on August 6, 1876, with Ludwig present, and the first cycle was performed between August 13 and 17. The event was proclaimed far and wide but Wagner and his music had by this time attracted at least as many critics as admirers. The verdict was by no means unanimous – Wagner himself was dissatisfied with certain aspects of the first festival – and the deficit was considerable. Nevertheless the achievement was undeniable and few composers before or since have matched him for tenacity of purpose; more than a third of his life had been devoted to a single project and for most of that time the prospects of a staging had seemed bleak.

No sooner was the festival behind him than Wagner turned to the legend of Parsifal, which had inspired a prose sketch in 1865. This last work was composed in Bayreuth between 1877 and 1879; the scoring was completed three years later, and the first performance given in the July of 1882, under Hermann Levi. Wagner himself distinguished *Parsifal* from his other music dramas by calling it a *Bühnenweihfestspiel* (lit. stage-dedication-festival-play) and it has certainly acquired a quasi-religious aura which has divided critics and disciples alike: is it the final testimony of an artist still at the

height of his powers; or is it the moral ramblings of senility? There
is perhaps more depth than at first appears in Ernest Newman's
immortal remark: 'In the great book of sex there are many chapters,
and *Parsifal* is simply the last of them for many people'; he has
perceived that the religiosity, whether genuine or of more symbolic
intention, is of less importance than the observations of human
behaviour.

The relationship between music and poetry is not precisely
comparable in any preceding work. At times, for example when
Kundry recounts the death of Herzeleide, and in the Good Friday
music, the orchestra follows quite closely the contours of the vocal
line. Indeed, the duplication in the latter, as in the *Liebestod* from
Tristan, enables it to be performed independently in the concert hall.
The tautology is not a return to the pre-*Ring* style, where there were
passages in which the orchestral role was virtually self-contained, but
yet a new solution to the problem of integration. The complexity of
symbolism demands a certain independence for the text, and gener-
ates an expressive line which is supported by the orchestra. Charged
with associations and cross-references, the orchestral polyphony
provides both the backbone to the drama and a commentary on it.
Occasionally, as in the long stretches of Gurnemanz's narration in
Act I, too great demands are made of a single recitative-like line, but
elsewhere the fusion is perfect.

The orchestration of *Parsifal* had been completed in Palermo, and
after sixteen performances in July and August, 1882, Wagner retired
with his family to Venice, where he died the following year. He was
buried in Bayreuth to the strains of the Funeral March from *Götterdämmerung*.

If *Parsifal* has been the cause of much controversy, there has been
equal disagreement as to the interpretation of Wagner's other works.
He has been embraced by Marxists, Nazis, Jungians, Freudians and,
more recently, even feminists. Whether or not we accept the full
Jungian exposition given by Donington, it is apparent that Wagner
probes deep into the subconscious, exposing levels of the psyche of
which we were previously only dimly aware. Such an explanation is
necessary to account for the extremity of reactions to his music, for
Wagner is noted for his liability to provoke either ecstatic fervour or
fierce revulsion, rarely dispassionate interest. Depending on one's
gut-reaction to the music is the extent to which one criticises the *man*
for his insensitive dealings with his fellow human beings. Those

inclined to be hostile make much of his cavalier attitude towards Minna and opportunist manipulation of friends – especially those with money or influence – while his sympathisers seek to justify Wagner by pointing to his genius and claiming its exemption from mere plebeian obligations. The divergence of viewpoint itself reflects the polarity of opinion about Wagner. It is a fascinating polarity, even unique, and should stimulate literature on the composer for some time to come.

DIE HOCHZEIT
(The Wedding)

——————— · ———————

A Fragment of an Opera

Libretto
Written in Prague, Summer, 1832.

Music
Introduction, Chorus and Septet completed, Würzburg, March 1, 1833.

Characters

Ada	Soprano
Lora	Alto
Arindal	Tenor
Harald	Tenor
Admund	Tenor
Cadolt	Bass
Hadmar	Bass

Chorus
Soprano, Alto, Tenor and Bass.

SYNOPSIS

A chorus of men celebrates in joyous song the end of a war between their ruler Hadmar and his enemy Morar; while a chorus of women welcome Morar's son Cadolt and his companion Admund, who, in token of the new friendship, have been invited to the wedding of Hadmar's beautiful daughter Ada to Arindal.

Cadolt, who appears disturbed at the prospect of this wedding, confides to Admund that he wishes they had not come. His friend assumes that this is because he distrusts Hadmar, but Cadolt says that the feeling in his heart is not hate but quite the contrary.

As the wedding procession approaches, the chorus pay tribute to the nobility of the bridegroom and the beauty of his bride. Evidently struck by Cadolt's appearance, Ada asks who he is, and Arindal replies that he is Morar's son – a former enemy who has now become his lifelong friend. In the ensuing septet, Hadmar welcomes Cadolt; Arindal looks forward to wedded bliss, and a female guest, Lora, bids her own heart be still, in view of the happiness of her friends, but Harald on the one side and Admund on the other are apprehensive of treachery; Cadolt expresses spiritual torment, and Ada is surprised at the disturbing effect upon her of his presence.

NOTES

Richard Wagner received his early education in Dresden but returned in 1827 to Leipzig, the town of his birth, where he had his first music lessons from Gottlieb Müller, a member of the Gewandhaus orchestra.

He had earlier shown an interest in German verse, writing a tragedy in Shakespearean style at the age of fourteen, called *Leubald und Adelaide*. Of this play, a mixture of *Hamlet* and *King Lear*, Wagner himself said 'I had murdered forty-two persons in the course of my piece and I was obliged to have most of them reappear as ghosts in the last acts for want of living characters.' On his return to Leipzig, however, he became more interested in music.

In 1831 he began to study composition under Theodor Weinlig and soon his earliest works were being both performed and published. Though these were mainly instrumental and orchestral, he composed the incidental music for a drama *König Enzio* by Raupach which was produced in Leipzig in March 1832.

In the summer of the same year, while staying at Pravonin near Prague, Wagner wrote the text of a tragic opera, *Die Hochzeit* (*The Wedding*) about which he says: 'I don't remember where I got hold of this mediæval subject: a love-crazed youth climbs through a window into the bedroom of his friend's bride, where she is awaiting the arrival of her bridegroom. She struggles with him, so that he crashes to his death in the courtyard below. During his funeral ceremony, the girl, with a shriek, falls lifeless upon his body.'

On returning to Leipzig he composed the first number – a septet, which was much admired by Theodor Weinlig.

Work on the opera was interrupted by his first engagement as a professional musician when, early in 1833, he became chorus master at the theatre in Würzburg where his brother Albert was a singer and the stage manager.

It was here that he completed the introduction, chorus and septet of *Die Hochzeit* but on the insistence of his sister, Rosalie, an actress at the Dresden Theatre, who strongly objected to the story of the opera, Wagner abandoned the work, eventually destroying the libretto. Consequently the only parts of the text that have been preserved are the words accompanying the musical score, the manuscript of which is dedicated: –

'To the Würzburger Musikverein with respectful gratitude. Introduction, Chorus and Septet. Würzburg, March 1st, 1833.'

It was eventually published in 1910 and has been broadcast by the B.B.C.

DIE FEEN

(*The Fairies*)

————— · —————

A Romantic Opera in Three Acts

Libretto

Based on Carlo Gozzi's *La Donna Serpente* (*The Snake Woman*).
Written in Leipzig, Winter, 1832–3.

Music

Sketched and completed in Würzburg, 1833–4.

Characters

The Fairy King	Bass
Zemina ⎤	Soprano
Farzana ⎬ Fairies	Soprano
Ada ⎦	Soprano
Arindal, King of Tramond	Tenor
Lora, his Sister	Soprano
Morald, her Suitor, Arindal's Friend	Baritone
Gernot, Arindal's Hunter	Bass Buffo
Drolla, Lora's Confidante	Soprano
Gunther, a Courtier at Tramond	Tenor Buffo
Harald, Arindal's General	Bass
A Messenger	Tenor
Voice of the Enchanter Groma	Bass
A Boy and a Girl, the Children of Arindal and Ada	

Chorus

Fairies, Morald's Companions, Citizens, Warriors, Earth Spirits,
Bronze Men, Groma's Invisible Spirits.

Scene

In the Kingdom of Fantasy.

ACT I SCENE 1 The Fairies' Garden.
       SCENE 2 A Wild and Rocky Wilderness.
       SCENE 3 The Fairies' Garden with Palace.

ACT II The Entrance Hall of a Palace in Arindal's Capital.
ACT III SCENE I A Banquet Hall.
       SCENE 2 The Underground Kingdom.
       SCENE 3 The Fairies' Palace.

FIRST PRODUCED. Hoftheater, Munich, June 29, 1888.

FIRST PRODUCED IN ENGLAND at the Great Hall, University of Aston in Birmingham, Birmingham, May 17, 1969 in a translation by Alison Murray and Terence Green by The Midland Music Makers Grand Opera Society (4 Amateur performances).

FIRST PRODUCED IN LONDON at Fulham Town Hall, Fulham, S.W.6. May 3, 1973 in a translation by Alison Murray and Terence Green by The Hammersmith Municipal Opera (3 performances).

No production in America is traceable.

DIE FEEN (THE FAIRIES)—CASTS

CHARACTERS	MUNICH 1888	BIRMINGHAM 1969	LONDON 1973
The Fairy King	Viktoria Blank	Derrick Hodgkins	Matteo de Monti
Zemina	Pauline Sigler	Jennifer Anscombe	Doreen Millman
Farzana	Margarethe Sigler	Sheila Moore	Lynda Day-Richardson
Ada	Lili Drebler	Patricia Nixon	Marie Hayward
Arindal	Max Mikorey	Ronald Hollins	Gunnar Drago
Lora	Adrienne Weitz	Iris Deathridge	Josephine Davis
Morald	Anton Fuchs	Kenneth Wilcox	Paul Riley
Gernot	Gustav Siehr	Robert Kirk	Emyr Green
Drolla	Emilie Herzog	Marie Austin	Rita Chard
Gunther	Hermmann	Leslie Deathridge	Geoffrey Pogson
Harald	Kaspar Bausewein	Harold Tomlinson	Michael Kallipetis
A Messenger	Max Schlosser		Arnold Chazen
Groma	Not named	Derrick Hodgkins	Michael Kallipetis
A Boy and a Girl	Not named	Susan Latham Jean Wood	Oliver Gibbs Malcolm Footer
Conductor	Hermann Levi	Colin Lee	Joseph Vandernoot
Producer	Carl Brulliot	Arthur Street	Max Miradin
Designer	*Scenery* Brioschi and Hermann Burghart *Costumes* Josef Flüggen	Lynda Kettle Ballet arranged by Patricia Heaven	Not named

*Extra character
A wounded soldier Frank Keyte

SYNOPSIS

SCENE 1   The fairies, led by Zemina and Farzana, are playing in a garden. They lament the loss of their beloved Ada who, by marrying a mortal, has jeopardised her own immortality, and they vow to separate her from her husband.

SCENE 2   In a rocky wilderness Morald and Gunther, from the Court of Tramond, unexpectedly meet the huntsman Gernot, whom they have not seen for eight years – since he disappeared in company with their Crown Prince, Arindal. After exchanging delighted greetings, Morald explains that he is journeying, at the request of the magician Groma, to find Arindal, who with the death of his father has become king. He is badly needed, as an enemy is besieging the country and claiming the hand of his sister Lora, Morald's betrothed. Gernot in turn tells how he and Arindal had followed a beautiful doe until it disappeared into a river. Springing in after it, they had found themselves in a castle owned by a lovely woman, who agreed to marry Arindal on the one condition that for eight years he would never ask who she was. So they had lived all the while in great contentment, and she had borne Arindal two children; but on the previous day, curiosity had led him to ask the forbidden question: suddenly the castle had disappeared, and the two men had found themselves alone in this solitary place. Gernot asks after his own wife Drolla, and hears that she is still alive and often weeps for him. The men go off, still talking.

Arindal, who is wildly seeking his lost love, beseeches her eloquently to return.

By every means Gernot tries to persuade Arindal to abandon the search. When the King angrily refuses, Gernot tells him the story of the ugly old witch Dilnovaz who, by means of a magic ring, contrived to appear young and lovely, until at last the King, her husband, discovered the deception.

Gunther now joins them, disguised as an aged priest. He solemnly tells Arindal that he has been deceived by a wicked woman, that all the wild animals in the neighbourhood are her ex-lovers whom she has enchanted, and that Arindal himself risks the same fate if he does not leave the place immediately. He is on the point of obeying, when there is a thunderclap accompanied by lightning, and Gunther's real identity is revealed.

Morald next appears, in the guise of the dead king, saying that he has died of grief at losing Arindal, and narrating all the troubles that have fallen upon the kingdom in the young man's absence. Conscience-stricken, Arindal feels it his duty to return; again there is thunder and lightning, and Morald stands revealed. He maintains, however, that everything he had said is true, and Arindal consents to accompany his friends home.

An alternative to this complicated scene, with its inherent absurdity, is given in the libretto. In this, Arindal's aria to his lost wife is followed by a simple scene in which he meets his friends, hears their news, and at once agrees to go back with them.

On the point of leaving, Arindal makes a last appeal to his wife to let him see her at least once and give her a farewell kiss. Overcome by drowsiness he falls asleep.

SCENE 3   A transformation scene then brings him back to the fairy garden. Ada, beautiful but sad at heart, comes from her palace, bewailing the loss of Arindal. There is a brief, passionate reunion, during which she declares that they can only remain together for a day and must then part for ever. Now Arindal's friends appear. Overcome by Ada's beauty, they sympathise with his reluctance to leave her, and despair of bringing him home.

But at this moment Zemina and Farzana, with a chorus of fairies, come to tell Ada that her father is dead (it has been explained that she is the daughter of a 'mixed marriage' between a fairy and a mortal), and that she has been elected their queen.

After a great many heartfelt regrets on both sides the husband and wife finally part, to take up their duties in their separate kingdoms; but not before Ada has made Arindal swear a solemn oath that, whatever may happen, he will never curse her. If he can keep this promise and remain true to her, she promises that they will be reunited in the end.

ACT II

In Arindal's palace the warriors and citizens are lamenting their defeat, when Lora, in armour, comes out and chides them for their cowardice. All are lamenting Arindal's absence, when a messenger brings the news that he has been found.

Amid the people's jubilation, Arindal enters with Morald. They then sing a trio, in which Morald and Lora, in their joy at being reunited, look forward to victory and happiness; while Arindal, depressed and lonely, wonders how he can bear all the troubles that he sees ahead of him.

Gernot and Gunther have passed a very bad night in the midst of thunderstorms that they take as a bad omen. Gernot asks after his wife, Drolla, and Gunther assures him that she is still young and pretty.

There follows a comedy duet between Drolla and Gernot, each suspecting the other of infidelity during the eight years that they have been separated. They go off on opposite sides, saying they never wish to see each other again, but soon return and fall into each other's arms, vowing that they will never part.

Ada comes, accompanied by Farzana and Zemina, who warn her that she must choose between a mortal's death on earth and immortality in fairyland. They then leave her, while she sings a long aria. She will test Arindal to the utmost: if in his despair he curses her, she will be turned into stone for a hundred years. Honour and unending life await her in fairyland, but she cannot face the prospect of living eternally without Arindal. Her choice is made: she will stay on earth.

All the other characters, with the warriors and citizens, come thronging back: the enemy is pressing hard upon them and they must risk all upon one final battle. Arindal, to whom they naturally turn, says he has no heart to fight, and Morald takes his place as commander.

Then Ada enters, bringing her two children who throw themselves into their father's arms. When Arindal says he will never give them up, Ada, by her magic powers, causes a fiery abyss to open and threatens to throw them into it. Amid the horrified protests of all, she does so, and the abyss closes again.

The general confusion is increased when stragglers from the defeated army rush in, declaring that all is lost and nothing remains but to flee. Even the gallant Lora is completely overcome when she hears that Morald is missing – presumably killed or captured.

Harald, whom they had hoped would bring reinforcements, then arrives with the news that his men have been dispersed by an army led by a beautiful woman who declared that she was Ada, Arindal's queen. Seeing Ada herself, he affirms that it was indeed the same woman.

Now at last Arindal's faith deserts him and he curses her. Farzana and Zemina appear, declaring that Ada now belongs to the fairy world and has become immortal. She herself bitterly reproaches Arindal: all this, she says, was only to test him. If he had remained true to her, she would have become a mortal and shared the rest of her life with him. Now she must resume her immortality – but first she must endure a hundred years as a figure turned to stone. Harald intended treachery, she declares, and his warriors whom she conquered would have gone to help the enemy. (After this accusation, Harald is seized and taken away under guard.) As for Morald, he is not dead but is in process of winning a victory.

'But what of the children?' asks Arindal. At a sign from Ada they reappear, unhurt, and again embrace their father, to whose care she entrusts them.

Morald then returns, announcing that the enemy is totally destroyed. Amid the general rejoicing, only Ada and Arindal are in despair – she, because she will soon be turned to stone, and he, at the prospect of losing her for ever.

ACT III

SCENE 1   In a hall of the palace Morald and Lora are enthroned. Grief has driven Arindal insane and the victorious Morald has been chosen to succeed him, with Lora as his consort. Everyone joins in praying that Arindal may soon recover. They then go off, and Arindal enters the empty hall.

In his madness Arindal imagines that he is out hunting, and that the beautiful doe which he has killed with an arrow is really his wife. Exhausted, he falls asleep on the steps of the throne.

Dreaming, he hears the plaintive voice of the statue-Ada; then that of the magician Groma, exhorting him to save her and himself. At his feet he finds a shield, a sword and a lyre.

Farzana and Zemina come to carry Arindal off to fairyland, lest he should rescue Ada. They are convinced that he will perish in the trials which await him, and Farzana hopes that he will, but Zemina has begun to pity him.

The mere sound of Ada's voice has restored Arindal to his senses, and, vowing he is ready to fight for her, he follows his two guides.

SCENE 2   In a fearful underground cavern, fairies and earth-spirits block Arindal's way. He is already faltering, when Groma's voice calls to him: 'The shield!' As he holds it out in front of him the spirits disappear. Groma sends his own friendly spirits to accompany Arindal.

In another part of the underworld, once more a band of bronze men challenges Arindal, and this time his shield is of no avail; but on Groma's advice he draws his sword, and again his enemies vanish.

At last in a grotto he sees the enchanted Ada. Farzana warns him that, if he weakens now, he himself will be turned to stone. He is in despair, when Groma orders him to take his lyre. Immediately recovering his strength and courage he begins to play it. His magic song brings Ada back to life, and she throws herself into his arms.

SCENE 3   In his cloud-palace the Fairy King sits enthroned amid his elves and sprites. He tells Arindal that the reward of his courage will be immortality; henceforward, renouncing his earthly kingdom, he will reign with Ada in fairyland.

Morald, Lora, Drolla, Gernot and Gunther are then brought in. Arindal bequeaths his kingdom to his sister and her husband, wishing them happiness; while with Ada he mounts the throne of the Fairy King.

REVIEW

Elizabeth Forbes in the *Financial Times*, May 4, 1973, wrote of the first London performance:

'In his introduction to *Wagner Nights*, first published in 1949, Ernest Newman wrote that "the reader is hardly likely ever to see a performance of *Die Feen, Das Liebesverbot* or *Rienzi*". Times have changed, and a new generation of British opera-goers has now had the opportunity of seeing performances of all three of Wagner's early works: *Das Liebesverbot* at University College, in 1965, *Die Feen* at Birmingham in 1969, *Rienzi* at Reading two months ago. Last night London received its first performance of *Die Feen* by the Hammersmith Municipal Opera.

'*Die Feen* was Wagner's first completed opera, though it did not reach the stage until 1888, five years after the composer's death. He wrote most of it during 1833, while working at Würzburg as chorus master, and while heavily under the influence of Weber and Marschner. The latter's *Der Vampyr* (produced in February this year at Nottingham) was one of the operas for which he had to prepare the chorus at Würzburg, and this work provides the most obvious and immediate inspiration for the music of *Die Feen*.

'It is an astonishingly mature score for the first effort of a boy of 20, full of pre-echoes of the operas to come as well as many reminders of the German romantic movement then in full flood. Wagner, already his own librettist, based the text on a fable by Gozzi, *La Donna Serpente*, altering the plot to suit his own purposes. The greatest change he made was to turn his half-human, half-immortal heroine, not into a serpent, as in the original, but into stone, more than 80 years before the Emperor in *Die Frau ohne Schatten* suffered a similar fate at the hands of Strauss and Hofmannsthal.

'Joseph Vandernoot conducted a vigorous, enjoyable performance. There was not a great deal of subtlety in his reading of the score, but Wagner, in his youthful enthusiasm, poured every kind of effect into the opera except perhaps subtlety. The overture is full of splendid tunes, including one from Elisabeth's Greeting in *Tann-*

häuser. This tune turns up again in the last section of the Weber-like aria that Ada sings in the second act. The opening chorus for the Fairies in the enchanted garden jumps straight to that other magic garden in *Parsifal.* The finales to both the first and second acts bring *Lohengrin* vividly to mind.

'As Ada, Marie Hayward sang vibrantly and managed her difficult aria with apparent ease, her voice rising splendidly to the very high tessitura. Gunnar Drago, the Russian–Swedish tenor, who made such a good impression in *Maria Padilla* the other day, also produced some fine, ringing tone as Arindal. His English was excellent, though the mad scene in the last act taxed his histrionic capabilities rather a lot. Rita Chard and Emyr Green provided light relief as Drolla and Gernot, attendants to Ada and Arindal.

'The chorus had a field day, and sang with much enthusiasm as fairies, spirits, courtiers and soldiers. The small parts were all well taken, including Ada's two children, whom she pretends to kill (shades of Medea), and who were played with perfect aplomb by Oliver Gibbs and Malcolm Footer. The Fulham Municipal Orchestra, encouraged by Mr. Vandernoot, managed not to drown the singers despite the thickish scoring. There were some very nice woodwind solos. Max Miradin produced the complicated story plainly and effectively. The English translation, by Alison Murray and Terence Green, sounded adequately singable.'

NOTES

During the winter of 1832, before going to Würzburg, Wagner adapted Carlo Gozzi's comedy *La Donna Serpente* (*The Snake Woman*) into an opera libretto, calling it *Die Feen* (*The Fairies*). This tells of a fairy who, through the fault of her mortal husband, is metamorphosed into a snake and can only be disenchanted when he is induced to kiss the reptile. For this situation Wagner substituted the more practical device of a statue brought to life by the sound of the husband's despairing song.

After he had abandoned *Die Hochzeit* Wagner went steadily to work, between his duties as chorus master at Würzburg, on the composition of *Die Feen* which was completed early in 1834.

The opera was accepted for production at Leipzig by Ringelhardt, the director of the theatre, but never produced, though Wagner himself introduced the overture at Magdeburg in 1834 during his term there as conductor.

The opera was not produced until after Wagner's death; neither was it published until its production at Munich in 1888.

Though it has been revived on a few occasions on the continent, there has been no fully professional English or American production.

An English translation of the libretto by T. Reuss and A. V. Sinclair (lyrics) was published in New York in 1894.

While at Würzburg Wagner also wrote and composed an Allegro for his brother to sing as Aubry in *Der Vampyr* by Heinrich Marschner, which was revived there on September 23, 1833. (The opera was first produced at Leipzig on March 29, 1828.)

This Allegro, inserted into Aubry's aria, was published in 1914.

Wagner also wrote and composed a *Romanze in G* for insertion in *Marie, Max und Michel* by Karl Blum (Riga 1837) and an aria of Orovisto for *Norma* by Bellini (Paris 1841), both of which were also published in 1914.

DAS LIEBESVERBOT oder DIE NOVIZE VON PALERMO

(Forbidden Love or The Novice of Palermo)

———— · ————

A Grand Comic Opera in Two Acts

Libretto

Based on William Shakespeare's *Measure for Measure*. Sketched at Teplitz, June 1834. Completed at Rudolstadt, Summer, 1834.

Music

Commenced Summer, 1834. Score completed at Magdeburg, Winter, 1835–6.

Characters

(as original German libretto)

Friedrich, a German, Regent during the absence of the King of Sicily	Bass
Luzio ⎫ Two young Noblemen	Tenor
Claudio ⎭	Tenor
Antonio ⎫ Their Friends	Tenor
Angelo ⎭	Bass
Isabella, Claudio's Sister ⎱ Novices in the Convent of	Soprano
Mariana ⎰ the Order of St. Elizabeth	Soprano
Brighella, the Police Chief	Bass Buffo
Danieli, an Innkeeper	Bass
Dorella (formerly Isabella's Chambermaid) ⎱ Employed	Soprano
Pontio Pilato ⎰ by Danieli	Tenor Buffo

Chorus

Judges, Policemen, Citizens of Palermo of all Classes, Countryfolk, Carnival Revellers, a Band of Musicians.

Scene

Palermo in the Sixteenth Century.

ACT I SCENE I A Suburb of Palermo: outside Danieli's Tavern.
      SCENE 2 Cloister-Garden of the Nuns of the Order of St. Elizabeth.
      SCENE 3 A Law-Court, with Platforms and Galleries.
ACT II SCENE I The Prison Garden.
      SCENE 2 A Room in Friedrich's Palace.
      SCENE 3 A Public Garden at the end of the Corso.

FIRST PRODUCED. Stadttheater, Magdeburg, March 29, 1836.
FIRST PRODUCED IN ENGLAND (in an abridged version) at the Collegiate Theatre, University College, London, February 16, 1965 in a translation by Edward Dent by the Music Society (4 Student performances)
No production in America is traceable.

DAS LIEBESVERBOT oder DIE NOVIZE VON PALERMO (FORBIDDEN LOVE or THE NOVICE OF PALERMO) – CASTS

CHARACTERS	MAGDEBURG 1836	LONDON 1965
Friedrich	Krug	Howard Bentley
Luzio	Freimüller	Graham Hale
Claudio	Schreiber	Terry Jenkins
Antonio	–	Philip Fryer
Angelo	–	
Isabella	Pollert	Wendy Davies
Mariana	Schindler	Pamela Jackson
Brighella	Unzelmann Jr.	Michael Kallipetis
Danieli	–	Paul Beech
Dorella	Limbach	Joanna Darlington
Pontio Pilato	–	Richard Virden
Conductor	Richard Wagner	George Badacsonyi
Producer	Richard Wagner	George Roman
Designer	–	George Roman
Costumes	–	Sue Yelland

SYNOPSIS

ACT I

SCENE 1   In a popular quarter of Palermo, a troop of police commanded by Brighella are raiding the taverns and bawdy-houses. There is tumult as people try to prevent them. Pushed out of Danieli's inn, the young nobleman Luzio and his friends Angelo and Antonio are half-laughing and half-indignant. When the innkeeper himself, his potman Pontio and barmaid Dorella, are brought out under arrest, Dorella calls for help to Luzio, who has flirted with her in the past and even promised her marriage. Backed up by the indignant populace, Luzio demands what authority Brighella has for his action. The police chief reads a decree signed by the Regent Friedrich – a German who in the King's absence is governing the country – ordering the closure of all houses of public entertainment, and declaring that drinking and wenching are crimes punishable by death.

This is greeted with derisive laughter by the gay Sicilians; but matters take a serious turn when Claudio is dragged in as a prisoner – the first to be condemned under the new law. He is to be executed next day. There is only one hope: he begs Luzio to visit his sister Isabella, who has recently become a novice, and persuade her to appeal to the Regent on his behalf.

SCENE 2   Isabella is sitting in the cloister garden with another novice – her friend Mariana. As they listen to the nuns singing, they rejoice in the peace and safety of their new life. Questioned by Isabella, Mariana confesses that unhappy love has brought her to the convent: she has been secretly married to a man who, through ambition, has repudiated her, and her unworthy husband is – the hypocritically virtuous Regent Friedrich!

An urgent knocking is heard at the outer door. Mariana slips away, while Isabella goes to admit the visitor. Startled to see a man, she veils herself and is about to escape, when Luzio detains her, giving her Claudio's message. Reluctantly, she agrees to go and appeal to Friedrich. In her agitation she has raised her veil, and

Luzio is overcome by her beauty. He begs her to leave the cloister for ever and marry him. Isabella indignantly rejects the proposal, but agrees to accept his escort.

SCENE 3 The people arrested on the previous day are being tried by Brighella – rather embarrassed by his new powers, but determined to keep in favour with the Regent. First, the terrified Pontio is condemned to banishment; but Dorella, knowing that Brighella has a weakness for her, laughs in his face, and her 'trial' ends in a scene of flirtation. Meanwhile, the other prisoners waiting outside grow impatient. With the help of the populace they break open the door, and the situation is getting out of hand when Friedrich appears and quietens the tumult. Unconditionally rejecting the people's plea to keep their Carnival (which he has banned), he proceeds to take charge of the trial himself.

Claudio is brought in, and Friedrich pronounces the death-sentence upon him and his absent partner in sin, Julia. At this moment Isabella appears with Luzio and makes her plea for mercy. Struck by her beauty, Friedrich has the court cleared and makes his proposal to her: in exchange for her favours, Claudio shall go free. Isabella, horrified, calls the people back, intending to unmask the hypocrite; but Ferdinand persuades her that no one will believe her story. When they ask what has happened, she remains silent and waves them back.

Isabella has a sudden inspiration: she remembers Mariana, Friedrich's secretly wedded wife, and sees a way of bringing the couple together and at the same time saving her own honour. Quickly, she gives the Regent the promise he requires, telling him that she will write later to give him the place and time of their rendezvous.

When the crowd return, Friedrich still declares that the death-sentence must stand; but Isabella only laughs and jests so wildly that they think she has gone mad.

ACT II

SCENE 1 Visiting her brother in the prison garden, Isabella tells him the bargain that she has made. He at first declares that he would rather die than see her dishonoured, but soon shows that this is only an attitude. Before long he is imploring her to save him at any cost; when she turns upon him indignantly he goes back into the prison, convinced that she will let him die. To punish him for his cowardice, Isabella decides to leave him all night in uncertainty as to his fate.

Dorella, set free through Isabella's influence, comes to thank her, and they decide to make use of Brighella's infatuation for the pretty servant-girl. Then Luzio comes to fetch Isabella, and, slyly, Dorella reveals his flirtation with herself and his promise to marry her. He too deserves punishment, decides Isabella; so she lightheartedly tells him of her assignation with Friedrich, leaving him frantic with rage.

A comedy scene in prose then follows between Luzio and Pontio, upon whom the young man works off his fury. As the servant calls for help, a band of policemen appear: Luzio escapes by leaping over a wall, so they take hold of Pontio and drag him off.

SCENE 2   Friedrich, alone in his room, is impatiently awaiting news, when Brighella brings in Dorella, bearing the longed-for note, in which Isabella tells him to meet her, in carnival disguise, on the Corso that night. Though angry and embarrassed at being thus obliged to break his own ban, Friedrich is willing to do even this; but he decides not to keep his side of the bargain. He decides that Claudio, in any case, shall die.

Brighella and Dorella then come forward and play a comedy love-scene. The girl induces him to agree to come to the forbidden carnival that evening disguised as Pierrot, promising that she herself will be his Columbine.

SCENE 3   Danieli has set up a refreshment tent at the end of the Corso. The gardens of the pleasure-houses are thronged by a motley crowd, many of them in fancy dress. All are determined to enjoy themselves, despite the ban. Antonio, Angelo and Danieli encourage them, and even the distracted Luzio sings a gay song.

When Brighella comes with his squad, the revellers disperse, followed by the policemen. He himself, remaining alone, quickly dons his Pierrot costume and looks around for Dorella.

Meanwhile, Isabella and Mariana, in identical costumes, step out. Mariana is tremulous, but her friend encourages her with the thought that she is at last going to celebrate her delayed honeymoon. Then she slips away. Friedrich appears in disguise, followed by Luzio who accosts him as a fellow-reveller, making a series of rude remarks about the Regent and his attempt to stop the carnival. Grudgingly,

Friedrich has to agree that he himself is a fool, a hypocrite and a scoundrel.

Seeing Mariana (whom he takes for Isabella) Friedrich breaks away and hurries after her. When Luzio tries to follow, he is detained by Dorella: they are watched from one side by the concealed Isabella and from the other by Brighella. In his rage at Isabella's supposed misconduct, Luzio renews his oath to Dorella, kisses her, and then rushes off in pursuit of Friedrich.

Isabella and Brighella then step out, the one feigning indignation and the other really enraged, and Dorella runs away in alarm.

Pontio then comes in, bringing Isabella the parchment which supposedly contains her brother's pardon. Suspicious, she opens it and finds that it is in fact a confirmation of the death-sentence. Indignantly, she once more calls the crowd to witness Friedrich's duplicity, and this time is not diverted from her purpose. Luzio, however, declares that she is telling lies, and the crowd remain in doubt, uncertain which to believe.

Coming out of the pavilion where they have been together, Friedrich and Mariana are seized and unmasked – to the great surprise of all present, and to that of Friedrich himself, who now for the first time recognises his lawful wife. The people, full of indignation, are ready to take violent action against him, but Isabella explains the trick that she has played. Friedrich himself is ready to pay the penalty under his own law, but the Sicilians are more merciful than he. They decide to let him go unpunished, and rush off to free Claudio and bring him back in triumph.

Meanwhile, Brighella and Dorella, in their disguises, are brought in by the policemen, to everyone's great amusement. Luzio now has pardoned Isabella, and will not hear of her proposal to go back to the cloister. Amid the general rejoicing comes the news that the King has unexpectedly returned, and the scene ends with a joyful carnival procession, led off by Friedrich and Mariana.

REVIEW

Colin Mason in *The Daily Telegraph*, February 17, 1965, wrote of the first English performance:

'Wagner's early opera "Das Liebesverbot" ("The Ban on Love", adapted from "Measure for Measure") was staged for the first time in this country last night at University College, London.

'It is more interesting for its relationship to the past than for glimpses of the future Wagner.

'The composer himself wrote in his autobiography of Bellini's "contribution" to it. Generally it is much closer to Italian models than to Wagner's German forebears, with surprisingly guileless florid flutings for the singers.

'Yet there are already hints of his mature "symphonic" method. Even in the heavily cut version performed here an instinctive mastery of operatic and theatrical craft could often be observed.

'The work is also enjoyable for its melodic freshness and fertility. Although much of the music, lacking anything specifically Wagnerian to replace the rejected Bellinian essence, is rather characterless (some of it might almost be Sullivan) it is all attractive enough.

'A complete version, well done, would certainly be worth hearing and seeing. Last night's student performance, conducted with immense gusto by George Badacsonyi, did not rise above the "heroic effort" class.

'But it was so full of life and fervour, as well as comedy, intentional and unintentional, and communicated the spirit of the work so zestfully, that all the indulgence needed was readily forthcoming.'

When the opera was revived at Bayreuth in August 1972, Peter Stadlen, in *The Daily Telegraph* (August 12), reported:

'I suspect it is because Wagner himself, later in life, strenuously disowned "Das Liebesverbot" ("The Ban on Love") that no one ever has a good word to say about it.

'The Bayreuth Festival is always eager to deepen our understanding of the master.

'It closed the gates of the Festspielhaus last night in order to focus attention on the revival of Wagner's second opera by this year's Bayreuth International Youth Rally at the City Hall.

'An aptly chosen set-up, for in his 21st year that phenomenally gifted theatre kapellmeister did not yet regard the Fatherland as the measure of all things. Hell-bent on success, he decided that a German composer's best bet was to try to beat the French and Italians at their own game.

'And indeed, the starkly undisguised styles of Bellini, Donizetti and Auber are often used with such verve and inventiveness that I would defy any devotee to tell this score from the genuine article. Except where Wagner's grand comic opera is rendered the more dramatic – and the more comic – through an occasional trailer of things to come, of Lohengrin's Elsa, for example, or Tannhäuser's Elisabeth in the big arias of Isabella.

'In Wagner's libretto, derived as loosely from "Measure for Measure" as Gounod's "Faust" is from Goethe's, Shakespeare merely provides the framework for a romantic tribute to the ideal of unhampered sensuality.

'The plot is also shot through with vaguely revolutionary Pan-European sentiments that yield lusty chorus clashes between the libertine populace and the forces of repression. The revelling Sicilians (not the Viennese) are ruled over not by Angelo but by the equally hypocritical German Friedrich – further proof of young Wagner's freedom from chauvinist prejudice.

'The Swiss designer, Roland Aeschlimann, very properly set out right away to deprave and corrupt through the choice of Michelangelo's "Leda and the Swan" for his first backcloth.

'A large cast of aspiring young singers, who included Martin Peters, as Luzio, and Horst Lorig, as Brighella, was led by Anne Conoley as Isabella, Elaine Watts (Mariana) and Anna Bernardin (Dorella), all three of them students at the London Opera Centre.

'The English conductor, John Bell, currently at Krefeld, worked wonders with the motley forces assembled for the occasion. Horst Reday gallantly stepped in for the Czech producer Emil Vokalek, who had failed to turn up.'

NOTES

After leaving Würzburg, Wagner commenced work on an adaptation of Shakespeare's *Measure for Measure* under the title *Das Liebesverbot* (*Forbidden Love*). The poem was sketched at Teplitz in June 1834 and completed at Rudolstadt in the following months. Wagner then commenced his engagement as conductor at the Magdeburg theatre and worked on the composition of the opera during the next year, eventually completing it early in 1836. It was announced for production at Magdeburg, under his own direction, for March 27, the Sunday of Holy week and caused Wagner's first clash with authority. Exception was taken to the title and that it was described as a 'Grand Comic Opera'. The police at once banned it, but after some discussion they were convinced that an opera, with a Shakespearean plot, must of necessity be highly respectable and the ban was lifted. A new title, *Die Novize von Palermo* (*The Novice of Palermo*) was substituted and the description 'Comic' dropped.

The first performance took place on March 29 and ended in chaos. For Wagner's benefit a second was announced for the following day but this did not take place. Just before the rise of the curtain, one of the members of the company accused another of having made advances to his wife; this resulted in a fight, in which most of the company joined, with the result that the performance was cancelled and the audience dismissed.

Wagner tried in vain to get the opera produced in Leipzig and Berlin and it was not revived until 1923, in Munich. The score and libretto had been published the previous year. In 1933 the opera was given in Berlin and later in some other German towns.* It has not been performed professionally in either England or America.

It was during Wagner's stay at Lauchstädt that he met Wilhelmine Planer (Minna), the juvenile lead in the company. When she left to

* It was revived as a 'fringe' attraction at the Bayreuth Festival in 1972 by the International Youth Festival at the City Hall. The London production in 1965 was a severely cut version (the original in two acts would run for some four hours). It was rearranged into 3 acts, dividing the original first act into two parts.

play at Königsberg, she arranged for Wagner to join this company as conductor and it was here that they were married in November 1836.

There are three overtures which date from this period: *Columbus* (for Apel's play, Magdeburg, 1835) *Rule Britannia* (written 1837 and performed at Königsberg, 1837) and *Polonia* (commenced 1832 and finished 1836) and an opera libretto (composed 1836–7) *Die Hohe Braut oder Bianca und Giuseppe* (*The Noble Bride or Bianca and Giuseppe*). This four act tragic opera (based on a novel by Heinrich König) was never set to music by Wagner himself, though a score was composed by Johann Kittl and the opera produced as *Bianca und Giuseppe oder Die Franzosen vor Nizza* (*Bianca and Giuseppe or the French before Nice*) at Prague on February 19, 1848.

The text was revised for Carl Reissiger at Dresden in 1842, but not used. Also at this period Wagner wrote the text of a two act comic opera *Männerlist Grösser als Frauenlist oder die Glückliche Bärenfamilie* (*Men are More Cunning than Women or the Happy Family of Bears*).

Early in 1837, the company at Königsberg failed and Wagner was appointed conductor of the newly formed Opera at Riga.

RIENZI DER LETZTE DER TRIBUNEN

(Rienzi the Last of the Tribunes)

——————— · ———————

A Grand Tragic Opera in Five Acts

Libretto

Based on the novel of the same title by Edward Bulwer-Lytton.
Sketched Leipzig, Summer, 1837.
Poem written in Riga, July 24–August 6, 1838.

Music

Commenced August 1838 and continued till September 12, 1839.
Laid aside until February 15, 1840, and completed in Paris, November 19, 1840.

Characters

Cola Rienzi, Papal Notary	Tenor
Irene, his Sister	Soprano
Steffano Colonna, Head of the Colonna Family	Bass
Adriano, his son	Mezzo-soprano
Paolo Orsini, Head of the Orsini Family	Bass
Raimondo, Papal Legate	Bass
Cecco del Vecchio ⎫ Roman Citizens	Bass
Baroncelli ⎭	Tenor
A Messenger of Peace	Soprano

Chorus

Ambassadors of the Lombard States, Naples, Bavaria, Bohemia, etc.;
Roman Nobles; Roman citizens, Male and Female; Messengers of
Peace; Priests and Monks of all Orders; Roman Police.

Scene

Rome in the Middle of the Fourteenth Century.
ACT I A Street in Rome.
ACT II A Great Hall in the Capitol.
ACT III A Square in the Ancient Forum.

ACT IV A Square in front of the Lateran.
ACT V SCENE 1 A Hall in the Capitol.
　　　　SCENE 2 A Square in front of the Capitol.

FIRST PRODUCED. Hoftheater, Dresden, October 20, 1842.
FIRST PRODUCED IN AMERICA. Academy of Music, New York, March
　　4, 1878. Sung in German by the Pappenheim Opera Company.
　　No production in English traceable.
FIRST PRODUCED IN ENGLAND. Her Majesty's Theatre, London,
　　January 27, 1879. Sung in English in a translation by John P.
　　Jackson, by the Carl Rosa Opera Company.
　　No production in German is traceable.

RIENZI DER LETZTE DER TRIBUNEN
(RIENZI THE LAST OF THE TRIBUNES) – CASTS

CHARACTERS	DRESDEN 1842	NEW YORK 1878 (in German)	LONDON 1879 (in English)
Cola Rienzi	Joseph Tichatschek	Charles R. Adams	Joseph Maas
Irene	Henriette Wüst	Alexandre Human	Helene Crosmond
Steffano Colonna	Wilhelm Dettmer	Heinrich Wiegand	George Olmi
Adriano	Wilhelmine Schröder-Devrient	Eugénie Pappenheim	Jennie Vanzini
Paolo Orsini	Michael Wächter	Alois Blum	Walter Bolton
Raimondo	Giovanni Vestri	F. Adolphe	Henry Pope
Baroncelli	Reinhold		Cadwallader
Cecco del Vecchio	Carl Risse	E. Cooney	G. H. Snazelle
A Messenger of Peace	Anna Thiele	Not named	Georgina Burns
A Herald	Not named		Muller
Conductor	Carl Gottlieb Reissiger	Max Menetzek	Carl Rosa
Producer	Wilhelm Fischer		
Designer	*Scenery*		*Scenery*
	Arigoni		Walter Hann
	Costumes		*Costumes*
	Ferdinand Heine		Ascoli

SYNOPSIS

Paolo Orsini, head of the great Roman family, has come with a band of followers to carry off Rienzi's sister Irene. Entering by a ladder, they seize the girl and bring her out, screaming for help. As they are about to drag her away, Steffano Colonna, with his son Adriano and several men, intervene. The Colonnas – hereditary enemies of the Orsini – think it good sport to snatch away their prize; but Adriano, recognising Irene whom he loves, assures her of his protection. Both parties come to blows, and the crowd that has gathered joins in the mêlée; but the fight is interrupted by the Papal Legate, Cardinal Raimondo, who sternly orders them to keep the peace. Orsini and Colonna defy him, and the brawl breaks out again – to be stopped immediately by the arrival of Rienzi, with his friends Baroncelli and Cecco. The Nobles are astonished at Rienzi's air of authority and the influence he obviously exerts over the citizens.

Irene hurries to her brother's side, and he, realising what has happened, bitterly reproaches the Nobles for their attempted abduction. They insult and jeer at him and then go off, arranging to settle their quarrel outside the city gates at dawn next day. Raimondo, Rienzi's friends and the crowd all urge him to take command and free the city from the tyranny of the great families, with their constant brawls.

Remaining alone with Irene and Adriano, Rienzi hears how the young Colonna has protected his sister. When Adriano asks why he desires power, Rienzi replies that it is to make Rome free and great, and to rescue its citizens from oppression. He tells how he has sworn to avenge his own young brother, murdered by a Colonna. Deeply ashamed, Adriano asks how he can make amends, and Rienzi suggests that the young man shall join him, as a free citizen of Rome. He then entrusts his sister to Adriano and leaves them together. They declare their love for each other in a duet, but the embrace that concludes it is cut short by a peal of trumpets.

The crowd comes back, greatly excited; an organ plays in the nearby Lateran church, and the congregation is heard singing a hymn to Freedom. They fall on their knees as the great doors open and Rienzi appears on the steps, declaring that Rome shall be free. When the people hail him as King of Rome he refuses the title: the city shall be governed by a Senate, he says, and he himself will be the People's Tribune. Baroncelli and Cecco lead the crowd in acclaiming him as such.

ACT II

This takes place in a great hall in the Capitol, and the curtain rises on a triumphal song by the patrician youths whom Rienzi has sent out to bear his message of peace throughout Italy. Clad in white, with wreaths in their hair and silver staves in their hands, they celebrate the success of their mission. As they file out, Colonna, Orsini and other Nobles enter, greeting Rienzi with grudging respect. He tells them sternly that they must dismantle their castles and abide by the laws, just as the plebeians do; then he invites them to a feast.

Colonna and Orsini have now banded together against their common enemy, Rienzi. Their plot to assassinate him is overheard by Adriano, who tries in vain to dissuade them. Colonna calls his son a traitor and curses him. Repulsed by all, the distracted Adriano hesitates whether he ought to save Irene's brother at the risk of his own father's life.

Escorted by a large crowd, Rienzi arrives with Baroncelli and Cecco. He greets everybody and graciously receives the foreign Ambassadors who have brought him messages from abroad. They and the Nobles are taken aback when he declares, in the name of the Roman people, that Rome has the historic right to elect the German Emperor.

While preparations are being made for the feast, Adriano takes the opportunity of warning Rienzi about the plot. The Tribune replies calmly that he does not fear assassination, as he is wearing steel under his doublet.

An elaborate ballet then takes place, with men in antique costumes performing gladiatorial combats, and military manœuvres. Threatened by a troop of mounted men, they are urged to resist by a performer representing Brutus, and they defeat the invaders. A bevy of maidens appears, some clad in ancient Roman costume and some in contemporary dress. The Goddess of Peace reconciles them, and they crown each other with festive wreaths, dancing in pairs – one ancient Roman with one modern; while the Goddess unfurls the colours of the new Rome – blue and white, with silver stars.

During this ballet Orsini, with some of the Nobles, has stealthily approached Rienzi. He suddenly draws a dagger and, despite Adriano's intervention, stabs him – harmlessly. Rienzi's guards rush in and overpower the Nobles.

Opening his tunic to show the breastplate beneath, Rienzi tells the disconcerted Nobles that he was prepared for their attack. He sends the crowd away, saying that the festivities are over and judgment must now be pronounced. His friends and Senators remain, to form a Court of Justice.

Baroncelli announces that Colonna's men have made a hasty and abortive attempt to seize the Capitol. The Senators agree that the Nobles are guilty of high treason and shall be executed. They are led, under guard, into an inner room.

While a choir of Monks chant the death-prayers within, Adriano and Irene plead for Colonna's life. At a sign from Rienzi the curtain hiding the inner room is lifted, showing the Nobles on their knees; while at the same time the crowd burst in, shouting 'Death to the Traitors!' Rienzi declares that vengeance belongs to Heaven, and that he will pardon the Nobles, on condition that they remain as hostages for their good behaviour.

The Act ends with an *ensemble*, in which Adriano and Irene praise Rienzi's clemency, his friends express their misgivings, the humiliated Nobles plan future vengeance, and the crowd hail Rienzi as a hero of Peace.

ACT III

Church bells are ringing a tocsin, and the ruins of the Forum are filled with an excited crowd calling for Rienzi: the hostages have fled and are expected to attack. The Tribune appears, expressing his surprise and anger at the revolt of the Nobles. He calls the people to arms, giving them the battle cry: 'Santo Spirito, Cavaliere!' Trumpets sound the alarm, as the people rush off to arm themselves.

Adriano, left alone, listens in deep distress to the tocsin. Faced with the alternative of fighting against his own father or of betraying Irene's brother, he decides to escape, seek out Colonna and try to bring about a reconciliation.

A grand procession then arrives. At the head is Rienzi, mounted, in full armour, with Irene beside him. Then come the Senators and the armed citizens; accompanying them are the women and girls, the children and old men. The warriors sing a battle hymn with the refrain: 'Santo Spirito, Cavaliere.'

Adriano beseeches Rienzi to send him as an ambassador to his father, but the Tribune fiercely refuses, saying: 'Let Fate take its course!' The men go off, singing, while Adriano remains behind with Irene and the other women. He says farewell to Irene, declaring that Death is calling him, but at last yields to her entreaties and stays with her. They join the women in praying for victory, and as they end their supplication they hear the song of the returning citizens.

Rienzi enters in triumph – his victory is complete. Orsini and Colonna have both been killed, and their bodies are borne back on litters. With a cry of despair Adriano flings himself on his father's body; then rises, curses Rienzi and rushes out, vowing revenge.

A triumphal chariot, on the ancient model, is brought for the Tribune, who mounts it and crowns himself with a laurel wreath, amid the plaudits of the crowd.

ACT IV

Cecco and Baroncelli, with a following of citizens, have been convened by a mysterious stranger to meet him in the square in front of the Lateran church. Meanwhile, they discuss the political situation. They are concerned because the Germans, angered at Rienzi's interference with the election of their Emperor, have withdrawn their Ambassador from Rome. The new Emperor is on good terms with the Pope, who, as Colonna's protector, is incensed against Rienzi because of his death. Cardinal Raimondo has also put himself under the protection of the Vatican. Baroncelli suspects that Rienzi intends to ally himself with the Nobles by offering his sister to Adriano as the price of a reconciliation. The crowd, regarding this as a betrayal, ask if there is any witness to confirm the statement.

'Yes!' exclaims Adriano, throwing off his disguise and stepping out from among the crowd: 'Colonna's son!' He declares that the Tribune is unworthy, is already out of favour with the Emperor and the Church, and spurs his listeners to be revenged on him. Rienzi has arranged a solemn Te Deum to celebrate his victory, and this will be the ideal opportunity.

As the conspirators turn to go, they are amazed to see Cardinal Raimondo entering the church, with a train of priests and monks.

Apparently, he has not only returned, but intends to perform the service himself.

Then Rienzi in festal garb, leading Irene by the hand, appears at the head of a jubilant procession. The conspirators have placed themselves in the church entrance, so that the entering procession must pass between their ranks; and Rienzi, seeing the waiting men, challenges them. Adriano, who cannot bring himself to kill the Tribune in Irene's presence, does nothing, and the others are won over by Rienzi's impassioned declaration that the men he has slain were their enemies and those of Rome. They throw their hats in the air and cheer him. Thus deserted by his allies, Adriano is nerving himself to strike, when the doors of the church open and, instead of the expected Te Deum, the priests and monks are heard chanting a solemn curse.

Raimondo appears on the steps and announces that Rienzi is excommunicated and may not enter the church, and the great doors are shut in his face. His followers, aghast, slink away, leaving the Tribune alone with his sister and Adriano. The young man begs Irene to flee with him, but she refuses and throws herself into her brother's arms. Exclaiming: 'Perish, then, with him!' Adriano rushes away. Brother and sister remain together, listening to the litany of the monks.

ACT V

SCENE I   Rienzi, kneeling at a house-altar, prays God to raise him from the depths into which he has fallen. When Irene joins him, he says he has been deserted by all: the Church, for whom his work was first begun; the citizens, whom he has tried to make free and happy; his fair-weather friends: she alone remains true to him. She reiterates her devotion, saying that she will not desert the last of the Romans, though it should cost her both life and love. He answers that his own love has been solely Rome; but he advises her to leave him and join Adriano. Irene proudly refuses and, after a fond embrace, Rienzi goes to put on his armour.

The rest of the scene is played against a background of increasing noise from the crowd outside; while the growing darkness is lit by the glare of their torches. Adriano, muffled in his cloak and grasping a drawn sword, enters in a state of great excitement. Once more he implores Irene to escape, and again she refuses. He tries to drag her away by force, but she breaks away and runs out.

...ie Feen' – Designs by the Viennese ...ists Brioschi and Burghart for the first ...oduction in Munich, 1888 (Munich ...eatre Museum).

Playbill for the first production of 'Der fliegende Holländer' at the Court Theatre, Dresden in 1843.

...enzi' Act 2 – Illustration by D. H. Friston of the first production in England, by the Carl ...sa Opera Company, at Her Majesty's Theatre, London in 1879.

'Rienzi' – Wood-cut of the final scene of Act 4 from the first production in Dresden, 184

'Der fliegende Holländer' – Wood-cut of the final scene from the original Dresden produc

Illustration by D. H. Friston of a scene from the first English language production of 'Der fliegende Holländer' at the Royal Lyceum Theatre, London in 1876.

'Lohengrin' – Illustration (from the *Illustrierte Zeitung*) of the first performance conducted by Franz Liszt at Weimar in 1850.

'Tannhäuser' – Act 2 of the first production at Dresden in 1845. After a watercolour by Wilhelm Heine.

'Tannhäuser' – Design by Max Brückner for the 1891 Bayreuth production.

'Tannhäuser' Act 1 – Illustration by Theodor Tischbein of the first production at Dresden in 1845 with Wilhelmine Schröder-Devrient as Venus and Joseph Tichatschek as Tannhäuser (Richard Wagner Gedenkstätte, Bayreuth).

igns by Angelo Quaglio for the 1867 nich production of 'Lohengrin'.

Lohengrin' Act 2 – Illustration by Theodor Pixis from the 1861 Munich production.

'Das Rheingold' Scene 1 – On the Bed of the Rhine. Painting by Josef Hoffmann after hi[s]
designs for the 1876 Bayreuth production.

Lilli and Marie Lehmann and Minna Lammert as the Rhine maidens in the first scene of 'Da[s]
Rheingold' at Bayreuth in 1876.

'Das Rheingold' Scene 3 – Josef Hoffmann's painting of the *Nibelheim* after his original stage designs for the Bayreuth production, 1876.

'Die Walküre' Act 3 – The Ride of the Valkyries. Illustration by Theodor Pixis after the original Munich production in 1870.

'Die Walküre' Act 1 – Josef Hoffmann's painting of the 1876 Bayreuth production.

'Die Walküre' Act 2 – Painting by Josef Hoffmann.

SCENE 2   The scene now changes to a square before the Capitol, of which the great stairs rise in the background. Bands of citizens are rushing about with torches, among them are Baroncelli and Cecco. When Rienzi, in full armour but bare-headed, appears on a high balcony with Irene, they refuse to listen and prepare to stone him. Meanwhile, the building has been set on fire. In a last impassioned speech Rienzi declares that his fame will endure as long as the Seven Hills of Rome. Flames rise towards the balcony where he and Irene wait, clasped in each other's arms.

At the head of a troop of Nobles, Adriano drives back the citizens and attempts a rescue. But as he approaches the building it collapses, burying him with Rienzi and Irene in the ruins.

REVIEW

The Music Critic in *The Era*, February 2, 1879, wrote of the first English performance:

'Monday night will be a memorable one for opera-goers, and especially for those who patronise opera in English. The first performance in England of a work so important as Wagner's *Rienzi* naturally attracted all musical London, and everybody expressed the utmost admiration of the enterprise, pluck, and good taste Mr. Carl Rosa had shown in venturing to represent so elaborate a work for the first time in England, and at an establishment like Her Majesty's Theatre. . . .

'It was at Dresden in 1837 that Wagner, after reading Bulwer's story "Rienzi," first conceived the idea of making an opera upon the subject. He came afterwards with the score of this work to Paris in the hope of getting it produced there. He says of the work himself in after life – "Rienzi, with his grand thoughts in his brain and in his heart, living in an era of rudeness and depravity, excited and attracted all my sympathy and admiration; yet my plan for the opera sprang first from the conviction of a pure lyrical element in the atmosphere of the hero. The Messengers of Peace, the Call to Arms by the Clergy, the Battle Hymn, induced me to the composition of the opera of *Rienzi*. The work was conceived and executed under the influence of my earliest impressions received from Spontini's heroic operas and from the glittering *genre* of the Parisian Grand Opera as represented by Auber, Meyerbeer, and Halévy. I completed *Rienzi* during my first sojourn in Paris; I had the splendid 'Grand Opera' before me, and my ambition was not only to imitate, but, with reckless extravagance, to surpass all that had gone before, in brilliant finales, hymns, processions, and the musical clang of arms." . . .

'Wagner's own opinion of the music we may frankly state hardly does himself justice. We know, however, that, pinning their faith upon music of a different character, Wagner and his disciples attempt to repudiate *Rienzi* altogether, and date the first "music of the future" from *The Flying Dutchman*. Judging of the score apart from all theories, we are prepared to admire greatly some portions of the music. It would not be easy in modern operas to select a more expressive or legitimate melody than the beautiful Prayer of Rienzi, for example, the instrumentation of which is very charming indeed, and thoroughly expressive of the sentiment. The double chorus at the conclusion of the first act is another item which displays genuine dramatic power. No composer at any period of his career need be ashamed of having written such a movement, and the clearness in the division of the choral parts cannot fail to be much admired. The duet for Adriano and Irene is quite in the light Italian school, but the lovely chorus of the Messengers of Peace is equal to almost anything that Wagner has written since. The delicious flow of melody and the freshness and purity of the style must impress the dullest hearer. The solo also was very beautiful. The *finale* to the second act is, perhaps, the most ambitiously constructed piece in the opera, and, while reminding us of Meyerbeer, there is much in it exclusively Wagner's own. Especially powerful and effective are the choral combinations, and the individuality of the passages where the nobles continue their plotting against Rienzi, even after he has pardoned their attempt on his life, must be warmly praised for its dramatic as well as musical significance. The "Battle Hymn" of the third act is terribly noisy we grant, but all must allow that it is admirably suited to the situation. The march will be voted very meagre in idea when compared with Wagner's later efforts of a similar kind, but nevertheless it answers its purpose, and is sufficiently telling. Altogether the score is unequal as will readily be imagined when we remember that the composer was a beginner rather than an experienced composer when he wrote *Rienzi*. Few make such beginnings, and if such an opera were produced for the first time at the present day we should look forward to the career of the composer with the deepest interest. We may notice, ere we conclude our remarks upon the music, that we have in *Rienzi* the first hints of the prolonged recitative which he afterwards used so freely, and this recitative, with other passages hardly likely to captivate the public, Mr. Carl Rosa has with admirable tact and judgment pruned rather freely, as is shown by the compression of the five acts into four, which, as the opera lasted from half-past seven until half-past eleven, was found quite long enough for the most eager musical appetite. We must praise without reserve the manner in which the work was put upon the stage. The scenery was truly magnificent, especially in the concluding act. The view of the Capitol and the exciting scene of the conflagration so astonished and delighted the audience that the scenic artist was called before the curtain. In fact, everybody was similarly complimented, and Mr. Carl Rosa (never in haste to seek public compliments, although few men have done so much to deserve them), was compelled more than once to come forward and bow his thanks for the very flattering applause bestowed upon him. He conducted the opera with the utmost skill and care, and his orchestra and chorus could not have been better. Mr. Carrodus, as usual, lent valuable assistance as first violin, and Mr. Betjemann upon the stage proved his value. The ballet was charming, and many of the *tableaux* in the gorgeous scene in the second act displayed rare taste, especially that in which the group of gladiators was raised and borne round the stage upon the shields of the soldiery, while flags and trophies were displayed in profusion. It remains for us now to speak of the chief *artistes*. Mr. Joseph Maas as Rienzi was very successful, although he has hardly the physical power required for such an exacting part.

'The voice of a Tamberlik, Wachtel, or Duprez is needed to do the fullest justice to it, but in all other respects Mr. Maas deserved the warmest commendation. He delivered the exacting recitatives clearly, and sang the Prayer with charming expression; while his appearance was excellent and his acting far more intelligent and refined than that of most tenors. Mr. Walter Bolton had not the fullest scope for the display of his great ability, but he made the character of Orsini striking and effective, particularly in the scene where Rienzi is stabbed. Mr. Bolton sang admirably. Mr. George Olmi was efficient as Colonna; and Mr. Henry Pope was a careful representative of the Papal Legate. Mr. Snazelle, Mr. Cadwallader, and Mr. Muller all acquitted themselves well. Madame Helene Crosmond had some trying music to sing as Irene, for even in his earlier style Wagner showed little mercy to the vocalists. She may be fairly congratulated upon her success; while as Adriano, the lover of Irene, Madame Vanzini proved a great acquisition to the company, her voice being pure and powerful, while her acting had plenty of animation and energy. If anything, she was almost too anxious in the earlier scenes of the opera, and her voice became fatigued in consequence. But there could be no question as to Madame Vanzini's success. The singing of the beautiful solo of the Messenger of Peace, by Miss Georgina Burns, was really exquisite. She sang with the

utmost purity, and the effect was charming. The audience was large
and enthusiastic, and before the curtain rose the National Anthem
was given by the band and chorus. We think it cannot be doubted
that the night was, as we have already suggested, a memorable one.
Mr. Carl Rosa has our warmest congratulations.'

NOTES

During his engagement at Riga, Wagner decided that his only chance of success in the field of opera was to compose a grand tragic opera, in the manner of Meyerbeer, for production in Paris.

With this in mind, he chose as his subject the novel *Rienzi* by Edward Bulwer-Lytton, which had been published in England in 1835. Wagner worked on the libretto during the summers of 1837 and 1838, and commenced the music in August 1838, working on it until the autumn of the following year.

Meantime he wrote to Scribe in Paris suggesting a translation, with the condition of production at the Opéra! As this was naturally without result and his contract at Riga was ending, he decided to go himself to Paris, to see what he could do on the spot.

In July 1839 he left Riga by sea with his wife, en route for Paris via London. The voyage was exceptionally stormy and dangerous, they were forced to seek shelter in a Norwegian port and were nearly a month in reaching London. After a short stay they travelled on to Boulogne where Wagner met Meyerbeer, who gave him letters of introduction to musicians and publishers, and they eventually arrived in Paris in September.

During the months that followed, the composer was quite unable to make any headway or get his opera accepted and he and Minna lived in dire poverty; while she took in lodgers, he did hack work arranging dance music, preparing piano scores of other composers' operas (even Donizetti!), and writing articles for musical papers.

Eventually he completed *Rienzi* between July and November 1840 sending it hopefully to Dresden. When it was, at last, accepted for production there, Wagner left Paris in April 1842 to superintend rehearsals.

The opera was presented with great success in October and this led to Wagner's appointment as conductor of the Opera House in February 1843.

Rienzi, as already noted, a long opera, was produced in January 1843 in two halves, on successive nights, as *Rienzi's Rise* and *Rienzi's Fall*. It soon became recognised and was staged all over Germany, making Wagner's name known for the first time. The score was published in 1844. Though it reached America, in German, in 1878, it was in English that London first heard *Rienzi* in 1879. The Carl Rosa Company also revived it in later London seasons and it was in their touring repertoire for some years. The Moody-Manners Company produced a version, condensed into three acts, during a London season at the Lyric Theatre on August 27, 1901, also including it in their repertoire on tour. There does not appear to have been a production in this country in its original German.

DER FLIEGENDE HOLLÄNDER
(The Flying Dutchman)

A Romantic Opera in Three Acts

Libretto

Commenced in Paris, Spring, 1840, and finished at Meudon, May 1841.

Music

Sketched out at Meudon, July–August 1841. Score completed in Paris, mid-November 1841.

Characters

Daland, a Norwegian Sea-Captain	Bass
Senta, his Daughter	Soprano
Erik, a Hunter	Tenor
Mary, Senta's old Nurse	Mezzo-soprano
Daland's Steersman	Tenor
The Dutchman	Baritone

Chorus

Norwegian Sailors, Crew of the Flying Dutchman's vessel, Girls.

Scene

The Norwegian Coast.

ACT I In a Bay.
ACT II A Room in Daland's House.
ACT III A Rocky Bay. On one side, Daland's House.

FIRST PRODUCED. Hoftheater, Dresden, January 2, 1843.

FIRST PRODUCED IN ENGLAND. Theatre Royal, Drury Lane, London, July 23, 1870. Sung in Italian as *L'Olandese Dannato*, in a translation by S. de Castrone, in a Season of Italian Opera under the direction of George Wood.

FIRST PRODUCED IN ENGLISH. Royal Lyceum Theatre, London, October 3, 1876, in a translation by John P. Jackson, by the Carl Rosa Opera Company.

FIRST PRODUCED IN AMERICA. Academy of Music, New York, January 26, 1877. Sung in English in an unnamed (J. P. Jackson?) translation by the Kellogg English Opera Company.

FIRST PRODUCED IN AMERICA IN GERMAN. Academy of Music, New York, March 12, 1877 by the Pappenheim Opera Company.

FIRST PRODUCED IN ENGLAND IN GERMAN. Theatre Royal, Drury Lane, London, May 20, 1882, in a Grand German Opera Season, under the Direction of Hermann Franke.

DER FLIEGENDE HOLLÄNDER (THE FLYING DUTCHMAN) – CASTS

CHARACTERS	DRESDEN 1843	LONDON 1870 (in Italian)	LONDON 1876 (in English)	NEW YORK 1877 (in English)	NEW YORK 1877 (in German)	LONDON 1882 (in German)
Daland	Carl Risse	Sgr. Foli	A. Stevens	George Conly	Felix Preusser	Paul Ehrke
Senta	Wilhelmine Schröder-Devrient	Ilma de Murska	Ostava Torriani	Clara Louise Kellogg	Eugénie Pappenheim	Rosa Sucher
Erik	Reinhold Wächter	Julius Perotti	Fred C. Packard	Joseph Maas	Christian Fritsch	Joseph Wolff
Mary		Rinaldini	Lucy Franklein	Lancaster	E. Cooney	Josephine Schefsky
Daland's Steersman	Wenzel Bielczizky	Iginio Corsi	J. W. Turner	C. H. Turner	Lenow	Leopold Landau
The Dutchman	Micheal Wächter	Charles Santley	Charles Santley	W. T. Carleton	Alois Blum	Eugen Gura
Conductor	Richard Wagner	Luigi Arditi	Carl Rosa	S. Behrens	Adolf Neuendorff	Hans Richter
Producer	Wilhelm Fischer		Arthur Howell	C. D. Hess		Bernhard Pollini
Designer	*Costumes* Ferdinand Heine		*Scenery* Hawes Craven *Costumes* Mr. and Mrs. Stinchcombe			

SYNOPSIS

Daland, a Norwegian captain, has anchored his ship after a storm off a rocky coast. He himself has gone on shore to ascertain his position, and his crew are shouting and singing as they furl the sails for the night. The Steersman sings of his delight at coming back to the land where his beloved is waiting for him.

Now there appears the Flying Dutchman's ship, with blood-red sails and black masts. The Dutchman himself tells in soliloquy how, doomed to wander eternally over the oceans, once in every seven years he may come ashore. Here, if he can win the true love of a maiden, he will be released from the curse; otherwise, he must go back to sea again.

The Steersman, who is on watch, does not see the ship until Daland calls his attention to it. Then they hail the newcomer, who tells them that he is a Dutchman, and offers Daland all the treasures in his cargo in exchange for a friendly welcome to his home. Hearing that Daland has a daughter, he asks if she will be his bride. Daland agrees to both proposals, and the two men go off together, while the sailors continue to sing at their work.

ACT II

In Daland's house, his daughter Senta sits gazing at the portrait of a pale man in antique Spanish costume; while her old nurse Mary and the girls of the household are singing as they spin. Mary chides Senta for her idleness, and the girls tease her – saying that her hot-tempered lover Erik will soon grow jealous and shoot his painted rival on the wall. Angry at their jesting, Senta sings the legend of the Flying Dutchman – condemned for a reckless oath to go on sailing the seas for evermore. She prays that he may come to her house, so that she may be the one to set him free.

Erik enters in time to hear this. He is disturbed at Senta's obsession, and so is Mary, who declares that the Dutchman's portrait shall be burned as soon as Daland comes home. He is on the way, says Erik, who has seen the Norwegians' ship approaching. While Mary and the girls go to prepare food for the sailors, Erik appeals to Senta, begging her to forget her dreams and marry him as soon as her father returns. He has had a vision of the ghostly stranger embracing Senta, and it has alarmed him. When the girl declares that in fact she is seeking the stranger and will follow him anywhere, Erik realises that this was no mere dream but a true presentiment, and he rushes off in despair.

Now Daland enters with the Dutchman. At the sight of him Senta stands as if transfixed. Her father tells her to welcome the stranger as a prospective bridegroom, while to his new friend he praises his daughter's beauty and kindness. Meanwhile, the two are gazing at each other in mutual recognition. At last, when Daland has left them together, they speak – he to hail her as the angel of his salvation, for whom he has waited so long; and she to assure him that she asks nothing better than to share his fate. Daland returns to hear their decision and give his blessing on their marriage.

ACT III

The two ships are lying side by side in harbour – the Norwegian gaily lit, with her sailors shouting, singing and dancing; the Dutchman lying dark and still. From Daland's house the girls have come with gifts of food and drink for both crews, but when they can get no answer from the silent ship, they leave it all with the Norwegians. At last the crew of the Dutchman strike up a chorus, calling on the storms to fill the imperishable sails that Satan has provided. Their song startles the Norwegians, who are beginning to suspect that they are evil spirits.

Senta comes from the house, followed by Erik, who implores her to remember her vows of love and not to forsake him for the stranger. Seeing them together, the Dutchman believes her faithless, and, although she tries to hold him back, breaks away from her, insisting that he must go on board his ship. When Daland and the rest come out, he turns upon them and, to their terror, reveals himself as the Flying Dutchman.

Senta, crying that she will be faithful unto death, flings herself into the sea, whereupon the Dutchman's ship sinks with all her crew. In the glow of the sunset the spirits of the Dutchman and Senta, clasped in each other's arms, rise up towards heaven.

REVIEW

The Music Critic in *The Era*, July 24, 1870, wrote of the first English production:

'Sunday, Two A.M.

'It is, probably, more difficult in music than in any other art to escape from the beaten track. All who are familiar with the career of Beethoven will remember how slowly the public and the musical critics were brought to recognise the depth, originality, and power of his conceptions, simply because the *manner* was unfamiliar to them. A few who chose to think for themselves, and were prepared to judge of a work of art for its intrinsic merit without reference to what had gone before, sympathised with the manly independence of the composer's ideas, and felt a glow of admiration for his courage in defying conventional rules. They felt also that music which produced such good effect in performance could not be radically bad in theory. We have intentionally alluded to Beethoven's victorious attempt to open up new paths of musical composition because there can be little doubt that Wagner was stimulated in his early endeavours by the example, and also by the ultimate success of his illustrious predecessor. In his craving for originality, however, Wagner quitted the ancient landmarks altogether; and while Beethoven did not disdain to avail himself of the experience of Mozart, Haydn, and younger musicians of his own day, Wagner boldly challenged hostile criticism by discarding the traditions of centuries, and starting upon an entirely novel plan. What this sytem was, and the mode of carrying it out, let us briefly explain. Wagner, in addition to his musical acquirements, is a writer of no mean talent; and in order to impress upon the public mind the importance and value of his efforts, he has availed himself of the Press, and of separate publications, to explain, discuss, and extol his own creations. In doing so he has frequently been both unjust and dangerous to musicians of the highest class, and because Mendelssohn differed from him in some special points, Wagner has not scrupled to write and speak of this great composer in terms almost approaching contempt. It followed, as a matter of course, that the "musical idealist," as his admirers love to call him, made not a few enemies, who, by the choice of a happy phrase, made Wagner known to Europe as the "composer of the future," at the same time intending to imply that his chance of success would be deferred to a very remote future indeed. The system adopted by Wagner is directly opposed to that of Mozart and other great composers. In all Mozart's operas – *Don Giovanni*, for instance – the ear is delighted with a series of enchanting melodies, which, in many cases, may be heard with equal pleasure, apart from the opera itself, but Wagner, in obedience to his pet theory, dispenses with this element of attraction, and in place of a catching air, gives us a musical picture, from which, by the aid of unusual combinations of voice and orchestra, we are to receive our impressions of the story. As in nature, argues Wagner, we derive exquisite pleasure from sounds, which have no definite character, we have only to apply the same principle to art, and the result will be equally effective. If the human heart can be so moved by the ripple of a stream, by the sighing of the wind in autumnal woods, by the joyous twitter of the birds in spring time, by the murmur of the insect, the roar of the ocean, the sudden hail, or the roll of distant thunder, "why," inquires the enthusiastic composer, "should we not carry musical art, and especially the lyric drama, into a loftier region than heretofore, and appeal to the mind rather than to the ear?" We might go at greater length into the composer's theory, but what we have already said will be sufficient doubtless to indicate to the amateur what has been Wagner's aim. It will thus be seen that if we judged the composer of *The Flying Dutchman* from the same point of view as an opera of Auber or Flotow, we should be manifestly doing him an injustice, and we hold that the cause of good music will not suffer in the end by meeting new ideas half way. Therefore, we maintain that it is wise to examine before we condemn, and we take the composer's own statement as a standpoint from which to pass an opinion. Judging the composer then by his own standard, we cannot but admit that he has a very strong feeling for dramatic effect, and there is a unity and consistency in the management of the story which prove a poetical element in his nature. But we fear the want of melody will prevent his ever becoming a popular composer in England, where pleasing tunes have ever been eagerly sought for and appreciated. In some points *The Flying Dutchman* insensibly calls to mind the *Der Freischütz* of Weber, and this may be accounted for by the prevailing gloom of the story. But Weber, unlike Wagner, distributed throughout the opera some of the very loveliest phrases of melody ever written – melodies which, while they satisfied the severest musical critic, also delighted the merest novice. It is only this kind of operatic composition that will ever gain a firm hold upon the taste of the English public. If, as has been stated, Wagner himself chiefly wrote and arranged the libretto when the opera was originally produced, he is certainly entitled to very high praise, for the story is intensely dramatic. Let the opponents of the composer say what they will, we defy them to witness the opera unmoved. The drama is compact, the incidents closely interwoven, and for the first two acts moves onward to the catastrophe with striking power; but in the third act there is an evident falling off both in the music and in the plot. The excitement with which the second act closes is not sustained, and there is an anti-climax almost as soon as the third act commences, which goes far to destroy the good effect produced by what has been already heard. Evidently Signor Arditi had foreseen this, and had cut out some portion of the act. But the flaw could not be overcome by the most skilful management or by the most exquisite singing and acting. Those who had witnessed the first and second acts with genuine enjoyment began to feel a want of variety in the music. That was just the time when a good stirring melody, either as a solo or chorus, would have been heartily welcomed, even, we fancy, by Wagner's warmest advocates.

'Our space will not permit a detailed account of the performance, which was extremely fine. The singing of Mr. Santley as the Dutchman could not possibly be better, and we have certainly never heard Mdlle. de Murska in better voice. She sang the difficult music to perfection, and looked the part probably better than any other *prima donna* that could be found. A special round of applause also rewarded Signor Foli, for his fine declamation at the beginning of the second act. The band, under Signor Arditi, it is hardly necessary to praise. It is enough to say that the overture was encored. We must not quit the subject, however, without a word of praise for the liberality of the Management in providing some of the best scenic effects ever witnessed at Drury Lane.'

NOTES

The legend of The Flying Dutchman had been on Wagner's mind for some years and on the stormy voyage from Riga in 1839 the idea for an opera was finally conceived. During his period of poverty in Paris, after commencing upon his libretto, he was forced to sell the scenario to the Paris Opéra for setting by another composer, for which he received five hundred francs. Having finished *Rienzi* he used the money to live while he completed his own libretto for *Der fliegende Holländer*. This he did at Meudon, near Paris, where he was then living, during May 1841. Work on the score immediately followed between July and August, the whole work being completed by mid-November.

Der fliegende Holländer was accepted for production in Berlin, on Meyerbeer's recommendation, but the performance did not materialise. Offers to other German theatres were also unsuccessful.

Two dramatic sketches date also from this year, *Die Bergwerke zu Falun* (*The Mines of Falun*) and *Die Sarazenin* (*The Saracen Girl*) neither of which was developed substantially.

Then in April 1842 Wagner left for Dresden and *Rienzi* had its first performance, to such acclaim that the Directors of the Opera decided to stage *Der fliegende Holländer*. It was produced on January 2, 1843, a month before Wagner himself became conductor of the Ducal Theatre of Saxony where he remained until 1849. Meantime the synopsis, sold to the Paris Opéra, had been turned into a libretto by P. H. Foucher and B.-H. Revoil. The music was composed by Pierre Louis Dietsch (who was later to conduct the three tragic performances of *Tannhäuser* in 1861). This opera *Le Vaisseau Fantôme* was produced on 9 November, 1842, and vanished completely from view after eleven performances. Yet another version of Wagner's text was set by Ernst Tschirch in 1850 but never staged.

Wagner's own opera was published in 1844. It marks a step from the grandiose grand opera style of *Rienzi* to a fervent romanticism, one which was too long for the average critic and musician to take. It started the opposition to the composer which grew in intensity over the next twenty-five years. It is in fact the first Music-Drama.

The opera was given only four times at Dresden and not revived there until 1865, but it soon reached other German Opera Houses. It was the first Wagner opera to be staged in London, though it was sung in Italian, as *L'Olandese Dannato*, in 1870 and yet another translation at Covent Garden, in 1877, was called *Il Vascello Fantasma*.

It is worth noting that 'A Nautical Drama' *The Flying Dutchman; or, The Phantom Ship* by Edward Fitz-Ball with music by George H. Rodwell was produced at the Adelphi Theatre, London, in 1827, and revived several times. Another version by Douglas Jerrold was played at the Surrey Theatre in 1829. In both of these, which were published, the Dutchman was named Vanderdecken, the name he was given in the programme of the first English production of Wagner's opera at the Lyceum in 1876. The version of the story by W. G. Wills and Percy Fitzgerald which Henry Irving played at the Lyceum in 1878 was also called *Vanderdecken*. It had incidental music 'selected from the works of Eminent Composers, and also from Norwegian Airs'. Among the interval music is noted 'Selection from *The Flying Dutchman* by Wagner'. The story was also the subject for several burlesques.

It was the first complete Wagner opera to be televised in Great Britain. It was seen on B.B.C. 2 on November 9, 1975, in a new English version by Peter Butler and Brian Large, conducted by David Lloyd-Jones and designed by David Myerscough-Jones. The cast was:

Daland	Stafford Dean
Senta	Gwyneth Jones
Erik	Keith Erwen
Marie	Joan Davies
Daland's Steersman	Robert Ferguson
The Dutchman	Norman Bailey

TANNHÄUSER UND DER SÄNGERKRIEG AUF WARTBURG

(*Tannhäuser and the Song Contest at Wartburg*)

———— • ————

A Romantic Opera in Three Acts

Libretto

Commenced in Teplitz, June 1842, and finished in Dresden, April 1843.

Music

Commenced in Teplitz, July 1843. Second Act completed in Dresden, October 15, 1844, and Third Act on December 29. Score completed April 13, 1845. The Paris version, with revised Venusberg Scene, first performed March 13, 1861.

Characters

Hermann, Landgrave of Thuringia	Bass
Tannhäuser	Tenor
Wolfram von Eschenbach	Baritone
Walther von der Vogelweide	Tenor
Biterolf	Bass
Heinrich der Schreiber	Tenor
Reinmar von Zweter	Bass
Elisabeth, the Landgrave's Niece	Soprano
Venus	Soprano
A Young Shepherd	Soprano
Four Pages	Soprano & Alto

Wolfram von Eschenbach, Walther von der Vogelweide, Biterolf, Heinrich der Schreiber, Reinmar von Zweter — } Knights and Minstrels

Chorus

Knights, Counts and Noblemen of Thuringia, Ladies, Old and Young Pilgrims, Sirens, Naiads, Nymphs, Cupids, Bacchantes, Satyrs and Fauns.

Scene

Thuringia: the Wartburg. Beginning of the Thirteenth Century.

ACT I Scene 1 Inside the Hörselberg near Eisenach.

          Scene 2 A Valley below the Wartburg.

ACT II At the Wartburg. (The Hall of Minstrels.)

ACT III A Valley below the Wartburg.

FIRST PRODUCED. Hoftheater, Dresden, October 19, 1845.

FIRST PRODUCED IN AMERICA. Stadt Theater, New York, April 4, 1859. Sung in German.

FIRST PRODUCED IN PARIS (Revised Version). Académie Impériale de Musique, March 13, 1861. Sung in French in a translation by E. Roche, R. Lindau and C. Nuitter.

FIRST PRODUCED IN ENGLAND. Royal Italian Opera, Covent Garden, London, May 6, 1876. Sung in Italian in an unnamed translation.

FIRST PRODUCED IN ENGLISH. Her Majesty's Theatre, London, February 14, 1882, in a translation by John P. Jackson, by the Carl Rosa Opera Company.

FIRST PRODUCED IN ENGLAND IN GERMAN. Theatre Royal, Drury Lane, London, May 23, 1882, in a German Grand Opera Season, under the direction of Hermann Franke.

FIRST PRODUCED IN AMERICA IN ENGLISH. Academy of Music, New York, April 4, 1888, in an unnamed translation (J. P. Jackson?) by the National Opera Company.

FIRST PRODUCTION IN AMERICA OF THE PARIS VERSION. Metropolitan Opera House, New York, January 30, 1889. Sung in German.

FIRST PRODUCTION IN ENGLAND OF THE PARIS VERSION. Royal Italian Opera, Covent Garden, London, July 15, 1895. Sung in French.

TANNHÄUSER UND DER SÄNGERKRIEG AUF WARTBURG (TANNHÄUSER AND THE SONG CONTEST AT WARTBURG) – CASTS

CHARACTERS	DRESDEN 1845	NEW YORK 1859 (in German)	PARIS 1861 (Revised version)	LONDON 1876 (in Italian)	LONDON 1882 (in English)
Hermann	Wilhelm Dettmer	Graff	Cazaux	Capponi	Henry Pope
Tannhäuser	Joseph Tichatschek	Pickaneser	Albert Niemann	Fernando Carpi	Anton Schott
Wolfram	Anton Mitterwurzer	Lehmann	Morelli	Victor Maurel	William Ludwig
Walther	Max Schloss	Lotti	Aimès	Oliva Pavani	Ben Davies
Biterolf	Michael Wächter	Urchs	Coulon	Scolara	Hervey D'Egville
Heinrich	Curti	Bolton	Koenig	Sabater	Dudley Thomas
Reinmar	Carl Risse	Brand	Fréret	Raguer	Leahy
Elisabeth	Johanna Wagner	Sidenburg	Marie-Constance Sax	Emma Albani	Alwina Valleria
Venus	Wilhelmine Schröder-Devrient		Fortunata Tédesco	Anna d'Angeri	Georgina Burns
A Young Shepherd	Anna Thiele	Pickaneser	Reboux	Cottino	Irene Adams
Four Pages	Not named		Christian, Granier, Vogler, Rouaud	Not named	Not named

Conductor	Richard Wagner	Carl Bergmann	Pierre Louis Philippe Dietsch	Auguste Vianesi	Carl Rosa
Producer			Eugène Cormann		
Designer	*Scenery* Edouard Despléchin et Cie *Costumes* Ferdinand Heine		*Scenery* Act 1 Scene 1 Charles Cambon and Joseph Thierry Scene 2 Edouard Despléchin Act 2 Nolau and Auguste Rubé Act 3 Edouard Despléchin *Costumes* Alfred Albert	*Scenery* Dayes and Caney	

TANNHÄUSER UND DER SÄNGERKRIEG AUF WARTBURG (TANNHÄUSER AND THE SONG CONTEST AT WARTBURG) – CASTS (continued)

CHARACTERS	LONDON 1882 (in German)	NEW YORK 1888 (in English)	NEW YORK 1889 (Paris version in German)	LONDON 1895 (Paris version in French)
Hermann	Josef Koegel	Frank Vetta	Emil Fischer	Pol Plançon
Tannhäuser	Hermann Winkelmann	Eloi Sylva	Paul Kalisch	Albert Alvarez
Wolfram	Eugen Gura	William Ludwig	Alois Grienauer	Victor Maurel
Walther	Leopold Landau	Charles Bassett	Albert Mittelhauser	Charles Bonnard
Biterolf	Paul Ehrke	Alonzo Stoddard	Carl Muehe	Charles Gilibert
Heinrich	Joseph Wolff	Joseph Pachex	Martin Paché	Iginio Corsi
Reinmar	G. Noldechen	George H. Broderick	Jean Doré	Antonio de Vaschetti
Elisabeth	Rosa Sucher	Bertha Pierson	Katti Bettaque	Emma Eames
Venus	Elise Weidermann	Sophie Traubman	Lilli Lehmann	Ada Adini
A Young Shepherd	Martha Hartmann	Attalie Claire	Felicie Kaschowska	Mathilde Bauermeister
Four Pages	Not named	Not named	Not named	Not named
Conductor	Hans Richter	Gustav Hinrichs	Anton Seidl	Luigi Mancinelli
Producer	Bernhard Pollini		Habelmann	
Designer				

SYNOPSIS

SCENE 1 Inside the Venusberg, Nymphs and Bacchantes are cavorting on the banks of a beautiful lake. The minstrel Heinrich Tannhäuser kneels at the feet of Venus. He cannot tell how long he has been with her – for no seasons can be felt in this underground Paradise – but he has faintly heard the sound of church-bells from the outside world, and he is homesick for the feel of the fresh grass underfoot and the open sky above. He beseeches her to let him go back. Venus resists, accusing him of ingratitude. She warns him that he will meet with scorn and insult from his fellow-men, and, if he finds no salvation, will return to her in the end. Tannhäuser declares that his salvation is in the Virgin Mary – and that name breaks the spell. He finds himself back on Earth.

SCENE 2 Tannhäuser has not changed his attitude, but now he is kneeling at a shrine of the Virgin, situated in a beautiful valley below the Wartburg. He hears the sound of sheep-bells and the song of a young shepherd playing on his pipe, who celebrates the return of Frau Holda, the goddess of Spring. Some Pilgrims, on their way to Rome, halt for a moment at the shrine, and Tannhäuser, suddenly feeling remorse, prays to be forgiven.

The kneeling Tannhäuser is seen and recognised by the Landgrave and his minstrel-knights, Walther, Wolfram and Biterolf, as they return from a hunt. Tannhäuser, the best singer of them all, had left them long ago after a quarrel, and they are uncertain whether he has come back as friend or foe. When the Landgrave asks where he has been, he evades the question, answering only 'In distant lands'. Reassured by his humble attitude, they press him to return with them, but he refuses, saying that he must go further. However, when Wolfram tells him that the Landgrave's daughter Elisabeth has remained so much impressed by Tannhäuser's songs that since his departure she has no longer graced their contests with her presence, he decides to come back with the rest. The act closes as the Landgrave and his retinue mount their horses to ride home.

ACT II

Elisabeth, alone in the Hall of Minstrels, rejoices at the return of Tannhäuser.

Wolfram brings Tannhäuser into the hall and then leaves him alone with Elisabeth, who asks him where he has been. Once more he is evasive. After Elisabeth has expressed her joy at seeing him again, they join in a duet of mutual happiness.

Landgrave Hermann enters, glad to find that Elisabeth has once more come to preside over the musical contest. He realises that she is in love with Tannhäuser, but agrees to be silent about it until after the contest, when her hands shall bestow the victor's wreath.

The Knights and Ladies of the Court then enter and hail the Landgrave in song. He addresses them, announcing the theme for the minstrels: 'What is the nature of Love?'

The first singer is Wolfram, who upholds the chivalrous ideal of courtly love – pure and humble devotion to a lady set apart like a star. These sentiments are praised by his audience, but Tannhäuser breaks in, roundly declaring that anyone with such a cold and timid approach can know nothing of real love, which needs to be enjoyed for its fulfilment.

Biterolf, constituting himself a champion of female virtue, wishes to fight Tannhäuser, and the others encourage him, but the Landgrave sternly orders them to put up their swords.

In wild exultation, Tannhäuser then sings the praises of Venus, ending with the advice that all who wish to know true love should seek it in the Venusberg.

The revelation that he has been in that accursed underworld is greeted with horror by all present. The Ladies leave the hall. Only Elisabeth, pale and shaken, stays watching as the Landgrave and his knights close upon Tannhäuser with drawn swords. Then she throws herself between them and their quarry, declaring that they must kill her first – they shall not destroy him and rob him of his hope of heaven.

The Landgrave then pronounces sentence of banishment upon Tannhäuser. Only one path to redemption lies open to him: he must join the pilgrims who are just setting out for Rome – and he must not return unless he has obtained the Pope's pardon.

Elisabeth prays that he may be forgiven, and offers her own life to heaven as a sacrifice for his redemption.

Burdened by a sudden sense of guilt, Tannhäuser is in despair, when the chorus of pilgrims is heard singing outside. He then accepts his fate. 'To Rome!' he exclaims, and the others echo: 'To Rome!'

ACT III

In the Wartburg valley, Wolfram, who loves Elisabeth with the self-effacing devotion which he expressed in his song, watches while she prays at the shrine of the Virgin.

They hear the song of the returning pilgrims, happy because they have been absolved from their sins. But Tannhäuser is not among them. Elisabeth, in deep distress, vows to the Virgin that she will live and die a maid, and spend her time praying that Tannhäuser may find grace.

Dusk falls, and Wolfram is alone in the valley. He sings of the evening star, and of his love, who will soon escape from the earth to be an angel in heaven.

Tannhäuser enters, attracted by the song. Wolfram – who does not at first recognise him in his pilgrim's garb – is struck by his look of utter dejection. Tannhäuser tells how, of all the company, he alone has remained unabsolved. When the Pope heard that he had been with Venus, he declared that a man who had sinned thus could no more find forgiveness than could the dry staff in his own hand put forth fresh leaves and flowers.

So Tannhäuser, desperate, is now on his way back to the Venusberg. His friend does all he can to restrain him, but the goddess herself appears in answer to Tannhäuser's appeal, and he is on the point of surrendering to her, when Wolfram stops him by pronouncing the name of Elisabeth.

With the cry: 'Alas! He is lost to me!' Venus disappears. In the glimmering dawn, a torch-lit procession approaches. It is the funeral of Elisabeth, whose body is carried in on a bier by the Elder Pilgrims. Beside it walk the Minstrels: the Landgrave, with his Knights and Nobles, follows. At a sign from Wolfram the bearers set down the bier. With the prayer: 'Holy Elisabeth, pray for me!' Tannhäuser sinks down beside it and dies.

While the stage is flooded with light by the rising sun, the Younger Pilgrims enter, bearing joyful news: the Pope's staff has blossomed during the night, and he has sent forth into all lands to declare the Almighty's pardon for the repentant sinner.

REVIEW

The Music Critic in *The Era*, May 7, 1876, preludes the first production in England:

'The opera of *Tannhäuser*, remarkable in many ways for its own sake, although it was hissed from the Parisian boards, notwithstanding a few faithful disciples expressed the warmest admiration for the work, and a popular French poet, Charles Baudelaire, published a pamphlet upon Wagner and his *Tannhäuser*. The spirit and central ideas of the opera are unquestionably very fine. Wagner seeks to show the contrast and the opposition of the religious and the voluptuous element in human aspirations, and he has made an earnest and honest endeavour to express this in vigorous and stirring music. . . .

'The key to much that puzzles the musical student in the works of Wagner may be found in his own idea of what music should be – "Music, vocal or instrumental, in its highest development, must aim at, and is capable of, rendering all the emotions of the human heart; not essentially differing in this from poetry, to which it is inferior in the distinctness of its means of expression, but which it surpasses in immediate impulse." Here we have an explanation of what Wagner really would arrive at – *if he could*. We must, in common justice, admit the difficulty of accomplishing this aim, for Beethoven himself, with his vast and original genius, and with all the experience gained from years of anxious toil and study, confessed that he fell short of his aspirations in *Fidelio*, noble as that opera everywhere is in conception and execution. In conclusion, we believe that the introduction of *Tannhäuser* to the Anglo-Italian stage will be a new revelation of Wagner's genius. On the question of melody the writer from whom we have quoted says: "Weber's melody was founded entirely on the popular tune of the *Volkslied*, and to its close connection with the inexhaustible and ever-new creating power of popular feeling, it owed the charm of its delightful freshness. Every passion and sentiment within the range of this pure and simple language Weber expressed with incomparable beauty. Only when the grand pathos of dramatic action demanded a higher scope of musical conception the limits of his power became obvious." It is his belief that Wagner made that step forward which he here indicates as desirable. We shall know by the reception of *Tannhäuser* what English amateurs think of this theory.'

After the first night *The Era* for May 14 continues:

'We have now to deal with the actual performance of Saturday last. As we suggested, the work was calculated to give a more genial impression of Wagner than anything of his previously produced in this country. Besides containing much really grand and effective music, the story of *Tannhäuser* has been treated by Wagner in a truly poetical spirit. His command of the orchestra is also very remarkable, and in many instances he rises to actual grandeur in his musical interpretation of the story. It is true the opera is terribly long. It did not conclude until nearly one o'clock in the morning; but it is decidedly interesting, and, being placed upon the stage with the utmost splendour and completeness, and being supported by *artistes* capable of doing it justice, it must be confessed Wagner had the best possible chance of being judged fairly by English amateurs. The performance of the principals was admirable, Mdlle. Albani adding to her laurels by one of the most delightful impersonations possible to imagine. Her first solo, "Salve d'amore," and the prayer of Elisabeth were efforts which no lover of genuine vocal art could possibly forget, and in many other portions of the music her lovely voice and pure style gave a charm impossible to resist. Her acting was on a par with her singing, and raised this gifted young lady higher than ever in the estimation of the opera-goer. Mdlle. D'Angeri has a less grateful character as Venus. She worked zealously, and with great effect; and Mdlle. Cottino was deservedly applauded for her graceful rendering of the Shepherd's Song, which is difficult, and, having no accompaniment, requires no ordinary skill on the part of the *artiste*. The tenor has hard work in *Tannhäuser*, and this is one reason why so few Italian vocalists are found willing to undertake it. Signor Carpi needed perhaps greater animation as an actor, but we can understand the necessity of husbanding his resources. He sang the music uncommonly well, and was much applauded. M. Maurel, as Wolfram, was also excellent. His two solos were admirably given. Signor Capponi, as the Landgrave, delivered some fearfully long recitatives with great energy; and Signor Pavani sang the solo of Walther carefully. Splendid new scenery was painted by Messrs.

Dayes and Caney; and the dresses were very picturesque. Signor Vianesi conducted, and merited great praise for his energy and skill. *Tannhäuser* has unquestionably enhanced Wagner's position as an operatic composer in this country.'

NOTES

The legend of Tannhäuser and Venus had interested Wagner as the subject for an opera during his stay in Paris and while he visited Thuringia on his way to Dresden in April 1842 for the production of *Rienzi*.

He commenced work on the poem at Teplitz in June 1842 but it was laid aside while he was occupied with the production of *Rienzi* and *Der fliegende Holländer*, but directly after he was appointed *Hofkapellmeister* to the King of Saxony at Dresden on February 2, 1843, he again set to work on the libretto of *Tannhäuser*, which was completed there in April. The full score was eventually finished by April 1845. Before it was produced Wagner made his first prose version of *Die Meistersinger* while at Marienbad in July and began on the idea for *Parsifal*.

Tannhäuser was staged on October 19, 1845. Wagner revised the ending for a later performance and the score was published in 1846.

Wagner also worked at this time on a dramatic sketch, *Friedrich Rotbart* (*Frederick Barbarossa*) to which he returned in 1848 but did not develop further.

Production of *Tannhäuser* in other German towns gradually followed and by 1859 the opera had even reached New York, seventeen years before it was first heard in London.

It was in 1861 that *Tannhäuser* was given its ill-fated production at the Paris Opéra.

For this performance Wagner had to make revisions to include the traditional ballet in the Venusberg scene in the first act. Other changes were also made. Of the adaptation of the libretto into French, Roche has told of the troubles he had with the composer:

'He came at seven in the morning; we were at work without rest or respite until midday. I was bent over my desk, writing, erasing, "cherchant la fameuse syllabe qui devait correspondre à la fameuse note, sans cesser néanmoins d'avoir le sens commun," he was erect, pacing to and fro, bright of eye, vehement of gesture, striking the piano, shouting, singing, for ever bidding me, "Go on! go on!" An hour or even two hours after noon, hungry and exhausted, I let fall my pen. I was in a fainting state. "What's the matter," he asked. "I am hungry." "True, I had forgotten all about that; let us have a hurried snack, and go on again." Night came and found us still at work. I was shattered, stupefied, my head burned; my temples throbbed; I was half mad with my wild search after strange words to fit the strange music; he was erect still, vigorous and fresh as when we commenced our toil, walking up and down, striking his infernal piano, terrifying me at last, as I perceived dancing about me on every side his eccentric shadow cast by the fantastic reflection of the lamp, and crying to me ever, like one of Hoffmann's creations "Go on! go on!" while trumpeting in my ears cabalistic words and supernatural music.' (*The Era*, February 1, 1880)

The ballet, by Lucien Petipa, was danced by Rousseau, Troisvallets and Stöikoff, as the Three Graces, with Aline and MM. Lefèvre and Millot.

The story of the disastrous first night has often been told. The disturbance was on the whole political and also partly due to a hostile clique opposed to the placing of the ballet so near the commencement of the opera, an organised opposition by the Jockey Club.

The first performance was followed by Offenbach's ballet *Le Papillon*, its twenty-seventh representation.

Tannhäuser was withdrawn after three performances and not revived at the Opéra again until May 13, 1895. The revised version was first seen in Germany at Munich on August 1, 1867, and in New York in 1889 and London in 1895. The opera is now often performed in a mixture of the two versions.

LOHENGRIN

———— · ————

A Romantic Opera in Three Acts

Libretto

Commenced in Marienbad, Summer 1845. Completed and read aloud at the 'Engelklub', Dresden, November 17, 1845.

Music

Sketched at Gross-Graupe, Summer 1846. Third Act commenced in Dresden, September 9, 1846, finished March 5, 1847. First Act commenced May 12 and completed June 8, 1847. Second Act commenced June 18 and completed August 2, 1847. Score completed April 28, 1848.

Characters

Henry the Fowler, King of Germany	Bass
Lohengrin	Tenor
Elsa von Brabant	Soprano
Duke Gottfried, her Brother	Non-singing role
Friedrich von Telramund, Count of Brabant	Baritone
Ortrud, his Wife	Mezzo-soprano
The King's Herald	Bass
Four Nobles of Brabant	Tenor and Bass
Four Pages	Soprano and Alto

Chorus

Saxon and Thuringian Counts and Nobles, Counts and Nobles of Brabant, Ladies, Pages, Men and Women, Servants.

Scene

Antwerp. First half of the Tenth Century.

ACT I A Meadow on the Banks of the Scheldt.
ACT II In the Castle of Antwerp.
ACT III SCENE 1 In the Bridal Chamber.
       SCENE 2 A Meadow on the Banks of the Scheldt.

FIRST PRODUCED. Hoftheater, Weimar. August 28, 1850.

FIRST PRODUCED IN AMERICA. Stadt Theater, New York, April 3, 1871. Sung in German.

FIRST PRODUCED IN ENGLAND. Royal Italian Opera, Covent Garden, London, May 8, 1875. Sung in Italian in a translation by Salvatore Marchese.

FIRST PRODUCED IN ENGLISH. Her Majesty's Theatre, London, February 7, 1880, in a translation by John P. Jackson, by the Carl Rosa Opera Company.

FIRST PRODUCED IN ENGLAND IN GERMAN. Theatre Royal, Drury Lane, London, May 18, 1882, in a Grand German Opera Season, under the direction of Hermann Franke.

FIRST PRODUCED IN AMERICA IN ENGLISH. Academy of Music, New York, January 20, 1886, in a translation by Natalia Macfarren.

'Die Walküre' Act 1 – The original production at the Court Theatre, Munich on June 26 1870 with Therese and Heinrich Vogl as Sieglinde and Siegmund.

'Siegfried' – With Melanie Kurt as Brünnhilde and Walther Kirchhoff as Siegfried at the Staatsoper, Berlin in 1911.

'Siegfried' – Heinrich Henke as Mime and Walther Kirchhoff in the title role – Berlin, 1911

'Siegfried' Act 3 – Painting by Josef Hoffmann for the 1876 production at Bayreuth.

'ötterdämmerung' Act 2 – Before the Hall of the Gibichungs. Painting by Josef Hoffmann
er his designs for the 1876 Bayreuth Festival.

'ötterdämmerung' – Group of vassals from the first Bayreuth production in 1876.

'Götterdämmerung' Act 1 – The Hall of the Gibichungs. Painting by Hoffmann after his 187
Bayreuth stage designs.

'Tristan und Isolde' – Max Brückner's design for the 1886 Bayreuth production with Heinric
Gudehus and Therese Malten in the title roles.

'Tristan und Isolde' – Design by Adolph Appia for the 1923 La Scala, Milan production.

'Die Meistersinger' Act 1 – Stage model by Angelo Quaglio for the first performance.

'Die Meistersinger' Act 1 – Etching by Michael Echter of the first Munich performance in 1868.

'Die Meistersinger' Act 3 – Etching Michael Echter after the first performa in Munich, 1868.

'Die Meistersinger' Act 2 – Illustration by Theodor Pixis of the original production in 1868.

...ifal' Act 2 Scene 1 – Stage model of ...gsor's Castle by Max Brückner for the ...Bayreuth production.

'Parsifal' Act 3 – Design by Christian Jank for a projected Munich production (1879).

...arsifal' Act 1 – Setting by Paul von Joukowsky for the Temple of the Holy Grail from the ...iginal Bayreuth production of 1882, which remained in use until Winifred Wagner's new ...oduction in 1934 (Bayreuth Archive).

View from the pit of the Festival Theatre, Bayreuth.

Interior of the Festival Theatre showing the setting for the Temple of the Holy Grail for 'Parsifal'.

LOHENGRIN – A ROMANTIC OPERA IN THREE ACTS – CASTS

CHARACTERS	WEIMAR 1850	NEW YORK 1871 (in German)	LONDON 1875 (in Italian)	LONDON 1880 (in English)	LONDON 1882 (in German)	NEW YORK 1886 (in English)
Henry The Fowler	Hoefer	Adolph Franosch	Seideman	George Conly	Josef Koegel	Myron W. Whitney
Lohengrin	Carl Beck	Theodor Habelmann	Ernest Nicolini	Anton Schott	Hermann Winkelmann	William Candidus
Elsa	Rosa von Milde	Louise Lichtmay	Emma Albani	Julia Baylord	Rosa Sucher	Emma Juch
Duke Gottfried	Agthe Hettstedt	Not named	Not named	Not named	Not named	Not named
Friedrich von Telramund	Hans Feodor von Milde	Joseph Vierling	Victor Maurel	William Ludwig	Emil Kraus	Alonzo Stoddard
Ortrud	Fastlinger	Marie Friderici	Anna d'Angeri	Josephine Yorke	Johanna Garso-Dely	Helene Hastretter
Herald	Pätsch	Wilhelm Formes	Capponi	Leslie Crotty	G. Noldechen	Edward O'Mahony
Four Nobles	Not named	Not named	Rossi, Manfredi, Fallar, Raguer	Not named	Not named	Not named
Four Pages	Not named	Not named	(8 named in cast) Parry, Pocchini, Estelle, Portaluppi, Ferrari, Vianello, Arbraham, Mardini	Not named	Not named	Not named
Conductor	Franz Liszt	Adolf Neuendorff	Auguste Vianesi	Alberto Randegger	Hans Richter	Theodore Thomas
Producer	Eduard Genast				Bernhard Pollini	
Designer	*Scenery* Carl Wilhelm Holdermann *Costumes* Ferdinand Heine		*Scenery* Dayes and Caney			

SYNOPSIS

ACT I

On the banks of the Scheldt near Antwerp, King Henry of Germany ('Henry the Fowler') sits under the Oak of Justice, surrounded by the Saxon Counts and Nobles. Opposite are the Counts and Nobles of Brabant, headed by Friedrich of Telramund, with his wife Ortrud by his side.

A Herald calls upon the men of Brabant to gather for a session of the court. They in their turn welcome the King and assure him of their allegiance and support. Henry tells them that a nine-year truce with Hungary has just ended: he expects an invasion by the Hungarians, which with their help he hopes to repel. However, he has found them divided by trouble at home, and he asks Friedrich to tell him the cause.

Friedrich explains that the late Duke of Brabant had left him as guardian of his heirs – Elsa and her brother Gottfried. One day the two young people had gone for a walk together; but Elsa returned alone, saying that her brother had disappeared and she had searched for him in vain. Friedrich, who had intended to marry Elsa, had turned from her in horror and taken Ortrud as his bride. Now he is charging Elsa, before the Court of Justice, with the murder of her brother.

All are shocked at this accusation, and the King asks what motive the girl could have for such an unnatural crime. Friedrich replies that he suspects Elsa of having a secret lover; no doubt she had reckoned that, with Gottfried out of the way, she herself would reign over Brabant with her paramour.

King Henry orders Elsa to be brought before him, and prays that he may judge the case rightly.

Summoned by the Herald, Elsa appears, looking so innocent and so beautiful that all hearts are touched. When the King asks what is her answer to the charge, she at first says nothing, and then sings of the champion, seen in a dream, who will come to vindicate her.

Reiterating his accusation, Friedrich challenges any man present to fight him in defence of Elsa. When King Henry asks if she is

88

willing to have her cause tried by single combat, she consents, offering her hand and the kingdom of Brabant to her defender.

The Heralds then call for a champion to come forward, but there is no answer. Elsa prays fervently that her dream-knight may come, and the women in the crowd join their supplications with hers.

Suddenly the men standing near the water's edge see a small boat approaching, drawn by a swan, and in it a knight in dazzling silver armour.

While the crowd hail the newcomer, Friedrich and Ortrud are seized with astonishment and dread. Seeing the stranger, Elsa recognises him with a cry of glad surprise . . . it is he of whom she had dreamed.

Amid a tense silence the knight steps from the boat and dismisses his swan with a song of thanks. He then greets King Henry and declares that he has come to defend Elsa. He and she plight their troth, the stranger making the sole condition that in no circumstances must she ask his name or his country. She willingly gives her promise.

The stranger then proclaims Elsa's innocence and challenges Friedrich of Telramund, calling upon God to prove the accusation false. The nobles of Brabant, impressed by the stranger's super-natural beauty, beg Friedrich not to take up the challenge; but he insists, ashamed to show himself a coward.

The Herald announces the contest, the lists are cleared, and the King, after solemnly praying that right may prevail, gives the starting-signal. Almost at once the stranger strikes down Friedrich, amid the plaudits of all present. The King joins with the rest in praising the victor, who, with Elsa, is borne away in triumph.

ACT II

In the Fortress of Antwerp Friedrich and Ortrud, poorly clad, are sitting gloomily on the steps of the Minster. As a result of the combat Friedrich has been stripped of his title and possessions, and ordered to leave the city by daybreak. He bitterly reproaches his wife for inciting him to make the false accusation against Elsa.

Ortrud protests that they can still retrieve the situation. Being a sorceress, she knows that if Elsa can be tempted to break her promise to the stranger, his power will be destroyed. She persuades Friedrich to stay on secretly and plot their revenge.

Elsa appears on the balcony above, and sings of her love and joy.

But her happiness is disturbed when Ortrud reproaches her with being the cause of her misfortunes. Moved to pity, Elsa comes down to speak to her; and meanwhile Ortrud calls on the ancient gods, Odin and Freyja, to grant her vengeance. To Elsa, however, she feigns humility and gratitude, when the girl generously forgives her and promises to intercede for them. She tells Ortrud to dress herself royally and come to the wedding, which is to be held later that day; then she takes her indoors . . . but not before Ortrud has planted the first seed of doubt in her heart, by suggesting that her magic lover may vanish as swiftly as he came.

Friedrich, left alone in the square below, swears that he will kill Lohengrin, the cause of his dishonour.

At daybreak, Warders call Reveille, and the nobles and retainers of the royal domain are astir. Concealing himself to watch, Friedrich hears the Herald pronounce his doom of banishment and forbid the citizens to help or harbour him. It is further announced that the un-known Knight has accepted the title of Guardian of Brabant, and that, immediately after his marriage to Elsa, he will set off to lead the King's forces into battle.

Elsa comes out, enthusiastically greeted by the crowd. But to her astonishment Ortrud quarrels with her over precedence, and taunts her with being unable even to name the man whom she is about to marry.

The King and his retinue arrive in the midst of this commotion, and the bridegroom sternly bids Ortrud begone. Suddenly Friedrich breaks from his hiding-place to accuse the stranger of sorcery. The King and the crowd take the part of the latter, and while the men rally round him, Friedrich approaches Elsa and whispers to her that, if a single drop of blood were drawn from her bridegroom, he would no longer be able to preserve his secret.

The agitated Elsa seeks shelter in the stranger's arms, and he angrily forbids Friedrich or Ortrud to speak to her again. Then he leads Elsa up to the King, and the bridal pair slowly ascend the steps of the Minster to their wedding. At the top Elsa looks back and notices with alarm a threatening gesture from Ortrud.

ACT III

SCENE 1 The married pair have been conducted to their bridal chamber – Elsa by the Court ladies, the stranger by the King and his nobles. All of them sing a wedding song and then leave the newly-wedded pair together.

A tender love-scene follows – but Elsa cannot conceal her longing to hear her husband's name. He gives her a solemn warning, saying that her love and trust must be his compensation for having abandoned the delights of his own realm for her sake. This only increases Elsa's doubts, for she suspects that he will one day tire of her and wish to return.

Despite his efforts to prevent her, she asks him the fatal questions: what is his name, and from where has he come? when Friedrich and four of his followers break into the room. Elsa snatches her bridegroom's sword and hands it to him; with one blow he strikes Friedrich dead, and the four others submit to him.

With a cry: 'Alas! our happiness is lost for ever!' the stranger bends over his fainting bride. Then he orders the four men to carry the corpse to the King's judgment seat, promising that next day, in the presence of all, he will tell Elsa everything that she wishes to know.

SCENE II Once more the scene is the Oak of Justice beside the Scheldt. It is dawn, and the King is presiding over a full conclave of the Saxon and Brabantine nobles. He summons them to battle with the slogan:

> 'For German land the German sword,
> Thus we the land shall surely guard.'

Suddenly they see the four nobles bearing the corpse of Friedrich. They are followed by Elsa, whose deep distress is interpreted as due to the approaching departure to war of her husband; and by the stranger himself, whom the King expects to give the word to start the campaign.

On the contrary, the stranger declares that he can no longer lead their forces into the field. Uncovering Friedrich's face, he states that he killed him in self-defence, having been treacherously attacked on his wedding night. The King and his nobles agree that the dead man has deserved his fate. And now, says the stranger, it is his turn to accuse – Elsa, his wife, who has broken her promise to him.

Since she has done so, he will no longer guard his secret: he is from Monsalvat, the Territory of the Grail, where his father Parsifal is King, and his name is – LOHENGRIN. It is the Grail that has sent him to help the falsely accused Elsa – and which now is summoning him home. If only his wife had trusted him for one year, he would have told her all . . . and her brother, whom she thinks dead, would have been released by the power of the Grail and brought home to her.

Promising the King victory over his enemies, Lohengrin bids his wife a solemn farewell.

Now Ortrud steps forward to declare with malicious glee that the swan is the missing Gottfried, whom she has enchanted by means of the gold ring round his neck. On the river bank Lohengrin kneels in prayer, and in answer he sees the Dove of the Grail hovering over his skiff. He rises and loosens the chain from the swan. At once it sinks, and out of the river there comes a handsome boy in shining silver garments – Gottfried, the new Duke of Brabant.

At the sight of him Ortrud shrieks and falls senseless. The young boy makes obeisance to the King, and then, through the ranks of the kneeling Brabantine nobles, rushes into his sister's arms.

Meanwhile, Lohengrin has harnessed the Dove to his boat, and, commending Gottfried to his people as their future leader, he glides away. With a great cry: 'My husband! My husband!' Elsa sinks lifeless to the ground. As the curtain slowly falls, Lohengrin is seen in the distance, leaning sadly upon his shield.

REVIEW

The Music Critic in *The Era*, May 9, 1875, wrote of the first English performance:

'The first performance of Wagner's romantic opera *Lohengrin* last night, at the Royal Italian Opera, was justly regarded as one of the most interesting musical events of the season. Only once before have we been permitted to judge of the compositions of the "musician of the future." At Her Majesty's Opera *The Flying Dutchman* was given on a single occasion,[1] but the real Wagner is far more discernible in *Lohengrin* than in the former work. New as Wagner's music will undoubtedly be to most English amateurs, in Germany it is becoming well known, and at Dresden, Munich, Berlin, Vienna, Frankfort, and elsewhere, *Lohengrin* has become a standard work in the *repertoire*. Wagner owes much to the enthusiasm of King Ludwig the Second for this opera, and some amusing stories are told how the young king, in the days before Wagner became a musical prophet in his own country, used frequently to have the opera performed for his sole gratification. The German tenor, Nachbaur, who has been the most successful representative of Lohengrin, is frequently invited to sing portions of the opera at Court. In Berlin the popular tenor Niemann takes the character of Lohengrin, and Frau Mallinger that of Elsa. The opera was first produced at Weimar in 1850 under the direction of Liszt, but for many years even the Germans, so much more tolerant of the romantic school than other nations, opposed it. But this antagonism has ceased in a great measure, and, as we have latterly seen, *Lohengrin* has found a circle of admirers who would have us believe that on such dramatic or original music was ever heard in opera before, and even in Italy it was received with rapture when performed at Bologna in the winter of 1871. Within a few months it had also been heard at New York, and in Boston it also created a sensation. It has at last reached England, where, whatever may be the ultimate verdict upon Wagner's music, it should certainly have been heard before. But better late than never. German critics tell us that in Wagner's operas it is not possible to judge the composer fairly

1. The Italian season was at Drury Lane in 1870, and the opera was actually given two performances.

without making ourselves first fully acquainted with the story. Wagner is, they say, as much a poet as a composer, and one of his greatest merits is that the character of his music clearly indicates the character of the story. In order to increase the dramatic significance of the music Wagner will not permit the action to be interrupted by separate melodies. All flows on in a continuous stream of sound, principals, chorus, and band all aiming at combined rather than isolated expression. There are instances, however, where the situations of the story compel the composer to treat them with individuality, and it is in some of these that Wagner's genius as a musician is most strikingly displayed. In the prelude, Lohengrin's song to Elsa, the music of the bridal procession, and the introduction to the third act, we find no extravagant departure from accepted models. The prelude has always awakened enthusiasm amongst musicians. It stands almost alone as an example of the power of music to express a mystical sentiment. The strange opening upon the high notes of the violins, afterwards blended with the softer wind instruments, then the repetition of the theme with the full power of the orchestra, and the gradual diminishing of the tone until it dies away in ethereal echoes, makes a powerful impression on an imaginative mind. . . .

'It was within five minutes of one o'clock when the curtain fell, and we are therefore necessarily prevented from giving full details, but we may say at once that Wagner was for the first time thoroughly appreciated in England by an operatic audience. The house was crowded as we never remember to have seen it before. The Princess of Wales, with a host of aristocratic visitors and all the musical celebrities in London, remained until the close of the opera, late as it was, and the enthusiasm manifested, especially by the German auditors, we have rarely seen equalled. Long as *Lohengrin* is they insisted upon having the famous prelude repeated, also the chorus where Lohengrin first appears, a magnificent movement, and, although it was nearly midnight when the third act commenced, the remarkable orchestral introduction was encored, and at last, when the curtain fell, a prolonged and deafening shout from the Wagnerites absolutely shook the house, while during the progress of the opera Mdlle. Albani had been recalled nearly a dozen times. We can hardly wonder at the enthusiasm in this instance, for a more delightful Elsa than Mdlle. Albani could not possibly be imagined. The grace and tenderness of her acting, the exquisite beauty of her voice, and absolute command of the most difficult and exacting passages could hardly be commended too highly. The lovely prayer on the balcony, and the scenes with Lohengrin and Ortruda, were absolutely perfect, and at the end of each act the audience went positively frantic with delight. The first appearance this season of Signor Nicolini was another interesting event. Signor Nicolini has returned in full possession of his beautiful voice, and his singing in the last act was superb, while his chivalrous bearing and acting as Lohengrin merited the utmost praise. Mdlle. D'Angeri acted and sang with great energy as the evil-minded Ortruda, and M. Maurel was a most satisfactory representative of Telramondo, singing and acting admirably throughout. Signor Capponi as the Herald did himself great credit. The new basso, Herr Seideman, was not in good voice, but exerted himself earnestly as the King. The choruses in some cases required more rehearsal, as the music is terribly exacting, and Signor Vianesi, who conducted, could not afford to be idle a moment. The scenery by Messrs. Dayes and Caney is splendid, and the costumes and *mise-en-scène* are worthy of the high reputation of the Royal Italian Opera. Indeed, we never saw anything better placed on the stage. Whatever may be the ultimate fate of "The Music of the Future", Wagner was positively triumphant at Covent Garden last night.'

NOTES

After completing *Tannhäuser* in April 1845, Wagner commenced work on the poem of *Lohengrin* while at Marienbad during the summer. It was finished by November 17, when he read it aloud to his friends in Dresden. Meantime *Tannhäuser* had been staged, and also while at Marienbad Wagner had made his first sketches for the poem of *Die Meistersinger*.

The music of *Lohengrin* was begun at Gross-Graupe in the summer of 1846; the third act was sketched first, followed by the first and, finally, by the second, the full score being finished by April 28, 1848. During this time Wagner also revised parts of Gluck's *Iphigénie en Aulide*, providing it with a new German translation. This was produced at Dresden on February 2, 1847.

The directors of the Dresden Opera did not care to experiment with the production of *Lohengrin* but the finale to the first act was performed at a concert celebrating the three hundredth anniversary of the Court Orchestra on September 22, 1848.

Undaunted by this setback, Wagner busied himself with his prose writings, when not conducting at the theatre. A dramatic sketch *Jesus von Nazareth* (*Jesus of Nazareth*), the enlarging of *Friedrich Rotbart* and a book on the Nibelungen Myths date from this period. This led to the writing of the poem *Siegfrieds Tod* which was eventually to become the opera *Götterdämmerung*.

Wagner began to realise that under the prevailing conditions at Dresden he could not hope to see his work and ideas fulfilled. He was met with both secret and open hostility and his unfortunate association and sympathy with the unsuccessful May Revolution in 1849 caused him to flee the city in order to escape arrest. He took shelter with Liszt, then conductor of the theatre at Weimar, who was at that moment rehearsing a production of *Tannhäuser*. With Liszt's assistance he quickly moved on to Paris but his second stay there was completely fruitless. He proceeded to Zurich in July 1849, and settled in Switzerland, a political exile, until 1861.

The unproduced *Lohengrin* was sent to Liszt from Paris, who produced it at Weimar on August 28, 1850. Wagner did not see it staged until the performance in Vienna in May 1861. *Lohengrin* marks the end of Wagner's second period, the romantic. The fully fledged Music–Drama came to life six years later with *Das Rheingold*.

Lohengrin was first heard in England in 1875 but translated into Italian, the necessary language for the Royal Italian Opera; it was the first of Wagner's works to be staged at Covent Garden. *Tannhäuser* followed the next year. New York was more fortunate, *Lohengrin* was heard there in 1871 and in the original language.

DER
RING DES NIBELUNGEN
(The Ring of the Nibelung)

—————— · ——————

A Stage Festival Play for three days and a preceding evening

    I Das Rheingold (The Rhinegold)
    II Die Walküre (The Valkyrie)
    III Siegfried
    IV Götterdämmerung (The Twilight of the Gods)

Libretto

Poem of the four operas completed in manuscript, 1853, and printed privately the same year. Published 1863.

Music

Commenced in 1853 and completed November 21, 1874.

Written in the following order:

GÖTTERDÄMMERUNG (as SIEGFRIEDS TOD) 1848–74
  (Produced 1876)
SIEGFRIED (as JUNG SIEGFRIED) 1851–71 (Produced 1876)
DAS RHEINGOLD, 1851–4 (Produced 1869)
DIE WALKÜRE, 1851–6 (Produced 1870)

      (For complete details see under each opera.)

FIRST PRODUCED AS A COMPLETE CYCLE. Festspielhaus, Bayreuth, August 13, 14, 16 and 17, 1876.

FIRST PRODUCED AS A COMPLETE CYCLE IN ENGLAND. Her Majesty's Theatre, London, May 5, 6, 8 and 9, 1882. Sung in German by Angelo Neumann's 'Richard Wagner Theatre'.

FIRST PRODUCED AS A COMPLETE CYCLE IN AMERICA. Metropolitan Opera House, New York, March 4, 5, 8 and 11, 1889. Sung in German. (Produced without DAS RHEINGOLD, January 30, February 1 and 3, 1888.)

Der Ring des Nibelungen

FIRST PRODUCED AS A COMPLETE CYCLE IN ENGLISH. Royal Opera House, Covent Garden, London, January 27, 28, 30 and February 1, 1908, in a translation by Frederick Jameson.

FIRST PRODUCED AS A COMPLETE CYCLE IN ENGLISH IN AMERICA. Opera House, Seattle, July 22, 23, 25, 27, 1975, in a translation by Andrew Porter.

For casts of these performances see under each individual opera.

NOTES

When he settled in Zurich in July 1849, Wagner realised that his operas were virtually outcasts from the stages of Europe and he commenced a vast literary output to defend himself against the attacks of prejudice, malice and ignorance, to which he felt his music subjected. During the next three years, there appeared a series of essays, explaining his aims and at the same time making his own purpose clear to himself for the Music–Drama of the Future.

After this activity he returned to work on the Nibelungen legend which he had commenced with *Siegfrieds Tod* in November 1848. On second thoughts he felt this needed a preceding poem as explanation.

He wrote *Jung Siegfried* during May and June 1851. Then, realising he must go back to the roots of German mythology, he worked backwards completing the poem *Die Walküre* in the summer of 1852. The prologue to the Trilogy, *Das Rheingold*, was finished by the following November and the whole cycle was privately printed in 1853 with the first two Siegfried poems revised and retitled *Siegfried* and *Götterdämmerung*.

Work on the music, of which some preliminary sketches dated from 1850, was then begun in earnest. The full score of *Das Rheingold* was completed by September 26, 1854.

During 1855 Wagner was conductor for the Philharmonic Society in London. On his return *Die Walküre* was completed by March 23, 1856; work on the composition of *Siegfried* followed.

Two dramatic sketches were also written during this year, *Wieland der Schmiedt* (*Wieland the Smith*), which Wagner hoped to have translated into French and then compose for the Paris Opéra, a project which did not materialise, and *Die Sieger* (*The Victors*), another unfulfilled idea.

In 1857 *Siegfried* was laid aside while the prose sketch of *Parsifal* was written and the poem of *Tristan und Isolde* was written at the height of his affair with Mathilde Wesendonck, which was to be the cause of his hurried departure for Venice in 1859. During the ensuing years of European travel *Die Meistersinger* was written and the music sketched between 1862 and 1867.

The four poems were published in 1863 as *Der Ring des Nibelungen* (*The Ring of the Nibelung*), Wagner having almost given up hope of ever completing the music, but in the following year Ludwig II of Bavaria invited Wagner to Munich, promising every assistance in carrying out the composer's projects.

Tristan und Isolde was produced with Hans von Bülow as conductor in June 1865.

Wagner recommenced work on the interrupted *Siegfried* but once again Court opposition forced him to quit Munich for Switzerland; it was at Tribschen, on Lake Lucerne, that he finished the score of *Die Meistersinger* in 1867 and it was produced at Munich in 1868.

The sketches of *Siegfried* were finished by August 1869 and the composition of *Götterdämmerung* followed immediately thereafter. The sketching of the music occupied Wagner until 1872.

The full score of *Siegfried* was finished by February 1871 and that of *Götterdämmerung* by November 1874. Meantime, *Das Rheingold* had been staged by von Perfall at Munich, against Wagner's wishes, in September 1869. *Die Walküre* followed in June 1870.

A two act comedy 'in ancient style' *Eine Kapitulation* (*A Capitulation*) was written by Wagner in 1871 while at work on *The Ring*.

The plans of King Ludwig for a special Wagner theatre in Munich having fallen through, in 1871 the composer decided upon Bayreuth as a home for his work.

The foundation stone of the Festival Theatre was laid on Wagner's birthday, May 22, 1872. The money to build the theatre was raised by private subscription, by Wagner Societies formed all over Europe and by a series of concerts arranged in many German cities. The 'Music of the Future' was rapidly gaining adherents and dividing musical opinion, for and against, to an almost alarming extent.

In the new theatre, Wagner put into practice his theories of construction, staging and design.

Founding his Theatre on the ancient Greek principle, he said:

'In the classical "orchestra", which was almost entirely enclosed by the amphitheatre, was the place for the tragic chorus, in the heart of the public, as it were: its singing, and instrumentally accompanied dancing, induced such enthusiasm in the public that the hero, appearing on the stage in his mask, had all the veracity of a spiritual apparition for the now perspicacious audience. The symphony orchestra will be rather similarly related to the kind of drama I have in mind as the Greek tragic chorus was to the dramatic plot. In the Greek theatre the element of music, which was the sole origin of the tragic work of art, took physical shape in the chorus or the orchestra: in the course of the changes which have taken place in the cultural destiny of modern Europe, the instrumental orchestra, a development of the original chorus, has evolved into our most original, in fact our only truly new, creation in the sphere of art, and one which is typical of our spirit. Hence: here the immeasurable potential of the orchestra, there the dramatic mime; here the womb of the ideal drama, there its manifestation, sounding from every side. . . .

'My demand that the orchestra should be made invisible immediately suggested to the famous architect, with whom I was lucky enough to discuss the project, the use to which the empty space thus created between the proscenium and the auditorium could be put; we called it the mystic abyss because it is intended to separate reality from idealism, and the architect enclosed it to the front in an enlarged second proscenium, the effect of which, in relationship to the rear, narrower proscenium, he expected would be the marvellous illusion of the actual scene moving further away; this consists in the spectator having the impression that the scene is at a great distance although he can at the same time see it with the clarity of real closeness; this, in turn, has the effect of producing another illusion, in that the figures in the scene appear to be of enlarged, superhuman dimensions.

The importance of the orchestra being invisible will be obvious to anyone who has been to one of our opera performances with the intention of gaining a true impression of a dramatic and artistic achievement, and who has then been made a witness to the mechanical movements attendant on the musicians' and their conductor's performance, to technical evolutions which should certainly be concealed from him almost as carefully as the strings, ropes, and boards of the scenery, which, when viewed from the wings, have a notoriously destructive effect on any illusion. Once one has realised how transfigured the tone of an orchestra is when heard through an acoustic screen, how pure, and free from all the added extra-musical noises which are unavoidable accompaniments to the playing of musical instruments, and if one then imagines the advantage to the singer if he has, as it were, direct contact with his listeners, and considers, for example, the greater ease in understanding his words, then one cannot but have the most favourable opinion as to the success of the acoustic-architectonic arrangement I suggest.'

After some delays the Festspielhaus was finally opened in August 1876, with the first complete performance of *Der Ring des Nibelungen*.

The Cycle was given three times with great artistic success, but with financial disaster. The scenery and costumes were sold and the theatre remained closed until 1882, when it reopened with *Parsifal*. *The Ring* was not seen again at Bayreuth until 1896. Meantime parts of the Cycle gradually achieved production in other opera houses. Large excerpts were heard in London at the Royal Albert Hall Wagner Festival in May 1877. Eight concerts were given under Wagner himself and Hans Richter, with singers from Bayreuth and Munich, including Amalie Materna, Friederike von Sadler-Grün, Babette Waibel, Elisabeth Exter, Georg Unger, Karl Hill, Max Schlosser and Chandon.

Later Angelo Neumann formed his 'Richard Wagner Theatre', under the composer's guidance, bringing *The Ring* to London in May 1882, and under Mapleson's management, giving three-and-a-half Cycles at Her Majesty's Theatre. It was announced that Wagner would be present but he did not arrive on this occasion.

The company toured Europe until June 1883. Their scenery and costumes were said to be those 'which have been so much admired at the Bayreuth festival-plays', and used 'by special permission of H.M. The King of Bavaria'.

London also saw *Tristan und Isolde* and *Die Meistersinger* for the first time, at Drury Lane, during Hermann Franke's season in May–June 1882, which also included the first German productions in England of *Der fliegende Holländer*, *Tannhäuser* and *Lohengrin*. These two months gave vast scope to the Wagnerites and to the opposition.

The Ring Cycle in its entirety was first seen out of London in February 1910, at Edinburgh, in English, under Ernst Denhof's management and in the provinces the following year.

The whole Cycle was not broadcast until 1950 (on the B.B.C. Third Programme from Covent Garden). America had to wait until 1975 to see a complete Cycle in English when it alternated with a Cycle in German at Seattle.

In 1976 Le Théâtre Magie, a puppet theatre founded by Charles Hamilton and Christopher Graham in a London railway arch, commenced the task of producing a complete Cycle performed by marionettes. *Das Rheingold* was presented on March 21 and throughout the summer performances to both German and English recordings were given. *Die Walküre* followed in September and the complete Cycle in April 1977. The conquest of the Music of the Future was complete!

REVIEW

The issue of *Punch* dated May 20, 1882, had some fun at the expense of the first London production.

'THE PRIZE RING DES NIBELUNGEN; OR, PANTO-MIME AND THE THREE MERRY MAIDENS OF THE RHINO. [By Alfred E. Watson]

'Few men have made more noise in the world than Herr Richard Wagner, and if anybody doubt it, let him try the *Ring des Nibelungen; or, Panto-Mime and the Three Merry Maidens of the Rhino*. The *Nibelungen* is made up of "motives," but Herr Wagner's motives are often hard to understand. "Blow it all!" says Herr Wagner (they have trombones, *and they all do it*), "here goes!" Herr Wagner's rule is, "When in doubt, play the drum." This raises a spirit of emulation in the bosom of the gentleman who has been entrusted with the cymbals. Bang they go! The violins tremble with indignation. Herr Seidl waves his arms to the ophicleides; at it go the horns, and the singers yell in another key, to show that they are not to be put down by the odds against them. Half-a-dozen "motives" have been going on – if one could only have picked them out.

'The *Nibelungen* opens with a view of some queer fish in an Aquarium. Here are the Rhine Maidens with Our New Patent Self-instructing Swimming Apparatus fitted on them, trying to remember that pretty little thing they heard last night. They don't recollect the proper words, so *Woglinde* sings the tune, which seems to be badly recollected from MENDELSSOHN, to the thrilling words:

"Weia! Waga! Waga la Weia!
Wallala, weiala weia!"

'Then "Gin a body meet a body coming through the Rhine." Everybody joins in chorus.

'These bodies are taking care of the Rheingold, or Rhino, as it is generally called, and a bad young man, *Panto-Mime's* brother, comes and walks about in the water; to which these bold young minxes do not object until he goes up the ladder, which has been incautiously left, from the bottom of the Rhine to the shelf on which the Rhino rests, and walks off with the treasure. Then they let off the steam – which, by the way, they do on every possible occasion. Before the steam has quite evaporated, and while there is still a good deal of Hot-bathy smell about the place, the gauze rises, and discovers about as coarsely a painted scene as we ever remember. Here *Wotan*, the King of the Gods, is in a very low state of mind, because the Giants have built him a palace and are coming to ask for their money. The *"Can't-pay-the-Rent-and-don't-know-what-I-shall-do-about-the-Taxes Motive"* expresses *Wotan's* sorrow, after which, to some good old pantomime music, in come the giants *Fafner* and *Fasolt*. You know they are giants directly, because it is stated so in the bill; though, as a matter of fact, dwarfs, giants, and gods are all the same size. To their *"Now-then,-Gov'nor,-are-you-going-to-weigh-in? Motive,"* *Wotan* replies that he really shall be very much obliged if they will kindly make it convenient to call again, and off they go, taking with them the goddess *Fry-a*, so named because she acts as a sort of plain cook and bakes the apples, which is all that keeps the gods young. For these gods are in a very bad way altogether. *Wotan*, who is a disreputable old man, then goes off on an expedition to steal the Rhino from *Panto-Mime's* brother, who is very good at conjuring tricks; and, at the bad old man's request, transforms himself into a crocodile, which makes the god very nervous, and he hits at him with his spear to the *"I-say,-you-know,-no-larks Motive."* The performer then changes himself into a toad, and to the *"Halloal-now-I've-got-you Motive,"* *Wotan* treads on him and steals the ring and the money. The Giants call again, *Wotan* settles their little account, and then, to the *"Schlog-him-on-the-kop Motive,"* *Fafner* settles his brother.

'Parts of the *Walküre* had better not be talked about; but it may be said that *Siegmund*, having been engaged in mortal combat for some hours with the brother of *Hunting* (a great sportsman), runs away, and takes refuge in *Hunting's* hut. *Hunting* asks him to supper, but *doesn't give him any*, and *Siegmund*, who hates being chaffed, accepts a challenge to settle it next morning after breakfast – that is to say, after *Hunting's* breakfast, for *Siegmund's* chances of getting any are remote. Wotan's wife drives in on her chariot drawn by rams to the *"Baa,-baa,-black-sheep Motive,"* and after letting the poor old god have it right and left, insists upon his seconding *Hunting*; and his daughter *Brünnhilde* backs up *Siegmund*, though her father distinctly tells her not to do so. Neither of the combatants has the least idea of fighting, and they both die apparently of fright, in spite of the fact that *Siegmund* has found a sword sticking in a tree which he has been assured will render him invincible; but that's the way it happens when Herr WAG-NER is to the fore. The Prize Ring they are all fighting about is not really the least good to anybody, and the all-conquering sword is smashed at the first go off. *Wotan* then proceeds to have it out with *Brünnhilde*, who has run away to her sisters, and finds them playing at horses, mounted on little wooden animals, to the "*Six-to-four-on-the-field,-two-to-one-bar-one Motive*." Up comes *Wotan* and condemns *Brünnhilde* to go to sleep for an indefinite period, only permitting her to have a fire lighted to prevent the bad effects of the night air, lest, when she does wake up, influenza should prevent her from expressing her gratitude to the gallant knight who rescues her. The fire is shown by much vapour with light thrown on it, but it is not very effective here, and can scarcely be called a *succès de steam*.

'This Knight is to be *Siegfried*, who is living in the forest with *Panto-Mime*, and, indulging in a good deal of bear-play – brings a bear in with him to help; but though the bear is evidently connected with *Panto-Mime*, that dwarf does not like it. *Wotan* is prowling about, and as he can't get anyone else to listen to him, and *Panto-Mime* is rather small, he keeps on obliging him with another stave, till *Siegfried* returns, joins together the fragments of the sword his father, *Siegmund*, made such a mess of, and goes for the giant *Fafner*, who is living in a cave hidden in a second-hand "property" dragon – that's the way *he* enjoys the Rhino he has got possession of. *Fafner* has caught a dreadful cold in his head, and greets *Siegfried* with the "*Aren't-you-frightened? Motive*," but *Siegfried* isn't in the least, and before *Fafner* can get out of the "property," he is pierced by the sword, and perishes to the "*Just-about-under-the-fifth-rib,-I-fancy? Motive*."

'Here is some graceful and melodious music. The ill-used strings have an innings, and make the most of it, and the flutes, brass, oboes, and clarinets take advantage of the opportunity. *Siegfried's* general appreciation of larks has taught him to understand the language of the birds, and one of them, to the "*Second-turning-to-the-right-and-then-keep-straight-on Motive*," tells him where *Brünnhilde* is sleeping. He goes, wakes her up, falls in love with her, and then begins the Grand Vocal Competition. "Nice voice you have," says

Siegfried. "Oh, do you think so? That's very kind of you," says *Brünnhilde.* "Not in the least. Can you sing A's?" "Certainly. Can you? I can sing B's." "Really! I can sing C sharp, if I want to. Let's see how long we can keep on at it? I'm a little out of practice, though. Why, I've been sleeping here since long before you were born!" "How strange! Never mind. Come on!"

'Advice to those who want to hear the Grand Vocal Competition: Go outside. Use your own judgment as to coming in again.

'There is one excellent thing about the *Götterdämmerung* – it is the last of the series.

'Advice to those who go to hear the *Götterdämmerung* (which begins at half-past six): – See the Prologue; go and dine quietly at your Club; come back and ask a friend to tell you all about *Gunter* – without the ices – and his relations. Here are *Siegfried* and *Brünnhilde.* He gives her the ring, she gives him her horse. To the "*Trifle-weak-in-the-forelegs,-but-otherwise-sound-enough Motive,*" *Brünnhilde* tells her husband to "uphold him well," (see Mr. Alfred Forman's ingenious translation of the book). Unfortunately, however, *Siegfried,* having got a good deal mixed up with all the conjuring business, forgets that he is married, commits bigamy, and is stuck in the back, when he isn't looking, by his brother-in-law, *Hagen,* who is probably rehearsing Clown's business for Christmas, as he waggishly directs *Siegfried's* attention to a couple of birds up in the air, and then sticks him. The "*Dirty-mean-trick Motive*" expresses natural abhorrence. Out of forty-five characters, forty-one are now dead, so the vocalists give in, and with a triumphant flourish in the orchestra it's all over.

'Honourable mention: Herr Niemann, voice a good deal worn, but good artist all round. Herr Heinrich Vogl, good singer, good actor. Herr Schlosser, very admirable performance of *Panto-Mime.* If Herr Wagner's music is in advance of his age (is he twelve?), his *mise en scène* is very far behind it.'

The following week (May 27, 1882) *Punch* followed through with another stinging, though less amusing diatribe.

WAGNER WAGGERIES.

'Of course it is utterly bad taste to declare that we would far rather hear *The Flying Dutchman* or *Lohengrin* than the whole of the *Ring des Nibelungen.* After four nights of the *Ring*, with the *Ring* of it still in our ears, – which makes us look and feel quite savage, – we deliberately say, "Never again with you, *Wotan, Siegfried, & Co.!*"

'It appears to our untutored and uncultivated taste that the *Ring*, taken as an "all round" work, is just what might be expected from an impulsive musician after seeing a melodrama and a pantomime for the first time, and struck by the happy thought of combining the effects and setting them to music. As to "Motives" – this is no marvellous creation of genius, as in every pantomime or ballet of action there has always been a certain phrase to indicate the arrival of every character possessing a marked individuality. When the Giant enters in *Jack the Giant-Killer*, there is the Giant Motive; and whenever *Blunderbore* is "heard without," this Motive recurs. The celebrated "Every Schoolboy" who has been to a Christmas pantomime knows by the music when a fairy is going to appear, and when *Old Mother Hubbard* is about to enter with her crutch-handled stick, also when *Pantaloon* is coming, by the conventional "hobble motive." Nay, in a pantomime there is a recurring Motive, we fancy, for a policeman, and invariably a rum-tum-tum-tum-tiddly-iddly-iddly-iddly Motive for the entrance of *Clown*. Of course genuine pantomime may be considered as the highest form of Dramatic Art; and this view must be seriously held by all Wagnerites, with whom in this instance we are inclined to agree.

'In melodrama the music is suited to the action throughout; and the repetition in Act III. of a strain that first occurs in Act I. is so invariably recognised as a connecting link for a train of thought that, on hearing it, the spectator can positively say, "Here she is again!" or "She's thinking of the parting with her lover in Act I."

'The Story of the Ring could be easily told in three, or, at the most, four Acts. As it is, several moderate "cuts" have been found necessary. How the audience brightened up whenever there was anything resembling a "tune"! How delighted they are when Herr Vogl acts and does something; and how pleased is everyone to get a laugh at the Dragon's expense!

'Our recipe for a Festival Play of this sort is: – Give a Composer plenty of rope and any amount of brass. We could do it ourselves if we only had brass enough; and we at once acknowledge that our Leading Motive would be the Pecuniary, or "Chink Motive."

'There is a greater chance for the Drury Lane German Opera, which commenced last week with *Lohengrin* and *Tannhäuser*. *Die Meistersinger* is advertised for the 30th May; Weber's *Euryanthe* for

June 6th, and Wagner's *Tristan und Isolde* for the 20th. Whatever the Wagner Motives may be for appealing to the British Public, whether der "chinken-motive" above-mentioned, or simply artistic, or a reasonable combination of both, we wish our musical Cousin-Germans success, and a blessing "on both their Houses." '

DAS RHEINGOLD
(The Rhinegold)

Prelude to the Trilogy
(In One Act and Four Scenes)

Libretto

Completed in Zurich by November 1852.

Music

Conceived at Spezzia, Autumn 1853. Sketched November 1, 1853–January 14, 1854. Score completed September 26, 1854.

Characters

Wotan	Gods	Bass-baritone
Donner		Bass
Froh		Tenor
Loge		Tenor
Fasolt	Giants	High Bass
Fafner		Deep Bass
Alberich	Nibelungs	Baritone
Mime		Tenor (Buffo)
Fricka	Goddesses	Mezzo-soprano
Freia		High Soprano
Erda		Alto
Woglinde	Rhine Maidens	Soprano and Alto
Flosshilde		
Wellgunde		

SCENE 1 In the Depths of the Rhine.
SCENE 2 An Open Space on the Mountain-Top.
SCENE 3 The Subterranean Caves of Nibelheim.
SCENE 4 An Open Space on the Mountain-Top.

FIRST PRODUCED. Hoftheater, Munich, September 22, 1869.

FIRST PRODUCED IN A COMPLETE CYCLE. Festspielhaus, Bayreuth, August 13, 1876.

FIRST PRODUCED IN ENGLAND. Her Majesty's Theatre, London, May 5, 1882, in a complete Cycle sung in German.

FIRST PRODUCED IN AMERICA. Metropolitan Opera House, New York, January 4, 1889. Included in a complete Cycle with the same cast, March 4, 1889. Sung in German.

FIRST PRODUCED IN ENGLISH. Royal Opera House, Covent Garden, London, January 27, 1908, in a complete Cycle. Translated by Frederick Jameson.

FIRST PRODUCED IN AMERICA IN ENGLISH. Carnegie Hall, New York, November 10, 1924, in a translation by Ernest Newman, by the English Grand Opera Company.

FIRST PRODUCED IN AMERICA IN ENGLISH IN A COMPLETE CYCLE. Opera House, Seattle, July 22, 1975, in a translation by Andrew Porter.

DAS RHEINGOLD (THE RHINEGOLD) – CASTS

CHARACTERS	MUNICH 1869	BAYREUTH 1876 (Complete Cycle)	LONDON 1882 (Complete Cycle in German)
Wotan	August Kindermann	Franz Betz	Emil Scaria
Donner	Karl Samuel Heinrich	Eugen Gura	Heinrich Wiegand
Froh	Franz Nachbaur	Georg Unger	H. Burger
Loge	Heinrich Vogl	Heinrich Vogl	Heinrich Vogl
Fasolt	Toni Petzer	Albert Eilers	Albert Eilers
Fafner	Kaspar Bausewein	Franz von Reichenberg	Robert Biberti
Alberich	Karl Fischer	Karl Hill	Otto Schelper
Mime	Karl Schlosser	Karl Schlosser	Max Schlosser
Fricka	Sophie Stehle	Friederike Grün	H. Reicher-Kindermann
Freia	Henriette Müller	Marie Haupt	Antonie Schreiber
Erda	Therese Seehofer	Louise Jaide	Orlanda Riegler
Woglinde	Anna Kaufmann	Lilli Lehmann	Auguste Krauss
Flosshilde	Wilhelmine Ritter	Minna Lammert	Maria Schulze
Wellgunde	Therese Vogl	Marie Lehmann	Katharina Klafsky
Conductor	Franz Wüllner	Hans Richter	Anton Seidl
Producer	Reinhard Hallwachs	Richard Wagner	Albert Petermann
Designer	*Scenery* Scene 1 Heinrich Döll Scenes 2 & 3 Christian Jank and Angelo Quaglio *Costumes* Franz Seitz	*Scenery* Josef Hoffmann *Costumes* Carl Emil Doepler	*Scenery* Josef Hoffmann *Costumes* Carl Emil Doepler

DAS RHEINGOLD (THE RHINEGOLD) – CASTS (continued)

CHARACTERS	NEW YORK 1889 (Complete Cycle in German)	LONDON 1908 (Compete Cycle in English)	NEW YORK 1924 (In English)	AMERICA 1975 (Complete Cycle in English)
Wotan	Emil Fischer	Clarence Whitehill	William Tucker	Noel Tyl
Donner	Alois Grienauer	Charles Knowles	Frank Dobert	William Taylor
Froh	Albert Mittelhauser	Walter Hyde	Oliver Stewart	Leonard Eagleson
Loge	Max Alvary	E. C. Hedmondt	Louis Dornay	Ticho Parly
Fasolt	Ludwig Mödlinger	Robert Radford	Dudley Marwick	Norman Smith
Fafner	Eugene Weiss	Francis Harford	Augusto Ottone	Frederick Guthrie
Alberich	Joseph Beck	Thomas Meux	Fred Patton	Malcolm Rivers
Mime	Wilhelm Sedlmayer	Hans Bechstein	George Gordon	Paul Crook
Fricka	Fanny Moran-Olden	Borghild Bryhn	Mariska Aldrich	Marvellee Cariaga
Freia	Katti Bettaque	Christine d'Almayne	Adele Rankin	Norma Lynn
Erda	Hedwig Reil	Edna Thornton	Devora Nadworney	Geraldine Decker
Woglinde	Sophie Traubman	Leonora Sparkes	Thelma Votipka	Patricia Cullen
Flosshilde	Hedwig Reil	Edna Thornton	Sheila Fryer	Carolyn Maia
Wellgunde	Felicie Kaschowska	Caroline Hatchard	Geraldine Marwick	Shirley Lee Harned
Conductor	Anton Seidl	Hans Richter	Ernst Knock	Henry Holt
Producer	Habelmann	E. C. Hedmondt	Andreas Dippel	George London
Designer	*Scenery* Hans Kautsky *Costumes* Dazien (after Carl Doepler)		Willy Pogany	John T. Naccarato

SYNOPSIS

SCENE 1 At the bottom of the river the three Rhine-Maidens, Woglinde, Wellgunde and Flosshilde, are playing beside the rock on which rests the sacred Gold that has been entrusted to their care. To them comes as a suitor the hideous dwarf Alberich. Each one in turn encourages him, and then cruelly mocks his ugliness.

The dwarf is raging, when suddenly his thoughts are diverted as the gold on the rock is magically lit by sunrays from above, and the three maidens sing a hymn in its praise. Alberich questions them, and they tell him the story of the gold: how he who obtains possession of it and shapes himself a magic ring will become master of the world – but only if he renounces love.

In his fury and humiliation, Alberich is quite ready to accept this condition. While the nymphs are laughing and jesting, he suddenly climbs the rock, grasps the gold, and disappears with it, leaving the Rhine-Maidens crying out for their lost treasure.

SCENE 2 Outside their new and splendid castle, Wotan, chief of the gods, and his consort Fricka are sleeping in a flowery meadow. Fricka rouses her husband and begins to reproach him for the agreement with the giants Fasolt and Fafner, by which he has promised to give them her sister Freia, the goddess of Youth and Beauty, as a reward for building his castle. Wotan points out that it was Fricka herself who asked for the new home, and she retorts that her main object in wanting it was to prevent him from straying outside. A domestic quarrel is developing, when Freia rushes in, crying for help. Closely pursued by the giants, she calls her brothers Donner and Froh to her aid. Wotan merely tells her that he is waiting for the cunning fire-god Loge, who will surely find a way to evade the contract.

Meanwhile, the giants arrive to claim their reward. All Wotan's efforts to temporise are in vain: they want Freia and nothing else. They are trying to seize her by force, when her brothers come to the rescue. Donner threatens the giants with his hammer; but Wotan forbids him to fight, saying that he must uphold the contract with his own spear. Freia, thus apparently abandoned to her fate, is in despair, when Loge at last arrives, to be reproached for his lateness. Donner and Froh turn their wrath on him, but again Wotan intervenes, asking Loge if during his wanderings he has found a substitute for Freia. In reply, Loge relates the theft by Alberich of the Rhinegold.

The giants listen eagerly, and Loge sees that their cupidity has been aroused. Fricka shows interest when Loge tells her that any woman possessing the Ring forged from it will be certain to keep her husband faithful. Wotan too desires the hoard, and also the power of the Ring, which Loge reveals has already been fashioned by Alberich.

After a private colloquy the giants have come to a decision: they will take Freia as a hostage, but will give her up in exchange for the Nibelung's gold. Despite her cries for help they carry her away.

Almost at once a mist begins to invade the scene, and the gods assume an aged and haggard appearance: even the turbulent Donner and Froh grow gloomy and inert; without Freia and her golden apples, the eternal youth of the gods must quickly wither.

Wotan decides on immediate action to seize the Rhinegold. As he and Loge plunge downward into the sulphurous depths of the earth, a black cloud rises and envelops all.

SCENE 3   In a subterranean cavern Alberich is scolding his brother Mime, whom he has charged with making out of the Rhinegold a 'Tarnhelm', or helmet, enabling the wearer to change his shape, or even become invisible, at will.

Mime pretends that it is not ready, but when Alberich violently shakes him, the work that he has been concealing falls from his hand. Alberich puts it on, disappears, and begins to rain unseen blows on his brother, whose screams and groans are heard by Wotan and Loge as they approach.

In answer to their questions Mime tells them how Alberich has used the power of the Ring to make himself master over the Nibelungs. He ill-treats them, forcing them to toil all day to mine gold for him and melt it into ingots. Mime had intended to keep the Tarnhelm for himself, hoping by its means to steal the Ring; but, not knowing how to use its magic properties, he has let Alberich take it. The gods roar with laughter at this tale, promising to set the Nibelungs free in exchange for Mime's help.

Alberich, visible now that he has removed the Tarnhelm, comes back, whip in hand, driving and cursing at a train of slaves laden with gold. He challenges the strangers, and Wotan replies smoothly that they have come as guests to witness the marvels of which they have heard. Suspiciously, Alberich taunts them with the threat of his rising power: Wotan gives an angry exclamation, but controls himself at Loge's warning. The fire-god suggests to Alberich that perhaps he is exaggerating the powers of the Tarnhelm. Can he give them a demonstration?

Yes, indeed, replies Alberich – and promptly transforms himself into a huge dragon. Loge pretends to be terrified; then, when Alberich is back in his normal shape, asks if he can also turn himself into something small – a toad, for example. Alberich falls into the trap: the gods grasp the toad and take away the Tarnhelm. Once more in his own form, Alberich finds himself their captive.

SCENE 4   On to the misty mountain-top emerge Wotan and Loge, dragging with them the pinioned Alberich, who curses and vows his revenge. As ransom Wotan demands his hoard and the Ring. Alberich is ready enough to part with the gold, which he knows he can replenish, but extremely reluctant to give up the Ring. At last, however, Wotan tears it from his finger by force. Loge then releases him and tells him to be off home; but before he goes Alberich lays a solemn curse on the Ring, that it may bring death to all who own it.

As the Nibelung vanishes again into the depths, Fasolt and Fafner appear to demand the gold. They have brought Freia back, and her return immediately dispels the mist and gives the gods back their look of youth. The giants agree to take, in exchange for Freia, a stack of gold equal in height and width to the young goddess as she stands in the midst of it.

Fafner watches as Loge piles it up, and his insistence to see that the gold is solidly pressed down angers Donner, who threatens him. Undeterred, he insists that the Tarnhelm and the Ring be added to the hoard. When Wotan insists on keeping the Ring for himself, the giants seize Freia and prepare to carry her away.

Then the Earth-spirit Erda rises from the ground to warn Wotan gravely that he had better give up the Ring, for only disaster will follow if he keeps it. Accordingly, as she sinks down again, Wotan throws it on to the heap of gold.

The giants then begin to quarrel over the Ring, one snatching it from the other, until in the struggle Fafner deals Fasolt a fatal blow with his staff. Callously ignoring his dying brother, he then throws the Ring into his sack and proceeds to gather up the rest of the gold.

Now that he has seen the effect of the curse, Wotan is deeply alarmed: he wishes to take counsel of Erda, but Fricka suggests he had better seek the safety of his new castle. This is still veiled in mist, but Donner clears the air with a thunderstorm, and with Froh builds a rainbow bridge over the valley to the castle, which Wotan now solemnly names 'Valhalla'. He and Fricka pass over the bridge, followed by Donner, Froh and Freia. Looking after them, Loge foresees their doom and is tempted for a moment to hasten it by fire; but finally he crosses the bridge in his turn.

On the threshold Wotan is halted by the complaint of the Rhine-maidens. He sternly bids them cease lamenting their gold; instead, they should rejoice at the new splendour of the gods.

REVIEW

The Music Critic in *The Era*, May 13, 1882, wrote of the first English performance:

'The first performance of a work so long anticipated and so much discussed, as the *Nibelungen Ring*, naturally attracted a large audience to Her Majesty's Theatre on Friday evening, May 5th, when this strange opera, or series of operas, was first heard in England. The story of this colossal production is as remarkable as the work itself and the composer who produced it, and it is impossible for the sturdiest opponents of Richard Wagner to withhold their admiration, when it is remembered how long the composer brooded over this pet idea, and with what undaunted energy and perseverance he at length placed it before the public. We shall reserve special comments respecting the system – or as some say want of system – adopted by Wagner in the composition of the *Nibelungen Ring* until we have made our readers more fully acquainted with the subject matter. The entire work is in a prelude and three dramas, and thus four nights are required for the performance. It is well known that Wagner's first ideas on the subject of taking the old Teutonic myths as the foundation of this gigantic operatic experiment exposed him to ridicule and opposition. There were, however, a few among his friends who admired the project, and one especially, Charles Tausig, the eminent pianist, who felt so much interested that he started societies in various European cities for the purpose of raising the necessary funds for the production of a work which he rightly calculated could not possibly appeal to the general public, but must be reserved for those capable of entering into the spirit of Wagner's ideas. The theatre at Bayreuth was the result of these endeavours, and in the month of August, 1876, the *Nibelungen Ring* was produced in the presence of a special audience, and under circumstances likely to give the work every possible advantage. Of course the idea of taking such a subject as the *Nibelungen Ring* was to give the musical public of the Fatherland something distinctively national. There was a great awakening of patriotic feeling after the triumphs Germany won over unfortunate France, and there were plenty of enthusiasts who wished that in music, as in everything else, Germany should assert herself as she had never done before. The weird forms of German mythology appeared to furnish subjects sufficiently large for the imagination and powers of the composer, who, in choosing these barbaric heroes, also chose to invent a new style of opera to introduce them. Consequently in the *Nibelungen Ring* we bid farewell to the old forms that served Mozart, Rossini, Meyerbeer, and a host of others. In the present work of Wagner he discards the chorus, he will have nothing to do with airs, duets, or other forms of concerted music, but his characters utter their loves, their hatreds, their pleading, or defiance in long – very long – recitatives, broken by constant and never-ceasing passages in the orchestra, and the subject of the entire work is carried out in this way. No sooner has one personage delivered in continuous recitative – frequently reminding one of murmured conversations rather than anything approaching to vocal effect – what he has to say than the wondrous tale is taken up by another, and so on until the curtain falls. In addition to this singular and frequently wearisome method there is another peculiarity which the disciples of Wagner are never tired of extolling. This is the system of separate musical phrases to characterise particular motives, incidents, or personages in the "music-drama," as Wagner calls it in preference to opera. Some of these "motives" profess to describe what in reality can never be described in music at all, while others merely follow a plan already freely used by other composers. Weber in his operas used special phrases to denote the appearance of the characters of the chief actors in his operas. Meyerbeer again does the same, and there is a greater example still in the *Fidelio* of Beethoven. Therefore we say that to give Wagner the credit of a system which had previously been so often adopted by other composers is sheer nonsense. But we freely admit that no other composer ever went so far in that direction, and for the simple and sufficient reason that the device is, after all, a mechanical one, and easily becomes tiresome. In one respect Wagner has made a true artistic advance in these works. He has given an importance to the orchestra it never had before. Merely to listen to the orchestra alone, in its varied changes, its novel effects, its wonderful colouring, has a charm for the musical student that causes him to forget much of the crudeness he sees upon the stage. The orchestra in Wagner's treatment is sometimes almost magical in its beauty and unexpected combinations of sound. When Wagner gets hold of a subject in his libretto that suggests beauty of treatment in the orchestra his genius shines forth resplendently. Then all harshness vanishes, and all that is far-fetched and pedantic, harsh and forbidden, is softened down into the most exquisite blending of instrumental sound imaginable. This great gift he possesses to an extent equalled by no other modern composer, and it will be for this, if for anything, that a future generation will listen to the *Nibelungen Ring*, and forgive the composer his fantastic theories. With regard to the libretto itself we shall have something to say, and that not of a complimentary nature. Truth to tell these old gods and heroes, these giants and dwarfs, were most abominable creatures, and nothing can be more immoral, more repulsive, more absolutely wicked than some of their doings, and not all the artistic skill of Wagner can make them otherwise. When we say that the principal hero is the offspring of an incestuous union with a brother and sister we ask if the modern stage, or indeed the stage at any period, ever witnessed a more horrible and revolting subject; and this is in no way softened down, for the glow and fervour of the music simply intensifies the scenes in which the hero and heroine appear. Nor is there any pretence whatever that the lovers are ignorant of their relationship. The excess of their passion becomes even more marked when this fact is known, and when the heroine laments the death of her brother she takes comfort in the promise that his and her son yet unborn will become a famous hero and avenge their fate. We shall dwell no longer at present upon incidents which were probably thought to be innocent because they were in another tongue. But books of the words were freely circulated with an English version. Yet do we not remember how, within a year or two, plays of childlike innocence compared with this have been prohibited. . . .'

After telling the plot the critic continues:

'Enough is shown even in the opening work of the repulsive character of the subject to make us regret that so much art, knowledge, ingenuity, and we will add genius, has been expended by Wagner on a story, or succession of stories, so far removed from human sympathies, and in too many instances thoroughly shocking and revolting to pure minds. We do not deny the beauty and musical interest of some portions of the *Rheingold*, but our pleasure in these items is procured at a sacrifice of self-respect. As we think of these Teutonic divinities we too frequently recall the old sea captain's opinion of the South Sea Islanders – "manners they had none, and their customs were beastly." This applies still more directly to operas yet to come. But let us meanwhile give due praise to the *artistes*, the orchestra, and the conductor, Herr Seidl. Herr Vogl, who represented Loge at Bayreuth, is an *artiste* in the best sense of the word. His vivacity reminds us of the French rather than the German school, and his acting in many instances was thoroughly brilliant and original. Herr Vogl's singing has some of the German peculiarities; indeed, the vocal art of Germany always had striking defects, especially in the production of the voice. This may be partially due to the uncouth language. Still the natural feeling and intelligence of the *artiste* made us forget all imperfections, and our verdict must be that Herr Vogl is one of the most remarkable members of the company, and in every way deserving of his reputation. Herr Otto Schelper as Alberich was another very able representative of the Wagner school. His rendering of Alberich had some admirable qualities. Of Herr Scaria as Wotan we shall speak further. He has the misfortune to impersonate one of the most abominable personages ever seen upon the stage. Every vice, defect, and frailty of human nature we see in an exaggerated form in that disgusting god Wotan. It is a comfort to know that poetic justice is dealt to this wretch and his brother monsters at the conclusion. Frau Reicher-Kindermann as Fricka had great merit; and Fraulein Schreiber as Freia, the Goddess of Youth, also deserved much commendation. The three Daughters of the Rhine were also well sustained. With regard to the orchestra, the combination of tone was admirable, particularly in the wind instruments; but we may note that the thin quality of the stringed instruments sometimes failed to give the fullest effect to the fine passages Wagner has written for them. The conductor, Herr Seidl, was warmly applauded, and there was as much enthusiasm as could have been expected. The scenic effects did not appeal greatly to the imagination. The concluding scene of the *Rheingold* was far inferior to some of our pantomimic transformation scenes.'

DIE WALKÜRE
(The Valkyrie)

———— · ————

First Day of the Trilogy

Libretto
Written in Zurich, May–June 1852.

Music
Commenced June 1854. First two Acts finished 1855, full score completed in Zurich, March 23, 1856.

Characters

Siegmund	Tenor
Hunding	Bass
Wotan	Bass-baritone
Sieglinde	Soprano
Brünnhilde	Soprano
Fricka	Mezzo-soprano
Gerhilde	
Ortlinde	
Waltraute	
Schwertleite	
Helmwige	Valkyries } Sopranos and Altos
Siegrune	
Grimgerde	
Rossweisse	

ACT I Inside Hunding's Dwelling.

ACT II A Wild Rocky Pass.

ACT III On the Summit of a Rocky Mountain. (The Valkyrie's Rock.)

FIRST PRODUCED. Hoftheater, Munich, June 26, 1870.

FIRST PRODUCED IN A COMPLETE CYCLE. Festspielhaus, Bayreuth, August 14, 1876.

FIRST PRODUCED IN AMERICA. Academy of Music, New York, April 2, 1877. Sung in German.

FIRST PRODUCED IN ENGLAND. Her Majesty's Theatre, London, May 6, 1882. In a complete Cycle. Sung in German.

FIRST PRODUCED IN AMERICA IN A COMPLETE CYCLE. Metropolitan Opera House, New York, March 5, 1889.

FIRST PRODUCED IN ENGLISH. Terato Nacional, Mexico City, April 14, 1891, in a Season by the Compañia In Glexide de Grand Opera under the direction of Carlos F. Locke.

FIRST PRODUCED IN ENGLAND IN ENGLISH. Royal Opera House, Covent Garden, London, October 16, 1895, in a Season under the direction of E. C. Hedmondt, in a translation by H. and F. Corder.

FIRST PRODUCED IN ENGLISH IN A COMPLETE CYCLE. Royal Opera House, Covent Garden, London, January 28, 1908, in a translation by Frederick Jameson.

FIRST PRODUCED IN AMERICA IN ENGLISH. Indiana University, Bloomington, Ind., March 22, 1970, in a translation by Stewart Robb.

FIRST PRODUCED IN AMERICA IN ENGLISH IN A COMPLETE CYCLE. Opera House, Seattle, July 23, 1975, in a translation by Andrew Porter.

DIE WALKÜRE (THE VALKYRIE) – CASTS

CHARACTERS	MUNICH 1870	BAYREUTH 1876 (Complete Cycle)	NEW YORK 1877 (In German)	LONDON 1882 (Complete Cycle in German)	NEW YORK 1889 (Complete Cycle in German)
Siegmund	Heinrich Vogl	Albert Niemann	A. Bischoff	Albert Niemann	Julius Perotti
Hunding	Kaspar Bausewein	Joseph Niering	A. Blum	Heinrich Wiegand	Eugene Weiss
Wotan	August Kindermann	Franz Betz	Felix Preusser	Emil Scaria	Emil Fischer
Sieglinde	Therese Vogl	Josephine Schefsky	Pauline Canissa	Therese Vogl	Katti Bettaque
Brünnhilde	Sophie Stehle	Amalie Materna	Eugénie Pappenheim	H. Reicher-Kindermann	Lilli Lehmann
Fricka	Anna Kaufmann	Friederike Grün	Listner	Orlanda Riegler	Louise Meisslinger
Gerhilde	Karoline Leonoff	Marie Haupt	Frida de Gebel	Auguste Krauss	Sedlimayer
Ortlinde	Henriette Müller	Marie Lehmann		Antonie Schreiber	Felicie Kaschowska
Waltraute	Hemauer	Louise Jaide		Katharina Klafsky	Louise Meisslinger
Schwertleite	Therese Seehofer	Johanna Jachmann-Wagner		Maria Schulze	Lena Göttich
Helmwige	Anna Possart-Deinet	Lilli Lehmann		Therese Milar	Sophie Traubman
Siegrune	Walburga Eichheim	Antonie Ammann		Lina Wagner	Egenor
Grimgerde	Wilhelmine Ritter	Hedwig Reicher-Kindermann		Rosalie Zoller	Hartmann
Rossweisse	Tyroler	Minna Lammert		Orlanda Riegler	Emmy Miron
Conductor	Franz Wüllner	Hans Richter	Adolf Neuendorff	Anton Seidl	Anton Seidl
Producer	Reinhard Hallwachs	Richard Wagner		Albert Petermann	Habelmann
Designer	*Scenery* Act I Christian Jank, Act 2 and Act 3 Heinrich Döll *Costumes* Franz Seitz	*Scenery* Josef Hoffmann *Costumes* Carl Emil Doepler		*Scenery* Josef Hoffmann *Costumes* Carl Emil Doepler	*Scenery* Hans Kautsky *Costumes* Dazien (after Carl Doepler)

DIE WALKÜRE (THE VALKYRIE) – CASTS (continued)

CHARACTERS	MEXICO 1891 (In English)	LONDON 1895 (In English)	LONDON 1908 (Complete Cycle in English)	AMERICA 1970 (In English)	AMERICA 1975 (Complete Cycle in English)
Siegmund	E. C. Hedmondt	E. C. Hedmondt	Walter Hyde	William Shriner	Claude Heater
Hunding		Alex Bevan	Robert Radford	Peter Schuba	Leon Lishner
Wotan		David Bispham	Clarence Whitehill	Roy Samuelsen	Noel Tyl
Sieglinde	Emma Juch	Susan Strong	Agnes Nicholls	Elizabeth Mannion	Lorna Haywood
Brünnhilde		Lillian Tree	Borghyld Bryhn	Margaret Harshaw	Anna Green
Fricka		Rosa Olitzka	Maud Santley	Martha Lipton	Marvellee Cariaga
Gerhilde		Russell	Caroline Hatchard	Mary Joy Johnston	Norma Lynn
Ortlinde		Singo	Jenny Taggart	Leah Beth Frey	Joan Falskow
Waltraute		Gray	Maud Santley	Pamela Herbert	Barbara Coffin
Schwertleite		Treflyn	Maria Yelland	Barbara Lockhard	Geraldine Decker
Helmwige		Kate Lee	Leonora Sparkes	Carolyn Yeldell	Thelma Salveson
Siegrune		Clare Addison	Edna Thornton	Anne Davidson	Shirley Lee Harned
Grimgerde		McCusker	Phyllis Archibald	Christine Cook	Carolyn Maia
Rossweisse		Rosa Olitzka	Dilys Jones	Marlene Reininghaus	Jennifer Chase
Conductor	Adolf Neuendorff	George Henschel	Hans Richter	Wolfgang Vacano	Henry Holt
Producer		E. C. Hedmondt	E. C. Hedmondt	Hans Busch	George London
Designer				C. Mario Cristini	John T. Naccarato

SYNOPSIS

ACT I

The scene is Hunding's dwelling-house, built around the stem of a huge ash-tree. Exhausted, dishevelled and weaponless, Siegmund pushes open the door, staggers to the hearth and there collapses.

After a while Hunding's wife, Sieglinde, disturbed by the noise he has made, comes to investigate. She finds the half-conscious man, who asks her for a drink. When she has revived him with water, followed by a draught of mead, he offers to go – but she tells him to await the coming of her husband.

Hunding is surprised to find his wife in the company of a strange man, but when she explains the circumstances he also offers hospitality to the guest. Glancing from him to Sieglinde, he is struck by their extraordinary resemblance; both, as he says, have 'the dragon-look in their eyes'.

He bids his wife serve supper and they sit down to their meal. Asked to tell them about himself, Siegmund gives his name as 'Wehwalt' (the Woeful). His father, he says, was 'Wolf', and he had a twin sister; but while the man and boy were away hunting, enemies had burned down their house, murdered his mother and carried away his sister. Siegmund had grown up in the forest, until one day his father had disappeared, leaving nothing but a wolf-skin behind him.

Sieglinde listens raptly to this tale and Hunding is sympathetic. Matters change, however, when 'Wehwalt' relates the sequel: how, in defence of a maiden, he has killed her brothers. It turns out that the kin of the slain men have appealed for redress to Hunding. The laws of hospitality forbid him to attack his guest on the spot – but next morning they will fight. He goes with Sieglinde into his room and closes the door.

Siegmund, left alone, laments that he has lost his sword. The firelight shining on the ash-trunk reveals the gleam of a sword-hilt buried deep in the tree; then it dies down and the room is dark.

Quietly the door opens and Sieglinde, in a white gown, enters, telling the joyfully surprised Siegmund that she has drugged her husband so that he may sleep soundly. She calls his attention to the weapon in the ash-tree. On the evening of her wedding-feast, she says, when robbers had snatched her and brought her to Hunding as his unwilling bride, a mysterious old man had entered the hall and thrust the sword into the tree, saying that only the bravest hero of all could draw it forth. Since then, many men have tried and all have failed, but she feels that her new guest will succeed.

Full of gratitude, Siegmund finds love for his beautiful hostess rising within him. Suddenly the great outer door swings open and, momentarily startled, they draw in the fragrance of the moonlit spring night.

Siegmund sings of the Spring, who goes forth in search of Love – his sister and his bride. The same joy has come to him, when, friendless and alone, he has met the fond sympathy of Sieglinde. At the end of the song she falls into his arms in a passionate embrace.

Gazing into his eyes she seems to recognise him – as he recognises her – in a dream: once again she asks his name, and when he says that he is a Volsung, she bestows on him that of her lost brother, Siegmund.

'Siegmund I am!' he exclaims, and goes forward unhesitatingly to draw the sword – for 'Wolf' his father has promised him that he shall find one in his dire need. Christening the sword 'Nothung' (Needful), with a mighty effort he draws it out. Now understanding everything, the delighted Sieglinde flings herself into his arms, crying: 'You have won your sister as well as your sword!' The curtain falls on their embrace and Siegmund's proud challenge:

> "Bride and sister be to your brother –
> So blossom the Volsung line!"

ACT II

In a wild and rocky pass, Wotan, in full battle array and carrying his spear, orders his daughter Brünnhilde – also fully armed – to go to the help of Siegmund and see that he wins his coming fight against Hunding. Brünnhilde, on her way to fetch her horse, calls back to Wotan bidding him look to himself, for Fricka, his wife, is on the war-path.

And in fact the goddess soon arrives, full of indignation, prepared to uphold the sanctity of marriage (as personified by Hunding) against the guilty brother and sister, whom she knows to be Wotan's own children, begotten of a mortal. The god resists as best he can, but is at last overborne by his wife, to the point of agreeing to let Hunding win the combat.

Brünnhilde, on the point of leaving, finds Wotan in deep dejection and guesses that he has had the worst of his encounter with Fricka. To her, his favourite child (of the nine Valkyries whom Erda has borne to him when he went to seek her counsel), he unburdens himself, telling her the story of the Ring, and how Alberich's hate threatens the destruction of the gods. All that shields them is the fact that the Ring is still in possession of Fafner, who has turned himself into a dragon to guard it and the hoard of gold. Wotan, bound by his agreement with the giant, cannot take it from him, nor can any other of the Æsir; it may only be done by a human hero, working alone with no help from the gods.

When Brünnhilde suggests that Siegmund is such a hero, Wotan replies sadly that he must bow to Fricka's will and abandon the Volsung to his fate; this is the curse that still clings to him from having handled Alberich's Ring: he must destroy what he loves.

Brünnhilde is not in agreement with this change of mind: she pleads for Siegmund, who has always enjoyed Wotan's protection; but the god sternly bids her fulfil his command. Sadly she takes up her weapons and goes to fetch her horse.

Siegmund and Sieglinde are in flight. Exhausted though she is, she wishes to go farther, but her brother persuades her to sit down and rest. She is deeply remorseful at having brought shame and danger upon him, and when they hear the horn-call of the pursuing Hunding she sinks down unconscious.

Brünnhilde, leading her horse, appears before Siegmund, telling him that only fated men can see her, and that she has come to fetch him away to Valhalla. He asks if he will find his father there, and she assures him that he will. When he hears, however, that Sieglinde will never join him there, he firmly refuses to follow Brünnhilde: to stay with his love he will renounce all the joys of Valhalla and go down into hell – if necessary he will even kill Sieglinde sooner than lose her. So impressed is Brünnhilde with his devotion that she promises to stand by him and give him victory in the coming battle.

Siegmund gently kisses the sleeping Sieglinde; then, at the sound of Hunding's horn, he goes forth into the gathering storm to meet him.

The thunder-peals awaken Sieglinde, who hears the two men defying each other and calls to them in anguish not to fight.

In a flash of lightning Brünnhilde is seen protecting Siegmund; then suddenly Wotan appears, splinters Siegmund's sword and allows Hunding to kill him. Sieglinde drops unconscious, but Brünnhilde snatches her up and swings her on to her horse. Wotan then avenges Siegmund by killing Hunding, and announces his intention of punishing Brünnhilde for her disobedience.

ACT III

On the summit of a rocky mountain four armed Valkyries are watching their sisters return from earth, each with a slain warrior hanging over her saddle-bow. Brünnhilde alone is missing.

At last she comes, in haste and fear, her horse Grane falling exhausted as she arrives. On her saddle is no warrior but a woman – the unconscious Sieglinde. She calls to her sisters for help, telling them that Wotan is pursuing her in wrath. Briefly she explains what has happened, and the Valkyries are horrified that she has dared to disobey All-Father's commands. They refuse to help her defy him.

Sieglinde, recovering her senses, says curtly that she needs no protection; since she has lost Siegmund, she herself wishes for nothing but a speedy death. But when Brünnhilde tells her that she is carrying Siegmund's child, her attitude changes; she begs the Valkyrie to save her, so that she may live to bear it.

A heavy storm heralds the approach of Wotan, and swiftly Brünnhilde tells her to go eastward into the forest, where the dragon Fafner lies guarding Alberich's Ring: there most certainly Wotan will not follow her. Taking out the fragments of Siegmund's sword, she gives them to Sieglinde, telling her to keep them for her son and to name him Siegfried.

Sieglinde escapes just in time, for Wotan, raging, calls to Brünnhilde through the tempest. Her sisters hide her in their midst, and when the god appears they beseech him to pardon her. He chides them severely and calls on Brünnhilde to come out and take her punishment.

When she does, he declares that by her own action she has forfeited the right to be a Valkyrie. Henceforth he disowns her: never again will she ride to fetch the heroes to Valhalla. She must lie in an enchanted sleep until a man awakens her, and then she must go to serve him humbly, to sit and spin by the hearth as his mortal wife.

The horrified Valkyries scatter in flight, and, with a cry, Brünnhilde sinks to the ground.

Remaining alone with Wotan, Brünnhilde pleads for mercy, saying that she carried out his real desire – for his order to destroy Siegmund was given against his will to placate Fricka.

Sternly, Wotan tells her that her duty was to carry out his commands, not to interpret them according to her own imagination. She prophesies that, owing to her intervention which has saved Sieglinde, a hero greater than all others will spring from the Volsung line. But Wotan will not be turned from his purpose. One favour alone he will concede to her: the place where she sleeps shall be ringed around with flame, so that only a hero of heroes will brave it to awaken her.

Then, solemnly, he embraces her, and with a kiss takes away her divinity. She sinks down and falls asleep: he closes her helmet and covers her with the great steel shield of the Valkyrie. At his command a stream of fire bursts from the earth and surrounds the rock on which she is lying.

REVIEW

The Music Critic in *The Era*, May 13, 1882, wrote of the first English performance:

'There was less excitement on Saturday night, because those who were new to the subject had acquired some knowledge of what they were to expect by the previous night's experience with the *Rheingold*. In the case of ordinary dramas we are told how long a period elapses, but in the case of gods, time is not thus measured, and we are left in doubt. Of some of the events taking place we learn only by narratives in *Die Walküre*. . . .'

After outlining the commencement of the opera the critic continues...

'There ensues a scene which has been defended by the admirers of Wagner as necessary to the completeness of the plot, but which, in our opinion, is not only unnecessary, but is also so revolting, indecent, and impure that it ought never to have been tolerated on the English stage. The subject may be simply told. It is nothing less than a sudden impulse of sensual passion between brother and sister. There is no mistake about it, no excuse that the relationship is unknown, for the hero openly requests Sieglinde to become "his sister and his bride," which the lady consents to without the slightest hesitation, and the climax of the first act is when the guilty and incestuous pair agree to fly at once; the act closing with a duet, the music of which is evidently written to suggest animal passion in its utmost excess. We have told this brutal and degrading story in as few words as our disgust will permit, but it is not thus told in the scene itself. All the resources of musical, scenic, and histrionic art are employed to make this sensual incident more striking. It is not lightly passed over – not referred to as some painful but necessary incident introduced for the elaboration of the story, but it is brought forward in the most prominent manner possible, as we could prove if we chose to offend the taste of our readers by quoting the libretto.

A composer must have lost all sense of decency and all respect for the dignity of human nature who could thus employ his genius and skill to heighten and render more effective a situation which should never again, if our authorities exert their power, be witnessed upon the English stage. Let us hurry over the scene, for the recollection of it is sickening. Sieglinde drugs her husband's drink, so that they may be undisturbed, and the incestuous pair steal away, the musical effect being heightened by an address to the spring, the pure light of the dawn stealing into the cottage as the lovers cling to each other in unhallowed embraces. Rather should deepest night and utter silence hide such a scene. The second act shows that Hunding is bent upon punishing the guilty pair. . . . Long recitatives of the dullest kind fill up the time, and there is nothing of the slightest interest save the occasional fine passages in the orchestra. No matter what else may be tiresome, we are always interested in the orchestra.

'One of the most striking and effective of the musical pieces in this drama is the ride of the Walkyries. The music is weird and unearthly, but it is appropriate to the situation, and produced great effect. Wagner offends us but too frequently with his far-fetched theories and his lamentable want of taste, yet when a scene suggests and demands fine music he is able to supply it. Art, imagination, and inspiration go hand in hand, and the impression produced is strong. The general representation was good; but perhaps hardly as fine as might have been anticipated. Herr Niemann has unquestionably been a splendid *artiste*, with a powerful tenor voice. It has lost its quality, but Herr Niemann retains his artistic skill, and frequently displayed remarkable powers. His acting was also telling and effective, marred, however, by the peculiarly objectionable subject. Herr Wiegand, as Hunding, made the most of a deep bass voice; and Herr Scaria, as the hateful Wotan, got through his dismal recitatives with astonishing determination. How he could remember them is a mystery. Frau Sachse-Hofmeister, in representing the most odious female character ever seen on our stage, displayed great talent as an actress, and also sang the few passages that could be fairly called vocal in good style. Her voice is rich and sympathetic, and her attitudes very picturesque. Frau Therese Vogl was excellent as Brünnhilde, and Frau Reicher-Kindermann gave all due importance to the character of Fricka. The scenic and other effects were generally good, but hardly realised the expectations of the audience, stimulated as they had been by the extravagant announcements of the Wagnerites. Granting there are passages for the musician to admire in *Die Walküre*, we must again repeat that nothing can justify the representation of such a story in public. Immoral and unspeakably degrading, it should have no place in true art.'

SIEGFRIED

Second Day of the Trilogy

Libretto

Written in Zurich, May–June 1851, as *Jung Siegfried*. Revised 1852.

Music

First sketch commenced 1856, continued 1857, laid aside and re-commenced 1864, completed after intervals, August 1869. Score completed February 1871.

Characters

Siegfried	Tenor
Mime	Tenor
The Wanderer	Bass-baritone
Alberich	Baritone
Fafner	Deep Bass
Erda	Alto
Brünnhilde	Soprano
A Wood Bird	Soprano

ACT I A Cave in the Forest.

ACT II In the Depths of the Forest.

ACT III SCENE I A Wild Region at the foot of a Rocky Mountain.

SCENE 2 On the Mountain Peak by the Valkyrie's Rock.

FIRST PRODUCED. Festspielhaus, Bayreuth, August 16, 1876, in a complete Cycle.

FIRST PRODUCED IN ENGLAND. Her Majesty's Theatre, London, May 8, 1882, in a complete Cycle in German.

FIRST PRODUCED IN AMERICA. Metropolitan Opera House, New York, November 9, 1887. Sung in German.

FIRST PRODUCED IN AMERICA IN A COMPLETE CYCLE. Metropolitan Opera House, New York, March 8, 1889. Sung in German.

FIRST PRODUCED IN ENGLISH. Prince's Theatre, Manchester, September 30, 1897, by the Carl Rosa Opera Company, in a translation by H. and F. Corder. Subsequently produced by the same company in London at the Coronet Theatre, Notting Hill Gate, October 31, 1901.

FIRST PRODUCED IN ENGLISH IN A COMPLETE CYCLE. Royal Opera, Covent Garden, London, January 30, 1908, in a translation by Frederick Jameson.

FIRST PRODUCED IN AMERICA IN ENGLISH. Opera House, Seattle, March 7, 1974, in a translation by Andrew Porter.

FIRST PRODUCED IN AMERICA IN ENGLISH IN A COMPLETE CYCLE. Opera House, Seattle, July 25, 1975, in a translation by Andrew Porter.

SIEGFRIED – CASTS

CHARACTERS	BAYREUTH 1876 (In Complete Cycle)	LONDON 1882 (Complete Cycle in German)	NEW YORK 1887 (In German)	NEW YORK 1889 Complete)Cycle in German)
Siegfried	Georg Unger	Heinrich Vogl	Max Alvary	Max Alvary
Mime	Max Schlosser	Max Schlosser	T. Ferenczy	Wilhelm Sedlmayer
The Wanderer	Franz Betz	Emil Scaria	Emil Fischer	Emil Fischer
Alberich	Karl Hill	Otto Schelper	Rudolph von Milde	Joseph Beck
Fafner	Franz von Reichenberg	Heinrich Wiegand	Johannes Elmblad	Eugene Weiss
Erda	Louise Jaide	Orlanda Riegler	Marianne Brandt	Louise Meisslinger
Brünnhilde	Amalie Materna	Therese Vogl	Lilli Lehmann	Lilli Lehmann
A Woodbird	Lilli Lehmann	Antonie Schreiber	Auguste Seidl-Krauss	Sophie Traubman
Conductor	Hans Richter	Anton Seidl	Anton Seidl	Anton Seidl
Producer	Richard Wagner	Albert Petermann	Van Hiell	Habelmann
Designer	*Scenery* Josef Hoffmann *Costumes* Carl Emil Doepler	*Scenery* Josef Hoffmann *Costumes* Carl Emil Doepler	*Scenery* Hans Kautsky *Costumes* Carl Schaffell	*Scenery* Hans Kautsky *Costumes* Dazien (after Carl Doepler)

SIEGFRIED – CASTS (continued)

CHARACTERS	MANCHESTER 1897 and LONDON 1901 (In English)	LONDON 1908 (Complete Cycle in English)	AMERICA 1974 (In English)	AMERICA 1975 (Complete Cycle in English)
Siegfried	Barron Berthald	Peter Cornelius	Herbert Becker	James McCray
Mime	E. C. Hedmondt William Gillard	Hans Bechstein	Paul Crook	Paul Crook
The Wanderer	Seph Jones Lamprière Pringle	Clarence Whitehill	Noel Tyl	Noel Tyl
Alberich	Alex Bevan Charles Tilbury	Thomas Meux	Robert Petersen	Malcolm Rivers
Fafner	Arthur Deane Leslie Walker	Francis Harford	Leon Lishner	Frederick Guthrie
Erda	Sydney Poyser Lydia Care	Edna Thornton	Christine West-Robbins	Geraldine Decker
Brünnhilde	Anna Sutherland Rita Elandi* Lucile Hill	Perceval Allen	Anna Green	Anna Green
A Woodbird	Lily Heenan Lizzie Burgess	Caroline Hatchard	Patricia Cullen	Carol Webber
Conductor	Richard Eckhold Eugene Goossens	Hans Richter	Henry Holt	Henry Holt
Producer	E. C. Hedmondt	E. C. Hedmondt	George London	George London
Designer			John T. Naccarato	John T. Naccarato

*On the first night in Manchester, Rita Elandi was indisposed and the part of Brünnhilde

SYNOPSIS

In a rocky cave in the forest the dwarf Mime is unsuccessfully trying to hammer a sword. He regrets that his craft does not suffice to weld together the fragments of 'Nothung'.

Suddenly young Siegfried bursts in, leading a bear which he has bridled, and with shouts of laughter urges it to chase Mime round the cave. When, however, he sees the sword that Mime has forged for him, he loosens the rope and sends the beast back into the forest, commenting: 'You've saved your skin today!' Then he takes the sword to test it, but at his first stroke it flies to pieces on the anvil. Raging, he scolds Mime for his slovenly work.

The dwarf whiningly reproaches him with ingratitude, telling how he took him in as a 'squalling brat' and reared him for many years, but has received no affection in return.

Siegfried frankly admits that he can hardly bear the sight of Mime. He has evidently heard the story many times before, but now he wants to know more – he urges the dwarf to tell him more about his mother.

Mime at first refuses, but under threat of violence relates how he found in the forest a beautiful woman moaning in labour, and sheltered her while she gave birth to her child; how she then died, confiding the baby to his care. To Siegfried's further questions Mime (who really knows the whole story) will tell him only that his mother's name was Sieglinde, that his unnamed father died in battle, and that Sieglinde, giving him the fragments of the broken sword, told him that it was for her son and that he must be named Siegfried.

Upon this the young man declares that he himself will forge the sword anew and go out with it into the world to seek his fortune. He then rushes out into the woods.

Mime sits down dejectedly, knowing that he himself is incapable of re-making the sword. But he is not left alone long, for Wotan, in the guise of a Wanderer, comes and sits by his hearth. The god proposes a contest, in which each of them shall answer three questions asked by the other, staking his head upon it.

To the alarm of the dwarf, Wotan answers each of his questions correctly: that the race dwelling in the depths of the earth are the black Nibelungs ruled over by Alberich; those on the face of the earth are the giants; and those in the sky above are the Æsir of Valhalla, who own allegiance to Wotan, the Lord of the Spear. With this he strikes his spear on the ground and a slight peal of thunder is heard.

Wotan now challenges the terrified Mime in turn. First he asks: what is the race that Wotan deals harshly with, and yet holds most dear? Mime correctly answers that these are the Volsungs – the wild couple Siegmund and Sieglinde, and their son Siegfried.

Secondly, Wotan asks: with what sword must Siegfried kill the dragon Fafner? Again Mime gives the right answer: it is 'Nothung'. But to the third question: who shall forge the sword afresh? Mime gives no answer, knowing that he himself cannot do it. Wotan tells him – the only man who can restore the sword is he who has never known fear – and to him shall Mime's head be forfeit. So saying, the Wanderer turns away, laughing, and disappears into the forest.

Siegfried, returning, finds Mime cowering behind his anvil, terrified at the sunlight outside, which makes him think that Fafner has come to devour him. The young man asks why he is in this un-dignified posture, and when Mime says he is afraid, Siegfried interestedly asks what that may be. He is none the wiser when Mime describes the symptoms to him; but if fear is an art, he is willing to learn it.

In that case, says Mime, he had better go to the cavern where Fafner the dragon lies hidden. 'Does the world lie that way?' asks Siegfried, and when Mime assures him that it does, he has only one thought – to take his sword and go out into the world with it. Furious that Mime still has not yet mended it for him, he decides to do it himself.

Throughout the rest of the scene Siegfried is first grinding down the metal to powder, then smelting it, then shaping and cooling the blade, and finally putting it into a sword-handle. Meanwhile, he questions Mime, who tells him the name of the sword: Nothung.

Taking advantage of his abstraction, Mime prepares a poisoned draught. His plan has now taken shape: Siegfried the fearless shall kill the dragon for him, enabling him to seize the hoard and the Ring. Having fulfilled the purpose for which Mime has brought him up, he will become superfluous and can be eliminated by poison; while Mime with the Ring can subdue his brother Alberich and become master of the Nibelungs.

Siegfried, hammering and sharpening the sword, continues to sing of its virtues; finally he tests it, and with a tremendous stroke cleaves the anvil in two.

ACT II

At the entrance of Fafner's gloomy cavern, Alberich is keeping watch. Wotan comes to him, still disguised as the Wanderer. Though in dread, Alberich jeers at the god, knowing that Wotan can neither kill him nor take back the hoard, being still bound by the contract written in the runes on his spear.

Wotan warns him that Mime is coming, bringing with him a youth who will kill Fafner. He suggests that Alberich, in exchange for warning the dragon, shall claim back his Ring; then, laughing, he disappears into the wood.

Alberich does, in fact, attempt to warn Fafner, and then goes to hide in a cleft of the rocks, as dawn breaks and Siegfried enters with Mime.

Once more Mime seeks to make the young hero afraid, by telling him all the ways in which Fafner can harm him; but Siegfried roughly bids him begone, saying he will drive his sword into the dragon's heart before any of these tricks can be played on him.

Mime then retreats and Siegfried remains alone, listening to the song of the birds and wishing he could understand it. He blows a merry note on his silver horn, and at the sound Fafner comes out to challenge him. In a quick struggle the dragon is mortally wounded and, dying, warns Siegfried that Mime is plotting treason against him. His blood, spurting on the young man's hand, scalds him, so that he puts his finger in his mouth to suck it off. Suddenly he realises that now he can interpret the language of the birds, and he hears one of them advising him to take the Tarnhelm and the Ring. He goes into the cavern to find them.

Slinking back to find out if Fafner is really dead, Mime is intercepted by Alberich. A wrangle ensues between the brothers, each claiming the Ring; but when Siegfried returns, holding both it and the Tarnhelm, the two hide themselves to watch him. Uncertain what to do with his prizes, he listens again to the bird, who warns him to beware of Mime.

The dwarf now returns to offer him the poisoned draught; but Siegfried, with his new insight, interprets the hidden meaning of his words as he proffers the drink, and with one stroke of his sword smites him dead. A peal of mocking laughter comes from Alberich in his hiding place.

Removing the body of Mime and the carcass of the dragon, Siegfried stretches himself under the lime-tree to rest. The bird sings to him of love – of the beautiful Brünnhilde, who can only be won by a fearless suitor. Delighted, Siegfried follows the bird, which will show him the way to find her.

ACT III

SCENE 1   On a stormy night Wotan the Wanderer rouses Erda from her sleep in a rocky cavern. She is reluctant to give him any advice, suggesting that he had better get it either from her daughters the Norns, or from his favourite child Brünnhilde.

Wotan tells her of Brünnhilde's disobedience and punishment, and adds that Siegfried the Volsung, whose innocence and fearlessness may disarm Alberich's curse, has taken the Ring and will soon awaken and win Brünnhilde.

As Siegfried appears, Wotan releases Erda and she sinks down out of sight.

Following the bird which sang to him of the sleeping maiden, Siegfried finds his way barred by Wotan, but is not in the least overawed. In answer to the god's questions, he narrates the story of his upbringing, his making of the sword, and his fight with the dragon. Rather impatiently he asks the old man to make way. Wotan warns him of the fire that guards Brünnhilde's rock, but Siegfried, unheeding, tries to push past him in the gathering darkness.

Opposing him with his spear, Wotan declares that this weapon has already once shattered his sword-blade.

'Then my father's foe faces me here!' cries Siegfried, and with a single stroke severs the spear. A terrific clap of thunder resounds; the Wanderer disappears, and the scene is flooded by a rolling sea of fire. Blowing his horn, Siegfried fearlessly plunges into it.

SCENE 2   On the rocky peak Brünnhilde still lies sleeping, covered by her shield, with her warhorse Grane near by. Siegfried gazes at her in astonishment, taking her for a warrior. He has never seen a woman before. But when he has removed the shield and helmet

he sees her lovely face and long curling hair. Removing her breastplate, he finds the flowing robes and soft bosom beneath, and
realises that this is in truth the bride whom the song-bird has
promised him. He wonders how to wake her, and does it at last with
a kiss.

Brünnhilde, sitting up still dazed, asks who has awakened her,
and is delighted to find that it is Siegfried, whom she had cherished
and protected even before his birth. They sing a rapturous love-
duet; but Brünnhilde, the inviolate virgin, still tries to hold Siegfried's passion in check for a while, until at last, as the curtain falls,
she surrenders and throws herself into his arms.

REVIEW

The Music Critic in *The Era*, May 13, 1882, wrote of the first English performance:

'On Monday evening there was again a brilliant audience at Her Majesty's Theatre, although in actual numbers there was a decided falling off as compared with the first night (of the Cycle). This was to be expected, for, although, like the late Earl Beaconsfield, the Wagnerites have done their utmost towards "educating their party," there are still hosts of "British Philistines" who cannot, and probably will not in any future however remote, appreciate the new operatic system. For these the work appeals in vain. Nevertheless, in high quarters much encouragement has been given. The Prince and Princess of Wales have been constant visitors, and the Duke and Duchess of Edinburgh have also attended, besides other royal personages; but the fact that there were four and twenty boxes empty on Monday evening, in addition to many vacant seats in other portions of the house, indicates the difficulty there will be in making the *Nibelungen Ring* popular. Possibly, remembering the high mission our German teachers have set themselves, they disdain all considerations of paltry lucre. If so all is well, because without popularity profit can hardly be expected. Turning to the third performance, *Siegfried*, the hero of which "music-drama" is, as we have already shown, the offspring of an incestuous union between brother and sister, we are repelled at the very outset, and cannot feel that sympathy for the deeds of this personage which would otherwise be readily accorded. We have spoken plainly as to the horrible and revolting character of the previous drama, and have expressed the astonishment that will be shared by our readers that such an immoral subject should have been permitted without protest on the English stage. Although some portions are fine, there is much in it that comes within the scope of pantomime, and which, considered as an operatic libretto, is silly in the extreme. . . .'

After telling the plot the critic continues...

'In reality the only incidents are the mending of the sword, the fight with the dragon, and the love scene with Brünnhilde. All the rest is mere "padding" so far as the spectator is concerned, and this is the fatal weak point of Wagner's system, that the most trifling incidents have the same importance given to them as the leading events. If one of the characters comes upon the stage to ask a simple question it is sure to lead to twenty minutes of recitative, accompanied by an avalanche of orchestral passages. In this process all real interest is completely crushed out. Take the cream of this gigantic work, for example, and compress it into a four-act opera, and it would be a masterpiece, but the dead weight of the eternal recitative wearies the listener until sympathy is lost for the fine passages when they occur. As for all the business with the dragon, it is childish nonsense, fit only for a nursery tale, and to present it seriously upon the stage, and call it "grand opera," is an outrage upon the common sense of any audience not recently released from Hanwell or Colney Hatch. The gravity with which it was received by the apostles of the new school of music was, perhaps, the most comic element of all. To watch sombre disciples following every movement of the scaly monster, and listening to his diabolical ugly noises, striving all the while to find out some deep under-current of meaning intended by the composer, was funny beyond anything we have ever seen at an operatic performance. Some considerable defects were to be noted in the representation, and we cannot say that the scenery was at all impressive. It was frequently raw, glaring and coarse. Herr Vogl, as the hero Siegfried, was entitled to hearty commendation for the spirit and energy with which he acted and sang. He had conceived the character in the true spirit, and, although at times more physical power was required, the general rendering had some admirable points. Herr Vogl was both chivalrous and tender, and at all times did justice to the difficult music. Herr Schlosser, as the crawling and deceitful dwarf Mime, also showed the utmost intelligence. The part is an uphill one; but the talent of the artist made it interesting, even when the scenes in which Mime appeared were disagreeable. Herr Scaria we have all along praised, and here also commendation was his due, for it was a triumph on his part that he succeeded in preventing that contemptible wretch Wotan from being hooted from the stage. Every kind of human vice and frailty may be seen in the character of Wotan in an exaggerated form. Brünnhilde was well represented by Frau Vogl, who sang her share in the love duet at the close with good effect. Herr Schelper, as Alberich, had little to do in this portion of the *Nibelungen Ring*, but there was enough to prove his value; and Fraulein Riegler, as the Goddess of Earth, executed her task skilfully. Herr Seidl conducted admirably; but on this occasion the orchestra was certainly inferior to that of the Royal Italian Opera. The strings were weak in tone and poor in quality.'

GÖTTERDÄMMERUNG

(The Twilight of the Gods)

------- · -------

Third day of the Trilogy

Libretto

First written as '*SIEGFRIEDS TOD*, A Grand Heroic Opera,' November 12–28, 1848. Revised as GÖTTERDÄMMERUNG, late 1852.

Music

Commenced at Lucerne, October 1869. Sketched, 1869–72. Score completed, November 1874.

Characters

Siegfried	Tenor
Gunther	High Bass
Hagen	Deep Bass
Alberich	Baritone
Brünnhilde	Soprano
Gutrune	Soprano
Waltraute	Mezzo-soprano
The Norns	Soprano and Alto
Woglinde ⎫	
Flosshilde ⎬ Rhine-Maidens	Soprano and Alto
Wellgunde ⎭	

Chorus

Men and Women.

PROLOGUE   On the Valkyrie's Rock.
ACT   I SCENE 1 Gunther's Great Hall on the Rhine.
           SCENE 2 The Valkyrie's Rock.
ACT II In Front of Gunther's Hall.
ACT III SCENE 1 A Wooded Spot by the Rhine.
           SCENE 2 Gunther's Hall.

FIRST PRODUCED. Festspielhaus, Bayreuth, August 17, 1876, in a complete Cycle.

FIRST PRODUCED IN ENGLAND. Her Majesty's Theatre, London, May 9, 1882, in a complete Cycle in German.

FIRST PRODUCED IN AMERICA. Metropolitan Opera House, New York, January 25, 1888. Sung in German. (The Norns and the Waltraute scene omitted.)

FIRST PRODUCED IN AMERICA IN A COMPLETE CYCLE. Metropolitan Opera House, New York, March 11, 1889. Sung in German. (The Norns and the Waltraute scene omitted. The first complete performance took place January 24, 1898.)

FIRST PRODUCED IN ENGLISH. Royal Opera House, Covent Garden, London, February 1, 1908. In a complete Cycle, translated by Frederick Jameson. (No previous separate production recorded.)

FIRST PRODUCED IN AMERICA IN ENGLISH. Opera House, Seattle, January 30, 1975, in a translation by Andrew Porter.

FIRST PRODUCED IN AMERICA IN ENGLISH IN A COMPLETE CYCLE. Opera House, Seattle, July 27, 1975, in a translation by Andrew Porter.

GÖTTERDÄMMERUNG (THE TWILIGHT OF THE GODS) – CASTS

CHARACTERS	BAYREUTH 1876 (Complete Cycle)	LONDON 1882 (Complete Cycle in German)	NEW YORK 1888 (In German—Incomplete)	NEW YORK 1889 (In German—Cycle Incomplete)
Siegfried	Georg Unger	Heinrich Vogl	Albert Niemann	Max Alvary
Gunther	Eugen Gura	Heinrich Wiegand	Adolf Robinson	Joseph Beck
Hagen	Gustav Siehr	Otto Schelper	Emil Fischer	Emil Fischer
Alberich	Karl Hill	Robert Biberti	Rudolph von Milde	Omitted
Brünnhilde	Amalie Materna	Therese Vogl	Lilli Lehmann	Lilli Lehmann
Gutrune	Mathilde Weckerlin	Antonie Schreiber	Auguste Seidl-Krauss	Louise Meisslinger
Waltraute	Louise Jaide	Hedwig Reicher-Kindermann		
First Norn	Friederike Grün	Orlanda Riegler		
Second Norn	Johanna Jachmann-Wagner	Therese Milar		
Third Norn	Josephine Schefsky	Katharine Liebmann		
Woglinde	Lilli Lehmann	Auguste Krauss	Sophie Traubman	Sophie Traubman
Flosshilde	Minna Lammert	Maria Schulze	Louise Meisslinger	Emmy Miron
Wellgunde	Marie Lehmann	Katharina Klafsky	Marianne Brandt	Felicie Kaschowska
Conductor	Hans Richter	Anton Seidl	Anton Seidl	Anton Seidl
Producer	Richard Wagner	Albert Petermann	Habelmann	Habelmann
Designer				
Scenery	Josef Hoffmann	Josef Hoffmann	Kautscky	Kautscky
Costumes	Carl Emil Doepler	Carl Emil Doepler	Dazien (after Carl Doepler)	Dazien (after Carl Doepler)

GÖTTERDÄMMERUNG (THE TWILIGHT OF THE GODS) – CASTS (continued)

CHARACTERS	NEW YORK 1898 (In German – Complete)	LONDON 1908 (Complete Cycle in English)	AMERICA 1975 (In English)	AMERICA 1975 (Complete Cycle in English)
Siegfried	Jean de Reszke	Peter Cornelius	Jean Cox	James McCray
Gunther	Adolph Mühlmann	Frederic Austin	Archie Drake	Archie Drake
Hagen	Edouard de Reszke	Charles Knowles	William Wildermann	William Wildermann
Alberich	David Bispham	Thomas Meux	Robert Petersen	Malcolm Rivers
Brünnhilde	Lilian Nordica	Perceval Allen	Ingrid Bjoner	Anna Green
Gutrune	Frances Saville	Edith Evans	Joan Winden	Joan Winden
Waltraute	Ernestine Schumann-Heink	Maud Santley*	Dori Cole	Marvellee Cariaga
First Norn	Ernestine Schumann-Heink	Edna Thornton	Geraldine Decker	Geraldine Decker
Second Norn	Louise Meisslinger	Caroline Hatchard	Dori Cole	Audrey Glass
Third Norn	Olga Pevny	Leonora Sparkes	Dolores Strazicich	Norma Lynn
Woglinde	Olga Pevny	Leonora Sparkes	Patricia Cullen	Patricia Cullen
Flosshilde	Louise Meisslinger	Edna Thornton	Carolyn Maia	Carolyn Maia
Wellgunde	Molka-Kella	Caroline Hatchard	Shirley Lee Harned	Shirley Lee Harned
Conductor	Franz Schalk	Hans Richter	Henry Holt	Henry Holt
Producer		E. C. Hedmondt	George London	George London
Designer			John T. Naccarato	John T. Naccarato

*Owing to indisposition of this singer scene omitted. At second performance sung by Edna Thornton.

'Der fliegende Holländer' Act 3 – Wieland Wagner's 1959 Bayreuth production conducted by Wolfgang Sawallisch (Siegfried Lauterwasser).

'Tannhäuser' Act 2 – Wieland Wagner's production for the 1954 Bayreuth Festival conducted by Joseph Keilberth (Siegfried Lauterwasser).

'Lohengrin' Act 1 – Wieland Wagner's 1958 Bayreuth production conducted by André Cluytens (Siegfried Lauterwasser).

'Lohengrin' Act 2 – Wieland Wagner's 1958 production (Siegfried Lauterwasser).

'Lohengrin' Act 3 – Wieland Wagner's 1958 Bayreuth production (Siegfried Lauterwasser).

'Das Rheingold' Scene 4 – The Entry of the Gods into Valhalla from the 1960 Bayreuth production by Wieland Wagner (Siegfried Lauterwasser).

'Das Rheingold' – On the Bed of the Rhine.
Designs by Adolph Appia for the 1924 production at the Stadttheater, Basel.

'Die Walküre' – A Wild and Rocky Pl
Adolph Appia's design for the 1925 B
Stadttheater production.

'Das Rheingold' – The final scene from Götz Friedrich's 1974 production at the Royal Opera House, Covent Garden (Stuart Robinson).

'Die Walküre' – Josephine Veasey as Fri
in the 1974 production at the Royal Op
House, Covent Garden (Donald Souther

'Das Rheingold' – Clifford Grant as Fafner, Lois McDonall as Freia and Harold Blackburn as Fasolt in the English National Opera's 1973 production (Anthony Crickmay).

'Die Walküre' – Norman Bailey as W in the English National Opera's 1970 duction designed by Ralph Koltai (Anth Crickmay).

'Siegfried' Act 2 – Alberto Remedios in the title role of the English National Opera's 197 production by Glen Byam Shaw and John Blatchley (Anthony Crickmay).

'Siegfried' Act 3 – Alberto Remedios as Siegfried and Rita Hunter as Brünnhilde in the English National Opera production (Anthony Crickmay).

'Siegfried' Act 2 – Ragnar Ulfung as Mime and Helge Brilioth as Siegfried in the 1975 Covent Garden production designed by Josef Svoboda (Donald Southern).

'Siegfried' Act 2 – Matti Salminen as Fafner and Helge Brilioth as Siegfried in Götz Friedrich's production for the Royal Opera, Covent Garden in 1975 (Stuart Robinson).

'Götterdämmerung' Act 1 – Rita Hunter as Brünnhilde and Katherine Pring as Waltraute in the English National Opera production (Anthony Crickmay).

SYNOPSIS

PROLOGUE

At night on the Valkyrie's rock, the three Norns are singing as they spin the rope of Fate by which the destinies of men and gods are determined. The eldest sings of the world's ash-tree which once grew green and strong, until Wotan dealt it a death-wound by tearing from it the wood for his spear.

The second Norn tells how, when Siegfried destroyed that spear, Wotan gave orders that the withered stem of the ash should be cut down. The third and youngest describes how its faggots have been piled high around Valhalla, so that they may be set ablaze when the gods know that their end has come.

From one to another they fling the rope, singing and spinning, until suddenly it breaks and with cries of alarm they disappear, returning to their mother, Erda, their task ended.

The day breaks and Siegfried steps out from the Valkyrie's rock in full armour, followed by Brünnhilde leading her horse. He is returning to the mortal world in search of more adventures to prove himself worthy of the role of hero for which he has been chosen; but first they exchange gifts. Siegfried gives his bride the Ring that he has won from the dragon, and she presents him with her noble steed Grane. With many vows of fidelity they part.

ACT I

SCENE 1   In the council chamber of the Hall of the Gibichungs on the Rhine are Gunther, chief of the clan, his gentle sister Gutrune, and his half-brother, the sinister Hagen – son of Alberich by a mortal mother.

Hagen says that, if the Gibichung race is to continue, it is imperative that Gunther and Gutrune should find mates for themselves. He suggests Brünnhilde as a wife for Gunther, and Siegfried as a husband for Gutrune, telling them about his victory over the dragon. He warns Gunther of the fire that protects Brünnhilde, through which a hero as fearless as Siegfried alone can pass. When Gunther asks what is the use of telling him about a bride that he cannot win, Hagen suggests that Siegfried should be sent to fetch her – and that he can be induced to do this if he is made to fall in love with Gutrune by means of a magic draught.

While they are planning this, Siegfried's horn is heard, and shortly afterwards he arrives.

Siegfried challenges Gunther to fight him, or else be his friend; to which the Gibichung answers by bidding him welcome and undertaking to have his horse cared for.

To Hagen's questions about the Nibelung hoard, the hero replies that he has left it all in the cavern, except for the Tarnhelm, which he does not know how to use. Hagen explains that by means of it he can change his shape at will, and asks if he has taken anything else. Only a ring, says Siegfried, and that he has given away – to a woman. (Brünnhilde, guesses Hagen.)

Gutrune now enters, proffering a drinking-horn filled with the love-potion. Siegfried drinks it, toasting Brünnhilde; but as he returns it he gazes rapturously at the maiden and asks Gunther her name. The other two men notice with satisfaction that he is still gazing at her, spellbound, as she goes out again.

Siegfried then asks Gunther whether he is married, and hears, with a vague dream-like remembrance, the story of the bride who can only be won by passing through fire; but her name, Brünnhilde, means nothing to him. He volunteers to bring her to Gunther, on condition that he himself may marry Gutrune. They conclude the bargain and swear blood-brotherhood.

SCENE 2   Brünnhilde is sitting alone at the entrance of the cave by the Valkyrie's rock, gazing at Siegfried's Ring and kissing it, when she sees her sister Waltraute. Surprised, she asks: 'How did you dare to brave Wotan's wrath by visiting me in my banishment?'

Her sister replies that there is great trouble in Valhalla: Wotan, who all these years has been wandering on earth, has lately returned with his spear in fragments, ordering the Æsir to cut down the world's ash-tree and pile the faggots around Valhalla. Since then he has remained still and silent, grasping the splintered spear. At last Waltraute has induced him to say that, if Brünnhilde would only give her Ring back to the Rhine-maidens, gods and men would be redeemed from the curse. So Waltraute has come to beg her to do it.

Passionately, Brünnhilde refuses: Siegfried's bridal pledge means more to her than the fate of Valhalla. With cries of woe Waltraute rushes away.

Looking out into the gathering storm, Brünnhilde is surprised to see flames once more glowing around her rock. Enraptured, she hears Siegfried's horn sounding in the valley. She prepares to welcome him, but recoils in horror when she sees an unknown man. By means of the Tarnhelm, Siegfried has taken the shape of Gunther, and this is the name he gives when she asks who he is, telling her that he has come to wed her.

Brünnhilde thinks that this is some new punishment sent by Wotan. She resists fiercely, the Ring giving her superhuman strength, until at last Siegfried tears it from her finger and vanquishes her. But, true to his oath, he draws his sword to lay between them – he will not touch his brother's bride.

ACT II

Outside the hall of the Gibichungs, Hagen, with spear and shield, sits sleeping. Beside him crouches his father Alberich, whose words he hears dimly in his dream, telling him that Wotan's power has been broken with his spear, and has passed to Siegfried, who must now be destroyed. Alberich makes his son swear that, whatever happens, he will lay hands on the Ring and prevent it from being returned to the Rhine-maidens. As the sun rises, Alberich disappears and Hagen awakes.

Siegfried, having removed the Tarnhelm, appears in his own form, greets Hagen and tells him that Gunther and Brünnhilde are on their way. When Gutrune comes to welcome him he hails her joyfully as his promised bride. She asks anxiously how her brother has fared in the flames – and for the first time hears about the substitution. Obviously she is somewhat dubious about the arrangement, but accepts Siegfried's assurance that he has respected Gunther's rights.

The pinnace bearing the bridal couple is now seen approaching. Siegfried goes in with Gutrune to fetch the women, while Hagen calls the men together, and all prepare to welcome and feast the bride and bridegroom.

Gunther comes in, leading the reluctant Brünnhilde by the hand. When she sees Siegfried and hears that he is betrothed to Gutrune she almost faints. He supports her, calling Gunther to help her, and she realises that he does not even recognise her; but at the sight of the Ring on his hand she fiercely asks how it came there, since it was (as she thinks) Gunther who tore it from her finger. She demands explanations which neither the puzzled Gunther nor the oblivious Siegfried can give. Hagen makes the confusion worse by craftily suggesting that Siegfried has won the ring from Gunther by a trick; while, in the hearing of all, Brünnhilde loudly cries that the man who wedded her was Siegfried. Though he fiercely denies it, she persists in her story.

On the point of Hagen's spear Siegfried swears that he has not been false to his oath; but at the same time Brünnhilde too swears with equal conviction that she is speaking the truth.

The vassals by this time are in tumult, but Siegfried retrieves the situation as best he can, by suggesting that the 'wild mountain maid' needs time to settle down – probably she has guessed the Tarnhelm trick and wants to pay Gunther back for it, but her anger will soon pass. Laughing, he seizes Gutrune and goes with her into the hall to lead the revels.

Brünnhilde and Hagen are left with the shamed and deeply dejected Gunther. Hagen offers to help Brünnhilde be revenged upon Siegfried, and she tells him that though through her magic arts the hero is invulnerable when he faces his foe, he may be stabbed in the back, which she has not troubled to protect, knowing that he would never turn it in battle. She then pours scorn on Gunther for letting another man win her for him under false pretences. He in turn appeals to Hagen to avenge his honour, and all three decide that Siegfried must die.

They plot to go hunting next day, kill Siegfried, and bring his body home, saying that he has been slain by a boar. Calling upon Wotan as their witness, Brünnhilde and Gunther swear to be avenged, while Hagen appeals for the aid of his father, Alberich.

ACT III

SCENE I The Rhine-maidens are once more singing of their gold as they play. They hear the horn-call of Siegfried, who has been lured to the river-bank by an elf. When he appears, they tease him and ask for the Ring on his finger, reproaching him with miserliness when he refuses. He takes it off, half-inclined to give it to them, but thinks better of it. They solemnly warn him that it brings death to all its wearers, and that if he keeps it he himself will die that very day. He retorts that he fears no threats – and as for the rope of Fate woven by the Norns, he will cut it with his sword. With the parting thrust that his ring will pass into the keeping of a

woman who will do their bidding, they swim away. Siegfried rue-
fully reflects that if he were not bound to be true to Gutrune, he
would willingly have captured one of these pretty maidens.

Hunting-horns are heard, and Gunther, Hagen and their followers
arrive, carrying the game they have killed. They settle down on the
cool river-bank to feast.

To divert the gloomy Gunther, Siegfried proposes to tell his
life-story. While he does so, Hagen mixes a herb in his drink which
restores his memory, so that he relates his first finding and winning
of Brünnhilde. Hagen distracts his attention for a moment, and then
plunges the spear into his back. Siegfried falls, having only strength
to call on the name of Brünnhilde; he dies and his body is borne
away. The moon comes out, and the scene is filled with mist, during
which it changes to . . .

SCENE 2 . . . the river-bank outside the hall of the Gibichungs.
Gutrune enters, full of foreboding. She has seen Brünnhilde going
towards the Rhine, and guesses that something strange is happening.

Hagen and the other returning men announce Siegfried's death;
but Gutrune, disbelieving their story of a hunting accident, rounds
on her brother, and as the dead hero's body is carried in, passionately
accuses Gunther of having murdered him. He in turn lays the blame
on Hagen. The two men quarrel and draw their swords. In the ensuing fight Gunther is killed, and Hagen snatches at the Ring on
Siegfried's finger. But the dead man's hand rises menacingly, and
as the thief recoils in terror Brünnhilde steps in, claiming Siegfried
as her own husband. Gutrune in despair, now understanding everything, curses Hagen for giving the fatal draught which made
Siegfried play false to both of them. Deeply shamed, she turns from
his body to her brother's, leaving Brünnhilde alone with the corpse
in the centre.

Brünnhilde calls on everyone to build a funeral pyre. She sings a
lament over Siegfried and takes off the Ring, saying that it shall be
purified by fire, and then return to its rightful owners, the Rhine-
maidens. Then she seizes a torch and sets the pyre alight. Her horse
Grane is brought to her and, mounting it, she leaps into the flames.

The pyre is rapidly consumed, and as it falls to ashes the river
rises in flood and the three Rhine-maidens swim in, looking for the
Ring. Hagen plunges madly into the waves, trying to grasp it, but
two of the maidens twine their arms round him and drag him under

the water, while the third, Flosshilde, joyfully holds up the recovered Ring.

From the ruins of the half-burnt hall, the men and women look up, awestruck, at the light in the sky, where the gods and heroes in Valhalla are seen completely ringed by flame.

REVIEW

The Music Critic in *The Era*, May 13, 1882, wrote of the first English performance:

'Once more the trumpet sounds and we are called to arms – or, rather, to arm-chairs. This is no metaphor merely, for before the commencement of each section of the tremendous work the visitors are warned to take their places by the sound of the trumpet, and woe be to any unlucky Philistine who is not in his place when the curtain rises; for the Wagnerites expect their idol to be worshipped in awe and silence like an Indian god. It was rather a lengthy worship, too, for the devotees were called together at half-past six o'clock, and within a few minutes of that time a large audience, including the Prince and Princess of Wales and the Duke of Edinburgh, assembled, and heroically remained through the five hours of the performance. The title, dusk or twilight of the gods, refers to the decay of their power, and, in addition to the three acts, there are also two introductory scenes. . . . In the last act the scene changes to the Rhine. The music of this scene, coming after the weary and dreary monotony of much that had gone before, was delightful to hear. . . .'

After telling the plot the critic continues...

'Undoubtedly there are the materials of a grand tragic drama in these incidents, which, sombre as they are, have much of the power of a Greek tragedy, combined with the imaginative effects of nor- thern mythical subjects. The scenic effects, which had been so lauded, were by no means equal to what the audience had expected. Many of our pantomimes and spectacular pieces have made, and are making, a grander display than anything to be seen in the *Nibe- lungen Ring*. At the same time the scenery was sufficient for the pur- pose, and would have satisfied the spectators more if its merits had not been so loudly trumpeted forth. But nothing is done by our Teutonic friends in these days without a great flourish of trumpets. Respecting the performance of *Götterdämmerung* there was much to admire. The Siegfried of Herr Vogl was admirable in every way. We may feel horror at his parentage, but he is a true hero in Herr Vogl's hands. He is gallant, chivalrous, tender, and manly, and the tone and manner of the actor fully realised the character intended. Siegfried is the one, and, alas! the only one, lovable personage in all this batch of murderers, thieves, adulterers, liars, and brawlers. If our readers fancy this is too strong, we refer them at once to the plot itself. The deep bass voice of Herr Wiegand was effective in the character of the King; and Herr Schelperre presented the vile traitor Hagen with considerable power. As Brünnhilde, Frau Vogl acted and sang with fine dramatic feeling, and in the closing scenes deeply impressed her audience; and Fraulein Schreiber was graceful and pleasing as Gutrune. The three Rhine maidens were cleverly sustained. In the performance of Tuesday some omissions were made, certainly to the advantage of the audience, for the representation lasted for five hours as it was. For the first time in the four music-dramas, a chorus was employed; but the singing was rough and coarse, and the music hideous. The orchestra was generally effective, but the deficiency of power in the strings caused the wind instruments to predominate too much for the balance of tone requisite. A few remarks are necessary respecting the general effect of the work as a whole, and the impression it made. One of the most fatiguing elements in Wagner's system is the constant repetition of the special "motives" with which he announces the chief incidents and characters. When it is told that there are no less than ninety of these distinct "motives," and that many of them are repeated a score of times, it will be easily understood how the old-fashioned opera-goer must execrate the method Wagner has adopted. Then, in order to make a completely satisfactory opera the music should not be secondary, as it too frequently is in the *Nibelungen Ring*. It is astonishing also what opportunities Wagner sacrifices through his perversity in refusing to introduce the exquisite charm of vocal melodies. Interminable recitatives, even at the best, must soon weary the hearer, and when Wagner is at his worst they become truly awful in their depressing influence; nor can all the ingenuity and skill he has lavished upon the orchestra redeem their absolute ugliness. When the composer forgets his theories and writes on the plan adopted by other musicians he becomes interesting, and sometimes really grand. No composer that ever lived need be ashamed to own some portions of this colossal work; but these happy moments

are few and far between. The want of concerted music is another
fatal barrier to the popularity of the work. The contrasts afforded
in this way are of the greatest value and importance, and to reject
such aids is simply a blunder. That Wagner's works will have great
influence on the opera music of the future cannot be doubted; but
we have every reason to believe that these experiments will not
supersede those operatic forms which have been the growth of a
couple of centuries. If Wagner survives in the future, so also will
Mozart, Beethoven, Meyerbeer, and many others. There are, we see,
three other "cycles" announced; but before they are concluded we
shall await with some curiosity the official judgment respecting that
most obnoxious story of incest *Die Walküre*. That the *Nibelungen
Ring*, in spite of its occasional power and beauty, can ever be
popular, is more than we expect and certainly more than we hope
for.'

TRISTAN UND ISOLDE
(Tristan and Isolde)

—————— · ——————

A Lyric Drama in Three Acts

Libretto

Written in Zurich, August–September 1857.

Music

First Act sketched in Zurich, October–December 1857. Score written, February–April 1858. Second Act commenced in Zurich, May 4, 1858, completed March 9, 1859. Third Act completed in Lucerne, August 1859.

Characters

Tristan	Tenor
King Marke	Bass
Isolde	Soprano
Kurwenal	Baritone
Melot	Tenor
Brangäne	Mezzo-soprano
A Shepherd	Tenor
A Helmsman	Baritone

Chorus

Sailors, Knights and Esquires.

ACT I At Sea, on the Deck of Tristan's Ship, on the Voyage from Ireland to Cornwall.

ACT II In the Royal Castle of King Marke in Cornwall.

ACT III Tristan's Castle in Brittany.

FIRST PRODUCED. Hoftheater, Munich, June 10, 1865.

FIRST PRODUCED IN ENGLAND. Theatre Royal, Drury Lane, London, June 20, 1882. Sung in German in a Grand German Opera Season, under the direction of Hermann Franke.

FIRST PRODUCED IN AMERICA. Metropolitan Opera House, New York, December 1, 1886. Sung in German.

FIRST PRODUCED IN ENGLISH. Royal Court Theatre, Liverpool, April 15, 1898, by the Carl Rosa Opera Company in an uncredited translation, and in London at the Royal Lyceum Theatre, February 3, 1899, by the same Company.

FIRST PRODUCED IN AMERICA IN ENGLISH. Metropolitan Opera House, New York, November 20, 1920, in a translation by H. and F. Corder (with Improvements by Sigmund Spaeth and Cecil Cawdrey).

TRISTAN UND ISOLDE (TRISTAN AND ISOLDE) – CASTS

CHARAC-TERS	MUNICH 1865	LONDON 1882 (In German)	NEW YORK 1886 (In German)	LIVERPOOL and LONDON 1898/9 (In English)	NEW YORK 1920 (In English)
Tristan	Ludwig Schnorr von Carolsfeld	Hermann Winkelmann	Albert Niemann	Philip Brozel	Johannes Sembach
King Marke	Ludwig Zottmayer	Eugen Gura	Emil Fischer	Liverpool – Lamprière Pringle London – Arthur Winckworth	Robert Blass
Isolde	Malvina Schnorr von Carolsfeld	Rosa Sucher	Lilli Lehmann	Liverpool – Rita Elandi London – Lucile Hill	Margarete Matzenauer
Kurwenal	Anton Mitterwurzer	Emil Kraus	Adolf Robinson	Charles Tilbury	Clarence Whitehill
Melot	Karl Samuel Heinrich	Joseph Wolff	Rudolph von Milde	William Dever	Robert Leonhardt
Brangäne	Anna Deinet	Marianne Brandt	Marianne Brandt	Kirkby Lunn	Jeanne Gordon
A Shepherd	Simons	Leopold Landau	Otto Kemlitz	Frank A. Wood	Octave Dua
A Helmsman	Hartmann	Not named	Emil Sänger	Liverpool – George A. Fox London – William Gillard	Louis D'Angelo
			Also in cast list A Sailor's voice – Max Alvary		Also in cast list A Sailor's voice – Angelo Bada
Conductor	Hans von Bülow	Hans Richter	Anton Seidl	Liverpool – Richard Eckhold London – Hamish MacCunn	Artur Bodanzky
Producer	Eduard Sigl	Bernhard Pollini	Van Hiell		
Designer	*Scenery* Angelo Quaglio (Act 1 and Act 3) Heinrich Döll (Act 2) *Costumes* Franz Seitz		Carl Schaffel		

SYNOPSIS

In her tent on the deck of the ship that is bearing her from Ireland to Cornwall, Isolde lies disconsolately on a couch. Her devoted maid Brangäne tries in vain to discover why she is so unhappy.

Brangäne opens the curtains, revealing the length of the deck, where sailors are busy about their work, while groups of knights and their attendants sit talking. Only Tristan stands alone, apart from the others, gazing moodily out to sea. When Isolde asks Brangäne her opinion of him, she cuts short her maid's ecstatic praise by calling him coward and traitor. Her relation with Tristan is complicated and curious. He has come to fetch her as a bride for his uncle, King Marke of Cornwall; but this is not the first time they have met. Under the alias of 'Tantris' he had come to her previously (since she was renowned for her skill in medicine), to be healed of a grievous wound received in single combat. Noticing a notch in his sword, she had fitted it to a splinter in her possession, and realised that the man whom he had killed in that fight was Morold, her betrothed. This Morold had been sent to Cornwall to demand the tribute due to Isolde's father, the Irish King; but after Tristan had slain him, his head, with the sword-splinter still in the wound, had been sent back to Ireland, with the insulting message that this was the only tax that Cornwall would pay. Telling no one of her discovery, Isolde had taken Tristan's sword to avenge her lover – but had found that she could not strike a sick and defenceless man. In due course he had gone back home, cured, with many protestations of love and gratitude – but when he came again, it was in his own name, to woo her as proxy for his uncle. And during the whole voyage he had pointedly avoided her.

Thinking of all this, Isolde orders Brangäne to go and tell Tristan that she wishes to speak to him. When the girl delivers this message Tristan politely refuses, saying that he cannot leave the helm, now that they are approaching land. His squire Kurwenal, however, sends back an impertinent rejoinder, and, despite his master's efforts to stop him, sings – so loudly that Isolde cannot help hearing it – an insulting ditty about Morold's death, which is taken up in chorus by the crew.

Controlling her anger with a great effort, Isolde confides all her distress to Brangäne, who tries to reconcile her to the prospect of marrying King Marke – which she, as a Princess of Ireland, regards as a humiliating match. Bitterly, Isolde complains of Tristan's coldness. That can easily be remedied, says Brangäne, bringing the casket full of magic potions that had been a parting gift to Isolde from her mother. From it Brangäne selects a love-draught; but her mistress has other ideas – the phial that she intends to use will bring not love but death.

At this moment the sailors are heard singing: land is near.

Kurwenal comes to ask Isolde and her ladies to prepare themselves to go ashore; but she sends him back with the message that she will not meet King Marke until Tristan has come in person to beg her pardon and be reconciled to her.

Isolde embraces Brangäne and says a last farewell, bidding her pour out the poison when the time comes. Her maid's horrified protests are cut short by the arrival of Tristan.

To Isolde's reproaches, Tristan, honourably concealing the love he feels for her, replies simply that he has avoided her because in his country it is not the custom for the proxy who fetches another man's bride to seek her company. Isolde then reverts to the more serious feud between them, telling him that she has sworn to be revenged for Morold. In that case, says Tristan, quietly handing her his sword, she has only to strike him down – and this time without faltering. But this is not the way Isolde has chosen. Letting the sword-point sink, she asks him to drink a cup of reconciliation with her – and signals to Brangäne to bring the poisoned draught.

To the refrain of the sailors' chanting, Tristan, who has guessed her purpose, prepares to drain the cup which will bring an end of all his troubles; but Isolde snatches it before it is empty, and quaffs the rest. For a while they stand motionless, gazing at each other in bewildered rapture – and then fall into a close embrace. Brangäne, who could not bring herself to poison her mistress, has substituted a love-potion.

While she tries to dress Isolde in royal robes for her meeting with King Marke, the lovers remain conscious of nothing but each other. Dazed, horrified, and yet happy when she learns, by Brangäne's confession, what has happened, Isolde swoons in Tristan's arms, as the sailors outside hail the arrival of the King.

ACT II

On a summer night in the garden outside her chamber Isolde is eagerly awaiting her lover; while Brangäne listens anxiously to the hunting-horns which tell them that King Marke is not far away. She warns Isolde that Tristan's false friend, Melot, is spying upon them, and that the King's hunt may be seeking a nobler quarry than the deer. Treating her warning lightly, Isolde extinguishes the torch – the preordained signal to Tristan that it is safe for him to come. She orders Brangäne to keep watch outside.

At once Tristan appears, and after a fervent embrace he and Isolde sing a love-duet, and then sink down to rest on a flowery bank. From the turret above, Brangäne warns them that it will soon be morning, but they pay no heed. They would be glad to die here together, in the ecstasy of their love. Once more Brangäne calls to them, but in their hallucinated state it seems as if their joyful night will go on for ever.

A scream is heard from Brangäne, and at the same time Kurwenal rushes in with drawn sword, crying: 'Save yourself, Tristan!' Almost immediately King Marke, Melot and the courtiers in hunting costume invade the garden. Brangäne hastens to Isolde's side, and Tristan spreads his cloak as if to conceal her from view. 'You see that my accusation was justified,' says Melot to the King. In deep distress, Marke reproaches Tristan with his treachery; but he wishes to be just and to find out the hidden causes of the betrayal. The knight, however, will make no attempt to defend himself. Seeing death before him, he asks Isolde if she is prepared to follow him to the land of darkness. She replies that, wherever he may be, she wishes only to share his fate, and he solemnly kisses her on the forehead.

In high indignation Melot draws his sword. He and Tristan fight, but the latter, making no attempt to keep up his guard, soon sinks wounded into Kurwenal's arms.

ACT III

Watched by the faithful Kurwenal, Tristan lies sleeping on a couch under a lime-tree in the garden of his castle in Brittany. A young shepherd is playing mournfully on his pipe. He asks Kurwenal how his patient is faring, and is told that Tristan has lain unconscious since he was brought home from Cornwall. His only hope of life is that Isolde may arrive in time to cure him.

The sound of the shepherd's pipe rouses Tristan sufficiently for him to ask where he is and what has happened. Kurwenal describes how, after he was wounded, he carried him to a ship and brought him home. The news that Isolde is expected temporarily revives Tristan. He thanks and embraces Kurwenal; then he faints, but recovers consciousness and asks him to go and watch for Isolde's ship. Suddenly the shepherd's sad tune changes to a gay note, and Kurwenal knows from this that the ship is approaching. He goes to meet Isolde, while Tristan in his excitement has a sudden revival of strength. Tearing the bandage from his wound, he springs up and reels forward. But the sound of Isolde's voice calling to him from outside is too much for him: as she enters he falls dead.

Isolde, trying to persuade herself that Tristan has only fainted, has at last to face the fact that he is dead, and falls senseless on his body.

Kurwenal, gazing in consternation upon the motionless forms of Tristan and Isolde, is warned by the shepherd that another ship is weighing anchor. From it come King Marke and Melot, who call upon Kurwenal to open the gate; but he avenges his master by stabbing Melot to death. Then, summoning the castle retainers, he sets upon the King's party and drives them back.

Meanwhile, Brangäne has climbed the wall and hastened to the side of her unconscious mistress.

At last Marke and his followers have forced their way in, and the mortally wounded Kurwenal falls at his dead master's feet.

Brangäne has managed to revive Isolde, to whom King Marke tells how, having heard the true story of the love-potion, he had determined to set her free and unite her to her lover. But it is too late: Isolde hears nothing: she is conscious only of the seemingly sleeping Tristan, and in an ecstatic delirium sinks lifeless upon his body. As the curtain falls, King Marke makes a gesture of blessing on the dead.

REVIEW

The Music Critic in *The Era*, June 24, 1882, wrote of the first English performance:

'Drury Lane Theatre was largely attended on Tuesday evening, when Wagner's opera *Tristan und Isolde* was given for the first time with a success which will be no criterion of the future reception of the opera in this country, seeing that the audience was a representative one, such as is not likely to be present at any future performance. Most of the celebrities of the musical world were present, and among them Madame Patti, who appeared to be deeply interested in the performance. There was great enthusiasm, but that there would be every outward show of success was a foregone conclusion. The audience came prepared for victory, and victory must be proclaimed, and there were many opportunities – thanks chiefly to the merit of the *artistes* – for applause and recalls. At the end of each act the curtain continued to rise and fall about half-a-dozen times, and the principal *artistes* advanced and retired as if they were executing a figure in a quadrille; and so determined were the supporters of Wagner to keep up the enthusiasm that even at midnight they were ready for their work and on the alert, so that no chance should be lost of making the less enthusiastic visitors see what a glorious triumph it was. But we cannot enter upon the subject with quite the same eagerness. There are two sides to every question, and unquestionably there are two sides, and one a very ugly side, to *Tristan und Isolde*. We would not for a moment disparage the genius of Richard Wagner. From his point of view the opera is a great work, but then we very much doubt whether the theories upon which *Tristan und Isolde* are founded will ever become generally accepted as the true and only method of operatic composition. No matter what noise Wagnerites may make, and they do shout pretty loud the praises of their idol, we have the solid fact before us that great operatic works, and greater than Wagner is ever likely to compose, were written before he was born, and will probably be popular when the bulk of his works are forgotten. We shall point out as we proceed some of the instances where we consider Wagner has sacrificed musical beauty for the sake of his theories, and we shall not fail at the same time to draw attention to those passages where the genius of the consummate musician triumphs over the laws he has laid down. When these occur there is no longer any doubt about the wonderful skill, dramatic feeling, and creative power displayed. The auditor is spellbound, and listens with delight until repelled by some harsh sound or crude recitative in which all that is least captivating in tone and effect is forced upon the ear with painful persistence. Wagner boasts that in *Tristan* he has freed himself from the ordinary operatic airs, duets, choruses, &c., and trusts only to the virtue of "continuous melody." Now, as the opera lasts for four hours, the impossibility of writing a "continuous melody" to keep the attention from eight p.m. until midnight is obvious. If any composer could have accomplished such a feat it was Rossini, whose flow of tunes was remarkable. But in *Tristan und Isolde* the bulk of the music is not really melody at all. It is recitative, broken by phrases in the orchestra, the principal *artistes* having frequently to sing passages that would be trying for an instrument, and when rendered vocally are sometimes only shrieks and wails, rather than musical utterances. There is no concerted music whatever. Each *artiste* goes his own way, or the way the composer has pointed out, and it is perfectly astonishing that any operatic *artiste* can be found able to commit such passages to memory, and to devote attention to the acting at the same time. The nearest approach to concerted music is a kind of nautical chorus on the deck of the vessel in the first act, but so harsh and forbidding is this strain that we are sure no crew of sailors, even in the remote period when the opera is supposed to take place, would have sung so crude a composition. All through the remainder of the opera the chorus singers merely stand about like dummies, and have nothing to sing and nothing to do. It is strange indeed that Wagner, after showing such intense dramatic feeling as he does in the second act, should have wasted so fine an opportunity of musical contrast simply for the sake of adhering to a pet system which, in this instance, robbed his opera of some of the best effects. It must not be supposed, in spite of these great drawbacks, that *Tristan* was without interest or attraction. So far as the principals are concerned, it is splendidly dramatic, and the passion of the lovers finds scope in the second act for one of the most powerful scenes ever witnessed upon the operatic stage. The

orchestra also, in many instances, is more varied and rich than in
any other work Wagner has written. . . .'

After giving the plot of the first act, the critic continues. . .

'Here we pause a moment to give the praise that is due to Frau
Sucher as Isolde and Herr Winkelmann as the hero. Their representation of the excess of passion was striking in the extreme. Most
operatic *artistes* would have made such an incident absurd, but the
admirable intelligence and histrionic gifts of these talented per-
formers caused a "risky" incident to be literally a triumph. The
enthusiasm was extraordinary, but it could hardly be said that it was
due to the music, for nearly all the principals had to sing in the
first act was recitative blended with the orchestra. Fraulein Marianne
Brandt had done admirable service as Brangäne. . . .

'It must be allowed that the whole of the second act is dramatic
in the extreme. The one weak point is where the chorus singers
again stand idly by, mere spectators of the exciting scene going on
before their eyes. But the love scene between Tristan and Isolde and
the occasional notes of warning uttered by Brangäne, are as pathetic,
powerful, and passionate as any lover of Italian opera could wish
for, and the orchestra appears to melt into the vocal music in the
most musicianly, artistic, and poetical style imaginable. We must
frankly admit a feeling of the warmest admiration for the composer
who could produce such effects as these. The music might not be
beautiful according to ordinary standards, but it touched the heart
and satisfied the ear, while it was only necessary to read the score to
see what ingenious and novel forms the composer has given to the
various instrumental passages. From this point our interest in
Tristan waned. The composer could not again reach the height of
that great argument in which he had so deeply moved his audience
in the second act. . . .

'The third act is very tragical, and the music that accompanies
it is as stormy and rhapsodical as the most extreme Wagnerite could
desire. The entire act resembles portions of the *Nibelungen Ring*,
"only more so," and it will be thought by many musical readers
that Wagner went quite far enough in those operas. We cannot
imagine that *Tristan und Isolde* will ever be popular in this country,
but we cheerfully applaud the enterprise that enabled the musical

public to hear a work respecting which there was so much curiosity. As for the performance, that was worthy of the highest praise. It was almost perfect, regarded from the point of view intended by the composer. Herr Winkelmann in, perhaps, the most difficult tenor *role* ever written, came out of the ordeal with triumph. There are no sweet tenor melodies, yet the cranky passages were delivered with effect, and in his acting Herr Winkelmann realised the character fully. Herr Gura has little to do as King Marke, but what music there was he gave with effect, and his acting was manly and dignified. Herr Dr. Kraus as the rugged Kurwenal was efficient, and Herr Joseph Wolff and Herr Landau rendered good service as Melot and Hirte. But the great feature of the entire representation was the splendid impersonation of the heroine by Frau Sucher, and what is still more remarkable was that the gifted lady undertook the part for the first time. Difficult and exacting as it was, Frau Sucher, by her excellent singing and really splendid acting, was triumphantly successful, and none applauded her with greater warmth than did Madame Patti, who evidently appreciated to the full the extra-ordinary talent displayed. The passion and fervour of the love scene in the second act and the brilliant and intensely dramatic delivery of the passages with Tristan in the first were brilliant examples of her skill. As the faithful attendant, Fraulein Brandt was perhaps some-what more tragical than the part required, but her powerful voice and most elaborate attention to every detail proved her once more to be a great *artiste*. The band was splendid, and the conducting of Herr Richter as near perfection as possible. And now that the opera has been heard which is upheld as the masterpiece of the composer, we cannot refrain from making a protest against the worship of animal passion which is so striking a feature in the later works of Wagner. We grant there is nothing so repulsive in *Tristan* as in *Die Walküre*, but the system is the same. The passion is unholy in itself and its representation is impure, and for those reasons we rejoice in believing that such works will not become popular. If they did we are certain their tendency would be mischievous, and there is, there-fore, some cause for congratulation in the fact that Wagner's music, in spite of all its wondrous skill and power, repels a greater number than it fascinates.'

NOTES

During the period when Wagner had recommenced work on *The Ring* at Zurich, his relationship with Mathilde Wesendonck reached its height and in 1857 *Siegfried* and the first draft of *Parsifal* were laid aside while the love poem of *Tristan und Isolde* was written in August and September. Wagner had earlier read Gottfried von Strassburg's narrative poem *Tristan*, a thirteenth-century paean to erotic and adulterous love, and the dramatic situation which it contained struck a chord in his emotions, bearing as it did such a strong parallel. The music of the first act was sketched by the Christmas and scored early in the new year.

Wagner had known the Wesendoncks since 1852 and his affair with Mathilde flourished under Minna's nose for many years. He had written a sonata for her in 1853 and her husband Otto, had been generous to the exiled composer, even to the extent of lending him a house near to his own. In 1857–8 Wagner set to music five poems by Mathilde and when the whole affair came into the open in the summer of 1858 Wagner fled to Venice in August, where the second act of *Tristan und Isolde* was completed on March 9, 1859. Wagner then returned to Switzerland and the last act was composed at Lucerne, where it was completed in August. The poem had appeared late in 1858 and the score was printed the following year.

Wagner made numerous attempts in the next years to get the opera staged at many places including Rio de Janeiro, Strasbourg, Paris and Prague. In March 1863, a production was abandoned in Vienna after many fruitless rehearsals, the work being considered impracticable.

The opera was not performed until King Ludwig had summoned Wagner to Munich, when it was put into rehearsal under von Bülow, who was appointed Court Kapellmeister expressly for the purpose. The dress rehearsal took place on May 11, 1865, at the Hoftheater, but the first performance was postponed from week to week, owing to a singer's illness, and was finally staged on June 10. Meantime a parody by Rauchenecker called *Tristanderl und Süssholde* had been produced at the Isar-Vorstadt-Theater on May 29.

Schnorr von Carolsfeld, the first Tristan, died mysteriously a few weeks after the fourth performance of the opera.

Liszt saw *Tristan und Isolde* at Bayreuth, when it was first performed there in July 1886; he collapsed during the third act, dying a day or two later.

DIE MEISTERSINGER VON NÜRNBERG

(The Mastersingers of Nuremberg)

————— • —————

Opera in Three Acts

Libretto

Sketched in prose at Marienbad, July 1845. Two further rough drafts, October–November 1861. Completed in verse, Paris, January 1862.

Music

Sketches for Act I commenced at Biebrich, March 1862; Act II sketched at Tribschen May 9, 1866 – September 23, 1866; Act III October 2, 1866 – March 5, 1867. Orchestral score completed on October 24, 1867.

Characters

Hans Sachs, Cobbler		Bass-baritone
Veit Pogner, Goldsmith		Bass
Kunz Vogelgesang, Furrier		Tenor
Konrad Nachtigall, Tinsmith		Bass
Sixtus Beckmesser, Town-clerk		Baritone
Fritz Kothner, Baker	Master-	Bass
Balthasar Zorn, Pewterer	Singers	Tenor
Ulrich Eisslinger, Grocer		Tenor
Augustin Moser, Tailor		Tenor
Hermann Ortel, Soap Boiler		Bass
Hans Schwarz, Stocking-Maker		Bass
Hans Foltz, Coppersmith		Bass
Walther von Stolzing, a young Knight from Franconia		Tenor
David, Sachs's Apprentice		Tenor
Eva, Pogner's Daughter		Soprano
Magdalene, Eva's former Nurse		Mezzo-soprano
A Night-Watchman		Bass

Chorus

Townsfolk, Journeymen, Apprentices, Girls, Countryfolk.

Scene

Nuremberg, in the middle of the Sixteenth Century.

ACT I Inside the Church of St. Catherine.
ACT II In the street, Outside the Houses of Sachs and Pogner.
ACT III SCENE I Sachs's Workshop.
        SCENE 2 An open Meadow beside the River Pegnitz.

FIRST PRODUCED. Hoftheater, Munich, June 21, 1868.

FIRST PRODUCED IN ENGLAND. Theatre Royal, Drury Lane, London, May 30, 1882. Sung in German, in a German Grand Opera Season, under the direction of Hermann Franke.

FIRST PRODUCED IN AMERICA. Metropolitan Opera House, New York, January 4, 1886. Sung in German.

FIRST PRODUCED IN ENGLISH. Theatre Royal, Manchester, April 16, 1896, in a translation by H. and F. Corder, by the Carl Rosa Opera Company; and in London at the Garrick Theatre, January 22, 1897, by the same Company.

FIRST PRODUCED IN AMERICA IN ENGLISH. Music Hall, Cincinnati, March 20, 1936, in a translation by Frederick Jameson.

DIE MEISTERSINGER VON NURNBERG (THE MASTERSINGERS OF NUREMBERG) – CASTS

CHARACTERS	MUNICH 1868	LONDON 1882 (In German)	NEW YORK 1880 (In German)	MANCHESTER 1896 (In English)	LONDON 1897 (In English)	CINCINNATI 1936 (In English)
Hans Sachs	Franz Betz	Eugen Gura	Emil Fischer	William Ludwig	William Ludwig	Arthur Fear
Pogner	Kaspar Bausewein	Josef Koegel	Josef Staudigl	Lamprière Pringle	Charles Tilbury	Eugene Loewenthal
Vogelgesang	Karl Samuel Heinrich	not named	Dworsky	L. Benucci	William Gillard	Joseph Schenke
Nachtigall	Eduard Sigl	not named	Emil Sänger	Chapman	Pownall	Carl Abaecheri
Beckmesser	Gustav Hölzel	Paul Ehrke	Otto Kemlitz	Homer Lind	Homer Lind	Hubert Kockritz
Kothner	Karl Fischer	Emil Kraus	Philip Lehmler	William Paul	William Paull	Louis John Johnen
Zorn	Weixlstorfer	not named	Hoppe	De Pless Poll	Chapman	Walter Ryan
Eisslinger	Hoppe	not named	Klaus	R. Brooks	R. Brooks	Fenton Pugh
Moser	Pöppl	not named	Langer	P. Somers	P. Somers	Neil Franciss
Ortel	Thoms	not named	Doerfler	Charles Tilbury	Leslie Walker	Richard Fluke
Schwarz	Grasser	not named	Hermann Weber	A. Newman	A. Newman	Milton Sachs
Foltz	Hayn	not named	Anlauf	Albert Winckworth	Skinner	John Schmidt
Walther	Franz Nachbaur	Hermann Winkelmann	Albert Stritt	Barton McGuckin	E. C. Hedmondt	Frederick Jagel
David	Karl Schlosser	Leopold Landau	August Krämer	Frank A. Wood	Frank A. Wood	Franz Trefzger
Eva	Mathilde Mallinger	Rosa Sucher	Auguste Seidl-Krauss	Alice Esty	Alice Esty	Inez Gorman
Magdalene	Sophie Diez	Josephine Schefsky	Marianne Brandt	Julia Lennox	Kirkby Lunn	Frances Benner
A Night-watchman	Ferdinand Lang	not named	Carl Kaufmann	George A. Fox	George A. Fox	Gerald Egelson
Conductor	Hans von Bülow	Hans Richter	Anton Seidl	Richard Eckhold	Richard Eckhold	Eugene Goossens
Producer	Reinhard Hallwachs	Bernhard Pollini	Van Hiell	E. C. Hedmondt	E. C. Hedmondt	Robert Korst
Designer	*Scenery* Angelo Quaglio and Christian Jank (Act I Act II and Act III, Scene I) Heinrich Döll (Act III, Scene 2) *Costumes* Franz Seitz		Carl Schaffell			*Scenery* Reising Studios *Costumes* Stivanello-Culcasi

SYNOPSIS

ACT I

A service is in progress in St. Catherine's church at Nuremberg. Among the congregation is Eva, Guild-Master Pogner's beautiful daughter, with her former nurse Magdalene; watching her closely is the young knight, Walther von Stolzing. When the final hymn is ended and people are leaving, Eva, by sending Magdalene back to the pew for something she pretends to have forgotten, contrives to have a few words alone with Walther.

He at once asks her if she is free or betrothed. Returning in time to hear this, Magdalene replies that Eva's father has promised her hand to the winner of the Master-Singers contest, to be held next day. Though he has no experience in this type of singing, Walther, encouraged by Eva, decides to enter the competition.

They are now joined by David, the apprentice of Hans Sachs, the cobbler, with whom the still pretty Magdalene is in love. He is busy helping to put up the enclosure for the singing contest, the preliminary trials for which are to take place that evening.

Magdalene and Eva now leave, while Walther awaits the arrival of the Masters, and David, helped by several apprentices, prepares the place for them, meanwhile teasing the absorbed Walther. The apprentices in their turn make fun both of him and of David, who also has aspirations to become a Master-Singer.

The lads' high spirits are quelled to respectful silence when the Masters begin to take their seats. First to enter are Pogner, and the 'Marker', Beckmesser – a rival suitor for Eva's hand. Walther introduces himself, with the request that he may be admitted to the Guild. Pogner presents him to some of the other Masters, and agrees to his taking part in the trials.

By this time all are assembled, and after Fritz Kothner, the Baker, has taken the roll-call, Pogner, in his introductory speech, explains that his promise to give Eva to the winner is dependent upon her own consent; but if she refuses him, she cannot choose anyone else. Hans Sachs declares that the girl's choice should be in line with the popular vote; therefore he proposes that the concourse should be held out-of-doors, as part of the Midsummer Day celebrations, in front of the whole populace. This leads to a brief dispute between him and Beckmesser, who accuses him of wanting to profit by the manœuvre, since he himself writes clap-trap for the crowd.

The meeting then proceeds to test Walther von Stolzing. When they ask under what Master and in what College he has studied, he replies simply that he has learned from the books of Walther von der Vogelweide, studied in no college but the open summer woods. Only Hans Sachs approves: the rest consider the twelfth-century Minnesänger tradition, of which Walther von der Vogelweide was a leading exponent, quite outdated.

After Kothner has read him a list of the rules, Walther starts his song – a lyric in praise of springtime love. Before he has finished, Beckmesser interrupts, saying that his slate is full – he has no more space to mark down the singer's faults. But Sachs stands up for him, affirming his right to be heard to the end – and Walther, furious, concludes his test-verse with a sneer at the 'Master-Crows' and storms out of the building.

Sachs declares him 'a true-born poet-knight' . . . but the majority verdict is: "Rejected and failed."

ACT II

It is Midsummer Eve, and David is putting up the shutters of Hans Sachs's shop. The apprentices are singing as they do the same at other houses. Magdalene, coming out of Pogner's house, asks how Walther has done in the trials, and is distressed to hear that he has failed. She goes back again, and the apprentices tease David about her. Losing his temper, he is about to attack them when Sachs arrives, scolds him and sends him indoors.

Pogner and Eva return from an evening walk. She is hoping that Walther has been invited to supper, and is much disappointed when Magdalene tells her that his candidature has been rejected. She decides to ask Hans Sachs for details, but Magdalene persuades her to go in to supper.

Sachs brings his work outside, singing of his enjoyment of the lilac-scented evening air.

Before long Eva comes out again and, trying to get information from Sachs, flirts with him, as a grown girl can do with an elderly man who has been kind to her when she was a child. She brings the conversation round to Walther, and Sachs declares that his case is hopeless: born to be a Master himself, he can never be just one among the rank-and-file; therefore he had better go elsewhere. Putting this verdict down to jealousy, Eva retreats to her house in a huff but remains on the doorstep talking to Magdalene – one of them loitering in the hope of seeing David, the other of Walther.

Eva catches sight of Walther and runs out to him. Sadly he tells her of his rejection. Eva, however, declares that it lies in her own power to award the prize, and most certainly she will give it to him. That will be no use, says Walther, as only a Master-Singer is eligible for the prize.

The Night-Watchman comes along, and Magdalene draws Eva into the house, just as Walther is trying to persuade her to elope with him. Their conversation has also been overheard by Hans Sachs, from behind his shutters: he comes out and tells Walther that this elopement must not be.

Indoors, Eva has changed clothes with Magdalene, and she now comes out ready to escape; but Sachs shines his light full upon the eloping couple. Disconcerted, they are wondering what to do next, when they see Beckmesser sidling up the alley with his lute, on his way to serenade Eva.

To his great annoyance, Sachs comes to the door and begins to hammer at his shoes and sing at the top of his voice. Meanwhile, Walther and Eva are hiding, unable to cross the lighted street. They watch as Magdalene (whom the serenader takes for Eva) opens the window above.

Beckmesser begins to sing, but Hans Sachs – acting as his 'Marker' – distracts him by striking a blow with his hammer every time the singer breaks the rules.

Beckmesser's unskilful song has disturbed the neighbours, who gather round to protest. Still more incensed is David, who thinks that he is intentionally serenading Magdalene. In his jealousy he attacks Beckmesser and a fight ensues, incited by the neighbours and apprentices, who eventually join in a general brawl. Eventually, the Masters and older Burghers are alerted, but even they do not succeed in restoring order.

Walther sees the opportunity of escaping with Eva in the confusion; but Sachs seizes him by the arm and prevents it; then he pushes Eva (whom the onlookers mistake for Magdalene) into her father's house. With the arrival of the Night-Watchman the crowd breaks up: all escape from the street and go indoors.

ACT III

SCENE I   Hans Sachs, absorbed in reading, takes no notice of David, who is joyful at having received a present from Magdalene – a basket of ribbons and flowers for the feast.

Arousing himself from his reverie, Sachs tells David to put on his best clothes, and they will go there together. Left alone, he sings about the crazy happenings of the previous night, and how, on this Midsummer Day, he, Sachs, will:

'Turn the madness his own way.'

Walther, who has slept at Sachs's house, now comes to greet him and relates a wonderful dream which he has turned into verse. He tries over the song and Sachs gives him good advice about it. The two men retire to another room in order to dress for the festival, as Beckmesser arrives, limping after his mauling on the previous evening.

Seeing Walther's song (which he takes to be by Sachs) lying on the work-bench, he picks it up and slips it into his pocket. When Sachs returns, Beckmesser reproaches him with having fomented the riot; but Sachs passes it off as a Midsummer Eve's joke. His neighbour is not mollified, however, for he regards the widower Sachs as a possible rival for Eva's hand. The cobbler protests that he does not intend to compete. 'What about the poem, then?' asks Beckmesser, incautiously revealing that he has purloined it.

Unexpectedly, Sachs not only says that he will give the poem to Beckmesser, but also promises not to reveal himself as its author. In return, Beckmesser says that he will appoint Sachs as the 'Marker'.

As Beckmesser limps away, Eva comes to complain to Sachs that one of the shoes he has made for her is too tight. He takes it off to alter it, whilst Eva – to the delight of Walther who comes in at that moment – remains with her bare foot poised upon a stool.

While Sachs finishes the shoe and returns it to the girl, Walther sings a lyric in her praise, which Sachs hails as a Master-song. Eva, who has listened enchanted, bursts into tears of emotion on Sachs's shoulder, and he transfers her into Walther's arms.

Now Magdalene and David appear in their festive costumes, and Sachs calls them to witness that he is christening Walther's song: 'The Glorious Morning Dream's True Story'. Eva, as 'godmother', praises the song and prophesies that it will win a prize. All celebrate the song in a quintet and go off to the meeting-place.

SCENE 2 The whole population is gathered in a meadow beside the River Pegnitz. One Guild after another passes in procession, singing of their trade: the shoemakers, the tailors, the bakers. . . . Frolicking apprentices hail the arrival of a boat-load of pretty girls from a nearby village, and compete with the journeymen in claiming them as dance-partners.

Then come the Master-Singers in procession: first Kothner as standard-bearer, next Pogner leading Eva by the hand, then a train of attendants, including Magdalene; finally the other Master-Singers. They arrange themselves on a platform, with Eva in the place of honour and Sachs, warmly greeted by the people, as 'Marker'. He announces the conditions of the contest and calls upon Beckmesser to begin. He sings Walther's song that he has stolen from Sachs's shop, but the tune is entirely wrong and his effort is greeted with universal derision. Railing against what he believes is treachery, he hurls the manuscript at Sachs declaring that he is the author of this ridiculous poem and rushes away in a rage.

The Master-Singers demand an explanation from Sachs: he declares that the song, in fact, is not his but Walther's, and that the knight will now prove it by singing it correctly. Walther does so, and Masters and populace are captivated to the point of unanimously awarding him the prize.

Eva puts the victor's wreath on his head and leads him up to her father, before whom they both kneel to receive his blessing. But when Pogner offers to elect Walther as a Master-Singer, the young man refuses; he is still angry at his treatment the day before and having won his bride he feels he does not need the honour. Sachs advises the young man to restrain his temper and not despise the elaborate rules of the Master-Singers, which have, at least, maintained high standards in the past. Eva then takes the crown from Walther's head and places it on that of Sachs, who is enthusiastically hailed by all present.

REVIEW

The Music Critic in *The Era*, June 3, 1882, wrote of the first English performance:

'The first performance of Wagner's opera, *Die Meistersinger* by the German company, at Drury Lane, on Tuesday, must have greatly astonished those who had only made acquaintance with the composer through the medium of the *Nibelungen* series of operas. That there were occasional gleams of mirth even in those works could not fail to be remarked; but only those who had previously studied the score of *Die Meistersinger*, or who had witnessed its performance in Germany, had any idea that the composer of the future could be so gay, genial, and merry as we find him in this opera. "Wagner's comic opera" has a curious sound to those who fancy the composer is always as grim and uncouth as he shows himself at times in his later work. But we have a new Wagner in *Die Meistersinger*, and truly a very pleasant companion Wagner can be when he quits his masquerading with the personages of the Teutonic mythology and condescends to set to music the joys and sorrows, and the oddities and caprices, of ordinary mortals. We must first preface our notice with the remark that in Germany this opera, which was produced at Munich in 1868, under Dr. von Bülow, is one of the most popular, perhaps the most popular, of any of the composer's works in Germany. This is easy to comprehend after hearing, for it is German to the core. All its merits and such faults as it possesses are exclusively national, and it has the advantage of being literally steeped in the melodies of the people. These, if Wagner has not actually borrowed, he has imitated with extraordinary felicity, and, although the story is simple and homely, the score is enriched with some of the most masterly touches that ever came from the brain and pen of a man of genius. Let us first of all pay a well deserved compliment to the almost perfect manner in which the opera was placed upon the stage. As for the conductor, Herr Richter, no praise we could give would be greater than his due. Rarely in all our musical experience have we heard such a finished and refined rendering of a difficult and elaborate composition. The simplest phrases and the most complicated found the accomplished conductor always ready, never at fault, even in the slightest detail, and the greatest admiration was excited by the brilliant playing of the orchestra throughout. Passages of the utmost difficulty went smoothly, and upon the stage everything possible was done to secure the success of the work, which we fully expect will make a deep and lasting impression, opening up, as it does, new and attractive forms of musical art, in which past, present, and future can shake hands and forget all rivalries; for in this work Wagner, without departing from the system he has adopted, allows himself to be influenced chiefly by the musical suggestions such a story as *Die Meistersinger* evokes. Wagner's first idea in producing a comic opera was when he had just finished *Tannhäuser*. At first he imagined a kind of musical caricature; but as the story grew he saw that it would be throwing away a good subject to treat it in this fashion, and, therefore, without destroying the humorous element, which is so great a charm in the composition, he devoted to the work all the resources of his genius, and the result is nothing less than a masterpiece. The story is interesting from first to last, and the music is so thoroughly in harmony with it that it is easy to perceive how poetry and music grew together in the mind of the creator. The overture and some of the music of the opera has been heard at concerts, but Wagner is quite right when he declares that most of his music loses its significance when heard apart from the stage. The overture, as played on Tuesday evening, at once revealed the admirable condition of the band, and prepared the audience for a fine performance. The first scene of the opera takes place in the church of St. Catherine at Nuremburg, and it must be noted that the curtain rises upon the last bars of the overture without any pause whatever, and this Wagnerian innovation is worthy of being followed. . . .'

After telling the plot the critic continues...

'It will be seen that the story of the opera is well adapted for its purpose. It is pure, homely, natural, and humorous, and the music is not merely suitable, but in some instances its quality is very high indeed. Wagner does not go out of his way to force his pet theory upon the hearer, and the immense advantage of a chorus and of good concerted music gives the opera fine contrasts which in his

'Siegfried' Act 3 – Wieland Wagner's 1954 Bayreuth production conducted by Joseph Keilberth with Astrid Varnay as Brünnhilde and Wolfgang Windgassen as Siegfried (Siegfried Lauterwasser).

'Götterdämmerung' Act 2 – Siegfried Wagner's 1930 Bayreuth production conducted by Karl Elmendorff with Nanny Larsen-Todsen as Brünnhilde and Gunnar Graarud as Siegfried (Pieperhoff).

'Götterdämmerung' Act 2 – Wieland Wagner's production for the 1957 Bayreuth Festival with Astrid Varnay as Brünnhilde and Bernd Aldenhoff as Siegfried (Adolf Falk).

'Götterdämmerung' – The Funeral March scene from the English National Opera's 1971 production (Anthony Crickmay).

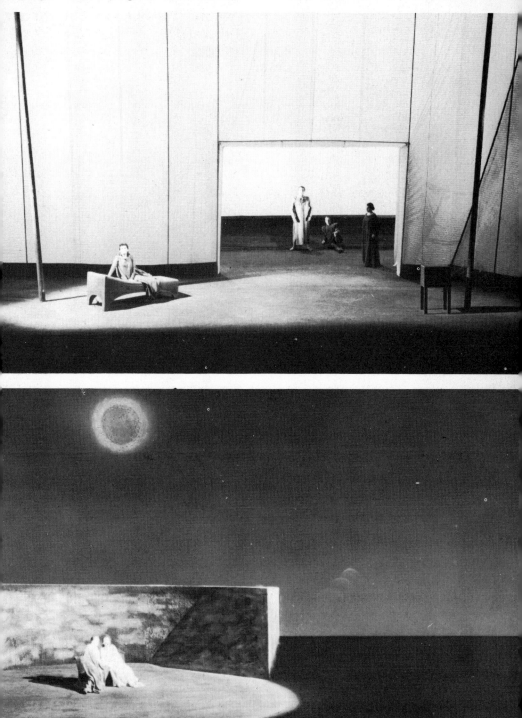

'ristan und Isolde' Act 1 – Wolfgang Wagner's 1957 Bayreuth production conducted by 'olfgang Sawallisch (Siegfried Lauterwasser).

'ristan und Isolde' Act 2 – Bayreuth 1957 (Siegfried Lauterwasser).

'Tristan und Isolde' Act 3 – Bayreuth 1957 (Heinz Evsell).

'Die Meistersinger' Act 3 – The 1930 Covent Garden Opera production with Rudolph Laubenthal as Walther von Stolzing and Lotte Lehmann as Eva.

'Die Meistersinger' Act 1 – Wieland Wagner's 1957 Bayreuth production conducted by André Cluytens (Siegfried Lauterwasser).

'Die Meistersinger' Act 2 – Bayreuth 1957 (Siegfried Lauterwasser).

'Die Meistersinger' Act 3 Scene 2 – Bayreuth 1957 (Siegfried Lauterwasser).

sifal' Act 1 – Wieland Wagner's 1951 duction conducted by Hans Knapperts-ch (Siegfried Lauterwasser).

'Parsifal' Act 3 – Bayreuth 1951 (Siegfried Lauterwasser).

sifal' Act 1 – Bayreuth 1954 (Siegfried Lauterwasser).

'Die Walküre' Act 3 – Gwyneth Jones as Brünnhilde and Donald McIntyre as Wotan in Patrice Chéreau's production for the 1976 Bayreuth Festival (Wilhelm Rauh).

'Götterdämmerung' Act 2 – Bengt Rundg as Hagen in the centenary productio Bayreuth conducted by Pierre Bo (Siegfried Lauterwasser).

'Siegfried' Act 2 – René Kollo in the title role – Bayreuth 1976 (Wilhelm Rauh).

later works are wanting. The representation was admirable in every way. The tender and passionate Eva was sustained by Frau Sucher with that grace and talent in acting, combined with charming vocal skill, which we have warmly commended on a previous occasion. Few *artistes* would have made so much of the part. In addition to the grand airs of the operatic *prima donna*, there are infinite little clever and natural touches which give the character reality and charm. The business of the clandestine meeting was admirably acted. The scene in Hans Sachs's room, where Eva stands motionless, gazing rapturously at her lover, while Hans Sachs is mending her shoe, has been, perhaps, extravagantly praised. Still the grace of the actress cannot be denied. Frau Sucher's voice told beautifully in the lovely quintet. It will sound strange to some to speak of "loveliness" in association with Wagner's music; but lovely it is, and so is a great deal in the opera. The method Wagner has adopted of giving individuality to his characters must be highly commended. Some of them stand before us like real personages, rather than as operatic lay figures. Hans Sachs, the poetical shoemaker, as indicated by Wagner and played by Herr Gura, is a veritable creation. The strong, manly, yet tender, nature of the man is brought out fully. We cannot help loving him. Herr Gura thoroughly understood the almost Shakespearean temperament of the shoemaker. Herr Winkelmann, as the hero, sang the beautiful music allotted to him with great power and effect, and acted extremely well. Herr Koegel, as Pogner, the rich goldsmith, was efficient; and the quaint humour of Herr Landau was well employed as David. As the defeated musical critic, Beckmesser, Herr Ehrke was seen to greater advantage than in anything he has yet appeared. He was quaint and droll in the extreme in the scene where he chalked down the faults in the knight's singing and where he delivers his own serenade. Dr. Kraus represented Kothner cleverly; and Fraulein Schefsky was an excellent Magdalene. The audience was a very large one, including the Duke and Duchess of Edinburgh.'

NOTES

In the autumn of 1859, Wagner left Switzerland to conduct a series of concerts, in order to support himself in his new circumstances. The aid from Otto Wesendonck had naturally ceased, but his wife Minna rejoined him in November in Paris which was to become his headquarters until 1862.

He conducted concerts in Brussels and with influence *Tannhäuser* received its fateful production at the Paris Opéra in March 1861.

The same year he received an amnesty and was allowed to return to Germany; visiting Vienna, he heard *Lohengrin* for the first time there on May 31. He also visited Liszt at Weimar, returning to Paris, where in October he recommenced work on *Die Meistersinger*, which he had sketched in prose in 1845, the poem being completed in January 1862 and published the next year. Wagner immediately started work on the sketches for the music but these had to be laid aside in May for more lucrative activities, which included concerts in Petrograd and Moscow and the publication of the poems of the Nibelungen cycle, for which he had lost hope of ever completing the musical setting.

Minna Wagner finally separated from her husband in 1861, going to Dresden where she died in 1866.

Wagner commenced his liaison with Cosima von Bülow, natural daughter of Liszt and wife of Hans von Bülow, in 1864, when King Ludwig invited the composer to Munich. Their daughter Isolde was born in 1865, the same year as von Bülow conducted *Tristan*.

Under Cosima's influence a period of feverish activity followed. *Siegfried* was recommenced and acts one and two of *Die Meistersinger* were completed by September 1866, but Wagner was forced to leave Munich on December 10, 1865, settling at Tribschen on the Lake of Lucerne with Cosima. He finished *Die Meistersinger* in October 1867, the score being published the following year.

Hans von Bülow remained faithful, in spite of everything, to the works of Wagner and the new opera was produced under his direction at Munich in June 1868, with the composer present in the audience.

Two more children were born to Wagner and Cosima, Eva in 1867 and Siegfried in 1869, and in July 1870 the von Bülows were divorced and on August 25 Wagner and Cosima were married.

After the first production in London of *Die Meistersinger* in 1882 it was not heard again in German for many years, the 'official' language of Covent Garden being Italian. It was as *Il Maestri Cantori di Norimberga*, in a translation by G. Mazzucato, that it was sung at the Royal Italian Opera on July 13, 1889. It was not until 1892 that Covent Garden became multilingual.

PARSIFAL

———— . ————

A Religious Festival Play in Three Acts

Libretto

First conceived in Marienbad, July 1845. First draft completed in Zurich, Good Friday, April 10, 1857. Written, January–February, 1877 and completed April 19, 1877.

Music

Sketch of Act I finished January 29, 1878. Act II completed October 13, 1878 and Act III, April 26, 1879. Score completed at Palermo, January 13, 1882.

Characters

Amfortas	Baritone
Titurel	Bass
Gurnemanz	Bass
Parsifal	Tenor
Klingsor	Bass
Kundry	Soprano
A Voice	Contralto
First and Second Knights of the Grail	Tenor, Bass
Esquires	Soprano, Tenor
Klingsor's Flower Maidens	Soprano, Alto

Chorus

The Brotherhood of Knights of the Grail	Tenor, Bass
Youths and Boys	Tenor, Alto, Soprano

Scene

In and near the Castle of the Keeper of the Grail – Monsalvat, Spain.

ACT I SCENE 1 A Forest.
  SCENE 2 The Vaulted and Pillared Temple of the Grail.
ACT II SCENE 1 Klingsor's Enchanted Castle.
  SCENE 2 The Enchanted Garden.
ACT III SCENE 1 A Meadow near the Castle of the Grail.
  SCENE 2 The Temple of the Grail.

Note

Scenery in the style of the Northern Mountains of Gothic Spain. Thus, Klingsor's Enchanted Castle should be considered as on the southern slopes of these mountains, facing towards Arabic Spain. The Knights and Squires of the Grail wear costumes suggesting the Order of the Templars – white surcoats and cloaks; but instead of the Red Cross, they wear the emblem of a hovering dove on their weapons and cloaks.

The original production used a panorama (moving scenery) for the transition between the two scenes of Act III.

FIRST PRODUCED. Festspielhaus, Bayreuth, July 26, 1882.

FIRST PRODUCED OUTSIDE BAYREUTH. Metropolitan Opera House, New York, December 24, 1903. Sung in German.

FIRST PRODUCED OUTSIDE BAYREUTH IN ENGLISH. Tremont Theatre, Boston, October 17, 1904, in a translation by John P. Jackson, and at the New York Theatre, New York, October 31, 1904, by the same Cast under the management of Henry W. Savage.

FIRST PRODUCED IN ENGLAND. Royal Opera House, Covent Garden, London, February 2, 1914. Sung in German.

FIRST PRODUCED IN ENGLAND IN ENGLISH. Royal Opera House, Covent Garden, London, November 17, 1919, in an unnamed translation by the Beecham Opera Company.

Concert Performances

The first performance of *Parsifal* in England took place in concert form at the Royal Albert Hall, London, November 10, 1884, given by Soloists and the Royal Albert Hall Choral Society. Sung in German.

The first performance in America took place at the Metropolitan Opera House, New York, March 3, 1886. Principal parts sung in German, with the Chorus of the Oratorio Society in English.

PARSIFAL – A RELIGIOUS FESTIVAL PLAY IN THREE ACTS – CASTS

CHARACTERS	BAYREUTH 1882	NEW YORK 1903 (In German)	BOSTON 1904 (In English)	LONDON 1914 (In German)	LONDON 1919 (In English)
Amfortas	Theodor Reichmann	Anton Van Rooy	Johannes Bischoff	Paul Bender	Percy Heming
Titurel	August Kindermann	Marcel Journet	Robert Kent Parker	Murray Davey	Foster Richardson
Gurnemanz	Emil Scaria	Robert Blass	Putnam Griswold	Paul Knüpfer	Norman Allin
Parsifal	Hermann Winkelmann	Alois Burgstaller	Alois Pennarini	Heinrich Hensel	Frank Mullings
Klingsor	Karl Hill	Otto Goritz	Homer Lind	August Kiess	Herbert Langley
Kundry	Amalie Materna	Milka Ternina	Kirkby Lunn	Eva von der Osten	Gladys Ancrum
First Knight	Anton Fuchs	Julius Bayet	Fracklyn Wallace	William Anderson	Sydney Russell
Second Knight	Stumf	Adolph Mühlmann	Albert Pellaton	Charles Mott	Arthur Wynn
Esquires (Four)	Galfy / Keil / von Hubbenet / Max Mikorey	Katherine Moran / Braendle / Albert Reiss / Willy Harden	Jennie Heller / Elsie van der Voort / Alfred Kappeler / William Kelly	Winifred New / Kate Holbrooke / Anton Hummelsheim / Frank Foster	Elsie Wynn / Mollie Mundle / Frederick Ricketts / Frederick Davies
Flower Maidens (Six)	Johanna André / Luise Belce / Galfy / Morson / Meta / Carrie Pringle	Isabelle Bouton / Braendle / Delsarta / Förnsen / Elsa Harris / Lillian Heidelbach	Pearl Guzman / Harriet Cropler / Celeste Wynn / Margaret Liddell / Florence Wickham / Charlotte George	Annie Puchmayer / Ada Davies / Bessie Jones / Rosina Buckman / Eveline Matthews / Elsie McDermid	Sylvia Nelis / Bessie Tyas / Doris Lemon / Lilian Stanford / Gladys Simmonds / Kathleen Moore
		Three additional Maidens in this production: Katherine Moran / Florence Mulford / Marcia van Dresser			
A Voice	Dompierre	Louise Homer	Florence Wickham	Franziska Bender-Schäfer	Not named

Conductor	Hermann Levi	Alfred Hertz	Walter H. Rothwell	Artur Bodanzky	Albert Coates
Producer	Richard Wagner	Anton Fuchs	Joseph Engel	Willi Wirk	
Designer	*Scenery* Paul von Joukowsky Act I, Act II, Scene 1, Act II, Scene 2, Act III; and Panorama Max Brückner *Costumes* Paul von Joukowsky		*Scenery* Walter and Albert Burridge (from German models)	*Scenery* Joseph Harker *Costumes* Attilio Comelli	*Scenery* Joseph Harker *Costumes* Attilio Comelli

PARSIFAL—CONCERT PERFORMANCES

CHARACTERS	LONDON 1884	NEW YORK 1886
Amfortas	Edward Schuegraf	Max Heinrich
Titurel	Henry Pyatt	Philip Lehmler
Gurnemanz	Emil Scaria	Emil Fischer
Parsifal	Heinrich Gudehus	August Krämer
Klingsor	Henry Pyatt	Philip Lehmler
Kundry	Therese Malten	Marianne Bennett
Knights	Bernard Lane	Not named
	B. Young	
Esquires	Hutchinson	Not named
	Norman	
	Bernard Lane	
	A. Thompson	
	Hutchinson	
Flower Maidens	B. Francis	Ford
	Thorndike	Dossert
		Klein
	H. Coward	Eshenbach
	Hirlemann	Bruni
	M. Fenna	Groebl
Conductor	Joseph Barnby	Walter Damrosch

SYNOPSIS

SCENE I   Under a tree beside a forest-lake, Gurnemanz – an old but
still vigorous man – and two young Squires lie sleeping. Roused by
reveillé from the nearby castle, they say a morning prayer; then the
two youths go to make preparations for their King Amfortas, who,
having received an incurable wound from the Sacred Spear that he
himself had incautiously taken to use against the enchanter Klingsor,
comes regularly to bathe in the holy waters of the lake in the hope
that it will relieve his pain.

Two Knights enter and are discussing the King's health, when
they are interrupted by the arrival of Kundry – a wild witch-like
woman, who has made a long journey in quest of a herb that might
cure the wound of Amfortas. Exhausted, she throws herself down on
the ground.

Amfortas then arrives, carried on a litter: he thanks Kundry for
her efforts and goes on towards the lake. The Squires, who look on
her askance, suggest that she should be sent to find the Spear, which
has remained in Klingsor's hands, and without which Amfortas
cannot be healed. Gurnemanz, however, declares that Amfortas has
learned in a vision that the only person who can help him will be 'a
pure fool'.

Suddenly the Knights and Squires are startled by the shooting of a
wild swan over the lake. They bring in the culprit – a young man
who can give no account of himself: he knows neither his name, nor
his parentage, nor his country of origin – having been brought up
by his mother in the heart of the forest. Kundry, who evidently
knows all about him, says that his father Gamuret perished in battle,
and that his mother is now dead. This news throws him into a faint,
and Kundry revives him with a drink of water.

Gurnemanz, guessing that this may be the 'pure fool' of the
prophecy, invites him to follow the company back to the Castle,
where the Knights take Communion every day.

SCENE 2   The scenery gradually changes into a vast hall, where two long tables are set with cups but no food. Amfortas, on a raised couch in the centre, has beside him the covered Shrine of the Grail. His father, Titurel, who though entombed still lives on, through the power of the Grail, orders him to uncover it. As Amfortas does so, the temple grows dark, while the cup remains illuminated by a ray of light; when the light returns, the Knights' cups have been filled with wine, and by each is a piece of bread. They then take part in the ritual of Communion. Gurnemanz has kept a place beside him for the unknown youth, who remains quite bewildered and dumbfounded.

Meanwhile, Amfortas's wound has broken open again. He gives a cry of agony and is carried away by his Squires.

When Gurnemanz realises that the young man has understood nothing of what he has seen, he is seized by anger and pushes him out of the temple. He kneels before the altar, and a voice is heard to repeat the prophecy of the 'Innocent Fool' made wise through pity, who will release Amfortas and the Knights from their anguish.

ACT II

SCENE 1   In Klingsor's enchanted castle Kundry is sleeping, but she wakes at his command. He reminds her that it was she who once lured Amfortas to the castle, and that – however much she may try to atone by helping the Knights of the Grail – he, Klingsor, has her in his power.

From the battlements they see the nameless youth approaching. Klingsor sends his henchmen out to oppose him; but the young man, disarming one of them, takes his weapon and fights his way through, wounding several of his opponents.

In surprise and delight he stands looking down at the castle, with its beautiful garden. Klingsor prophesies that he will fall an easy prey to Kundry's wiles and, once deprived of his purity, will be at the mercy of the enchanter himself.

SCENE 2   The scene changes to the garden, where the stranger stands gazing at a group of lovely, startled flower-maidens who bid him welcome, though with gentle reproaches for his ill-treatment of their lovers. They cover themselves with garlands and perfume themselves, till they seem to the young man like the flowers of the garden come to life. He is ready enough to amuse himself with them, but when they become amorous and dispute his favours he is alarmed and tries to escape.

All at once he hears Kundry's voice calling him by name: Parsifal
... and he remembers hearing his mother once speak that name in
her sleep. He sees Kundry – no longer a haggard witch, but an
alluring woman in diaphanous Oriental garments, lying on a couch
of flowers. She sharply bids the girls begone, and, remaining alone
with Parsifal, tells him that his father Gamuret, as he was dying in
Arabia, gave him that name while he was still unborn. Because she
wished to preserve him from his father's fate, Parsifal's mother had
brought him up far from the world, with no knowledge of feats of
arms; but he, as he grew up, wandered far and wide. It was his
absence, Kundry tells the young man to his great distress, that
broke his mother's heart and led to her death.

Kundry suggests that Parsifal can best find consolation for his
sorrow and remorse by learning about love, and she presses her lips
to his in a long kiss.

In terror, Parsifal leaps up, crying: 'Amfortas! The wound! The
wound!' ... He has realised that it was Kundry through whose
enchantments Amfortas was undone. He spurns her, though she tells
him that she is repentant and seeks redemption through his love.

She has been condemned to wander the face of the earth since the
time she had laughed at Christ on his way to Golgotha. Now she
believes she has found her redeemer in Parsifal. But he rebukes her
again and insists that he must return to Amfortas.

Enraged, Kundry calls upon the inhabitants of the castle to stop
him from escaping. Klingsor appears on the walls bearing the
Sacred Spear, which he hurls at Parsifal. But a miracle occurs. The
spear remains floating in mid-air above the young man's head.
He seizes it and with it makes the sign of the Cross; whereupon
the castle disappears and the garden withers to a desert. Kundry lies
motionless as Parsifal, departing, says to her: 'You know where we
shall meet again.'

ACT III

SCENE I   Gurnemanz, now very old, has become a hermit, and the
action takes place on a pleasant spring day in front of his hermitage.
Hearing Kundry groan, he draws her out of a thicket where she has
been sleeping during the winter. When he has revived her, he
observes that a great change has come over her. Gone is the old
haunted look. Her face has grown almost ethereal. She murmurs
softly, 'I must serve,' and falls silent. While she is filling a pitcher at

the spring she sees a Knight approaching, clad completely in black armour ... Gurnemanz tells him that it is Good Friday and therefore he should disarm. He obeys, and kneels down in prayer beside his discarded weapons.

In amazement, Gurnemanz recognises the Spear and the youth he expelled from the Temple years before. Parsifal says he is on his way to bring it home, but has been delayed by many battles and misfortunes. All are waiting eagerly for him, declares Gurnemanz, for Amfortas no longer has the strength to give his Knights Communion: Titurel is dead, and the other Knights are all weak and dejected.

Seeing that Parsifal is exhausted from his journey, Gurnemanz bathes his head and Kundry his feet. Parsifal, who says that he knows he will become Guardian of the Holy Grail that day, baptises Kundry with water from the spring, and kisses her on the forehead. Gurnemanz and Kundry clothe Parsifal in the mantle of the Knights of the Grail.

SCENE 2   The landscape has changed, as in the first act, and Parsifal now finds himself back in the Great Hall, where one train of Knights are bearing in the corpse of Titurel, while others bring Amfortas on his litter. The Knights implore Amfortas to uncover the Grail, but he refuses, tears aside his robes, exposing his terrible wounds, and begs them to put an end to his torment by killing him.

Meanwhile Parsifal, accompanied by Gurnemanz and Kundry, enters unperceived; and now, advancing, he stretches out the Spear, touching Amfortas's side with its point. Immediately his wound is healed.

Declaring that he himself is now their guardian, Parsifal opens the Shrine and takes out the Chalice. The Temple is mysteriously darkened, while the Grail shines with an unearthly light. A white dove hovers over Parsifal's head. Kundry sinks to the ground, and dies, her bondage at an end, while Amfortas and Gurnemanz kneel in homage to Parsifal.

REVIEWS

Of the first performance of *Parsifal* in England, in concert form, the Music Critic in *The Era*, November 15, 1884, wrote:

'There was very naturally great curiosity manifested respecting the first performance of Wagner's *Parsifal*. Those who had attended the Bayreuth festival were somewhat sceptical as to the results of transforming the opera, or music-drama as Wagner called it, into an oratorio, or, to speak more exactly, a cantata. Wagner is essentially a dramatic musician, and it is not so long ago that he refused altogether to have his music performed away from the stage. But amateurs remember that Wagner at length consented to break through a rule which was of decided advantage to his works, and the consequence was a series of concerts at the Albert Hall. These were by no means successful, save with a few enthusiasts, as the music heard apart from the stage lost much of its interest and significance. We fear the same result will happen in the present instance; but, of course, the first night of *Parsifal* had no little interest for those who had not previously heard any of the music. People wished to hear what the opera was like whether it pleased them or not, and as an element in satisfying musical curiosity there was justification in producing it, although we are bound to say it hardly realised under such conditions the intentions of the composer. *Parsifal* is the eighth of Wagner's music dramas, and his last. It was given for the first time at Bayreuth July 26th, 1882, and the following year, February 13th, 1883, the composer died at Venice. An opera written when the composer had reached the age of sixty-eight can hardly possess the freshness and vigour of earlier works, and the plain fact about *Parsifal* is that it is dull and destitute of inspiration. In other works the wonderful energy, dramatic feeling and novelty of ideas carried the hearer along and compensated for so much that was ugly, harsh, and crude. But the truth must be told that in this latest effort of Wagner, there is a feeling of exhaustion. The spring of inspiration has been pumped out. It is useless for the composer's admirers to account for its dullness on the score of its being heard apart from the stage. That is something, but it is not all. The depression attending the performance of *Parsifal* arises from the simple fact that there is nothing in the work to please the ear. It is very well to call it a "miracle play," a "mystery," and "sacred music drama," and so forth, but inventing fancy names will not conceal the dreariness and utter want of charm. Another fatal defect, considered as a modern opera, is the introduction of the sacred rites and forms of Christianity. Granted that these were necessary to the subject, then the work becomes an oratorio and not an opera. The ritual of the church cannot be dramatic, and when it is allied to scenes of human passion more will be offended than pleased by it. Not for a moment could *Parsifal* be tolerated on the English stage, yet without the stage the work loses all significance. Hence there are two rocks ahead for *Parsifal*. It goes wrong because of the religious element, and it goes wrong because it loses all interest in the absence of stage surroundings. . . . Regarding the performance, it is impossible to describe it as really successful, for the simple reason that the bulk of the audience got utterly weary of the endless "leading motives," containing, as they did, so little musical beauty. There was no sign of a melody throughout the three fantastic acts. The worst faults of the Wagner system are repeated in the work. Yet there are instances of musical effect which, if the composer had not tied himself to theory, might have been turned to still better account. The artists were Fraulein Malten, Herr Gudehus, Herr Scaria, Herr Schuegraf in the German list, and Mrs. Hutchinson, Miss Coward, Miss Fenna, Madame Hirlemann, Miss Thorndike, Miss Francis, Madame Norman, the excellent tenor Mr. Bernard Lane, and Messrs. Thompson, Young and Pyatt. Mr. Barnby conducted with his customary care and skill, and the chorus deserved great praise. But, after all, *Parsifal*, without scenery and spectacular effects, was a terrible trial, save to a few devoted adherents of the composer. We may safely predict that *Parsifal* will never find many admirers in this country, in spite of the occasional beauties of the composition. None could, for instance, deny the grace of the chorus of flower-maidens and the sombre effects of the ritual scenes, and the full choral passages, in which orchestra and voices were combined in masterly manner, and revealed the great powers of the composer, who was said to play with the orchestra as with a pianoforte. It is not necessary to dwell further on the efforts of the solo artists, as they were mostly occupied with dreary recitative. About the middle of the second act the audience began rapidly to disappear, and ere the close patient listeners were few and far between.'

The Music Critic in *The Times*, February 3, 1914, wrote of the first English performance:

'Queen Alexandra occupied the Royal box at the first performance in England of Wagner's *Parsifal*, which took place at Covent Garden last night before a very distinguished audience. The opera was heard with almost reverent attention. The request that visitors should be in their seats early was universally complied with; even the beginnings of applause at the end of an act were hushed by protests from the body of the audience.

'The huge audience which filled every seat in the Opera House from the stalls to the gallery was drawn there no doubt by every conceivable motive and interest, from a devotion bordering upon a religious enthusiasm to mere curiosity and the desire to share in an historic event. Yet for practical purposes it could be divided into two definite classes, those who knew or thought they knew what *Parsifal* is and those who had come to make the discovery. Most of the former were, of course, those who have frequented the Festspielhaus at Bayreuth; among the latter must have been many to whom at least portions of the music were as familiar as is the music of *The Ring*, but who came to fit together for the first time their fragmentary impressions.

'Both classes no doubt had one question uppermost in mind: the question how far what they were to see and hear would be the *Parsifal* which until this year has remained secluded at Bayreuth. The question, though inevitable, is destructive to the spirit which Wagner fought so hard to gain from his audience. He wanted what every artist wants and rarely gets, an attitude of concentrated sympathy freed from all exterior distractions. He wanted an audience without poses either of piety or cleverness to whom he could speak direct. The conditions of modern artistic production make the ideal unattainable, and while those who know *Parsifal* have by now answered the question each in his own way, it must be our business to answer it to some extent for the benefit of the newcomers.

'The management had done all that could be done to make up for the loss of all the special conditions which simplify the listener's task at Bayreuth by insisting on punctuality, on the lowering of lights in the auditorium some minutes before the performance began, and on closing the doors during the whole of each act. The stage itself offered more serious problems, some advantages, and many difficulties. The immense size of the Covent Garden stage necessarily makes the pictures something very different from the originals.

'The forest scene, into which Kundry rushes wild-eyed and breathless, bringing balsam for Amfortas's wound, and where the boy Parsifal strays and thoughtlessly shoots the swan, gives a far more spacious view of lake and mountain than can be shown at Bayreuth. The temple in which the mystery of the Grail is celebrated is, on the other hand, a very close reproduction of the Venetian architecture of the Bayreuth scene, but the point at which this production fails is the moving scenery which Wagner intended should link the two. The idea was one of Wagner's worst blunders in practical stagecraft. He directed that the whole scene should move gradually towards the right, and even when it is done perfectly it has some of the absurdity of the old-fashioned panorama show. But when the scene does not move at all, but is gradually obliterated by a canvas on a roll (which is what happens at Covent Garden), the absurdity is multiplied a hundredfold. If the management could have had the courage to prove Wagner wrong by omitting the moving scenery altogether, letting the journey to Monsalvat be pictured imaginatively in the magnificent music of the orchestra, as Siegfried's journey to the Rhine is pictured, a lasting service to Wagner's art would have been done.

'The second act contains altogether three scenes. It opens in the darkened vaults of Klingsor's Castle, the details of which have been closely copied from Bayreuth. Originally the transformation to the garden of the magician's flower-maidens was effected by the castle appearing to sink into the earth, but this has been modified in recent years; so has been the garish scene of the garden, which, as a Correspondent pointed out in *The Times* on Saturday, was an eyesore to the first visitors to Bayreuth. At Covent Garden the castle sinks to the earth in accordance with the original plan. The garden when it appears is certainly more brilliant than the present Bayreuth scene, and throughout Parsifal's temptation by Kundry it remains the same instead of being gradually softened by wreaths of green foliage closing in around the actors. When Parsifal signs the Cross with the spear there follows the final transformation to a scene of fallen leaves and bare tree stems which in last night's performance was rather clumsily managed.

'In the third act, the scene of the "Karfreitagszauber," there is again at Covent Garden both loss and gain. The beautiful spring scene, the fields strewn with crocuses, the white may and rose trees in full bloom, is in itself far more vivid than the comparatively simple picture at Bayreuth. Yet one misses the exquisitely mellow light which tones perfectly with Wagner's orchestral colour, and on the large stage one loses much of the intimacy of the action. The eye is distracted from the important things – Parsifal's forgiveness of Kundry and the preparation for his office. Again we have the same crude evasion of the difficulty of the moving scenery which leads back to the Temple of the Grail.

'But these things are really only the accessories. Every one realises now that the heart of Wagner's art lies in the music. The cast had been carefully chosen with this in view. Herr Hensel has sung the part of Parsifal in two Bayreuth festivals; Mme. Eva von der Osten is the possessor of one of the most beautiful mezzo-soprano voices of modern times, and in Herr Paul Bender, Herr Knüpfer, and Herr Kiess were secured three of the finest singers possible. Individually the work of the principal artists was of the highest order. But one looks for more than this, and through most of the performance we got more both in the careful *ensemble* and in the fine orchestral playing. The opening scenes were the least satisfactory. One realised to what an extent Wagner relied upon the preparedness of his audience, assuming that their absorption in the drama would carry them through the uneventful first scenes, the questions of the young men to Gurnemanz, and his long narration of the founding of the Order of the Grail by Titurel. There seemed to be some lack of cohesion, too, between the singers and the orchestra which prevented the thing from gripping the attention at once, and it was not until Parsifal's sudden entrance following the wounded swan that the work became fully vitalised. But the great scene of the Love-feast of the Grail was intensely impressive; had it not been for some flat singing by the chorus of Knights (a fault which appeared again in the last scene) we could have declared it to be unsurpassable. It was not only the majesty of the scene, the dignity of the ritual, and the excellent singing of the distant choirs which combined to produce a memorable effect, but in contrast to these things the human character of Amfortas as presented by Herr Bender stood out in strong relief.

'It is in his drawing of Amfortas that Wagner's genius reaches to its full height. It is dramatically stronger than Parsifal himself because it has light and shade, the struggle between weakness and aspiration. Parsifal in the first act is unawakened; in the last he is raised too high above human frailty for Wagner to dare to touch him strongly, or for the audience to enter into complete sympathy with him. It is only in the second act that he is quite a living personality. Herr Hensel, fine singer though he is, has not sufficient dramatic subtlety to be able to do all that can be done with the difficult part. He does not by a look or gesture fill in gaps which Wagner necessarily left to the artist.

'In the second act the singing of Mme. von der Osten was extraordinarily fine. From the first terrible wails with which she answered the call of Klingsor through the long scene of temptation her voice had the thrill of a wonderful musical tone. The one fault was that she was entirely commanding, too big a creature to suggest seductive art, but her singing was a joy to hear. The flower maidens' chorus was beautifully sung, and the whole of this act had the grip of reality which the beginning of the first had failed to get. If the third did not reach quite so high, that was largely owing, as we have suggested, to the conditions of the performance. The illusion, too, was broken by some small accident to that tiresome moving scenery which made it necessary for Herr Bodanzky to stop the orchestra for several seconds.

'The last scene contains what we feel to be the most beautiful piece of music in the whole opera – Amfortas's appeal to be allowed to die with Titurel, and Herr Bender's singing of this was most deeply felt. The ending in which Parsifal raises the Grail, illumined as in the first act, produces an anti-climax musically as well as dramatically. Wagner's attempt to give it additional significance by the descent of the dove produces no more than a cheap theatrical effect, and he has no new musical point to add to the score. In this as in much else one is reminded of the fact that *Parsifal* is the work of his old age. His strength was ebbing, but the sincerity of his purpose sufficed to produce a work which has created a deeper reverence for opera than any of his earlier masterpieces could achieve. Even if we do not feel *Parsifal* to be Wagner's greatest work, its unique beauty and the loftiness of its standpoint are incontestable.'

NOTES

After Wagner's marriage to Cosima in 1870, he continued to work on the, still unfinished, *Ring* tetralogy, of which *Das Rheingold* had been produced against his wishes at Munich in 1869 followed by *Die Walküre*, in 1870. *Siegfried* was finally completed in February 1871 at Tribschen.

The scheme for the founding of a Festival Theatre at Bayreuth was under way and the foundation stone was laid in May 1872, the Wagner family moving into the Villa Wahnfried, which had been built nearby, in April 1874. The final opera of the *Nibelungen Ring* cycle, *Götterdämmerung*, was completed in November.

The inauguration of the Festspielhaus took place with the first performance of a complete cycle of *Der Ring*, in August 1876. The financial failure of the enterprise caused Wagner once again to travel and give concerts of his works to recoup his fortunes; he was in London in May 1877 for an Albert Hall Festival. Before this visit he had taken up the draft of *Parsifal*, which he had written in Zurich in 1857. He worked on the poem during January and February. It was finally completed in April 1877 and published. The music was sketched between 1877 and 1879 and designs were made for a projected production at Munich but Wagner wished Bayreuth to be the scene of its birth.

Other literary work also occupied Wagner at this period. The first edition of his collected works, edited by himself, had appeared in nine volumes, from 1871 to 1873, and a second edition, with an additional volume, during 1882 and 1883.

His autobiography, *Mein Leben* (up to May 1864), was privately printed for friends between 1870 and 1875; the final version was not published until 1911.

It was not until January 1882 that the score of *Parsifal* was eventually completed, and the first performance took place at the re-opening of the Festspielhaus, Bayreuth, on July 26, 1882. The opera was given sixteen performances, under Wagner's direction, the vocal score was published and the composer made arrangements for a second series of performances the following year when ill health caused Wagner to seek a warmer climate and he went to Venice, for the winter, dying there suddenly on February 13, 1883. He was buried in the garden of the Villa Wahnfried at Bayreuth. Cosima continued to direct the Festival until 1906 and lived until 1930 when she died at the age of ninety. The Festival was directed from 1908 until 1930 by their son Siegfried, and after his death, his British wife, Winifred, maintained the traditions until 1944, when her sons Wolfgang and Wieland took charge. The latter died in 1966 after completely rethinking the production of the operas during the post-war years. Direction of the Festival has since been the responsibility of Wolfgang Wagner.

It was Wagner's wish that *Parsifal* should be performed only at Bayreuth as 'a religious festival play' (Bühnenweihfestspiel) but by special permission it was performed eight times in private between May 3, 1884 and April 1885 for King Ludwig, at the Court Theatre in Munich, the King and his retinue being the only members of the audience.

Parsifal was seen at Bayreuth again in 1883 and 1884, the full score was published in 1885 but there was no Festival that year. The next Festival in 1886 included also *Tristan und Isolde*, and that of 1888 had *Die Meistersinger* as the second opera; all three were seen in 1889. After that *Parsifal* remained the principal work, while most of the composer's other operas were staged at various times.

Other countries had to be content with *Parsifal* in concert form (London 1884 and New York 1886) but the laws of copyright were violated in the United States and *Parsifal* was given there, in German, in 1903 and, in English, the following year. Two unauthorised performances were given in Amsterdam in June 1905, in German, and one private performance took place on January 26, 1913, in Monte Carlo. The general copyright was due to expire at midnight on December 31, 1913, but as the Swiss copyright expired a little sooner, it was performed in Zurich on April 13. It was also produced in Buenos Aires and Rio de Janeiro in June and September, in Italian.

Barcelona was determined to stage the first European production after December 31, 1913, and commenced a performance, in Italian, at midnight. On January 1, *Parsifal* was produced in Berlin, Bremen, Breslau, Kiel, Prague, Budapest, Bologna, Rome and Madrid. London did not see it until February 2.

Strange prejudices against *Parsifal* long existed, even amongst staunch Wagnerians. John Runciman, in a monograph on the composer published as late as 1905, wrote: 'This disastrous and evil opera was written in Wagner's old age. . . . The whole drama consists in this: At Monsalvat there was a monastery and the head became seriously ill because he had been seen with a lady. In the long run he is saved by a young man – rightly called a "fool" – who cannot tolerate the sight of a woman. What it all means – the grotesque parody of the Last Supper, the death of the last woman in the world, the spear which has caused the Abbot's wound and then cures it – these are not matters to be entered into here. Some of the music is fine.'

A strange series of performances of *Parsifal* in 'tableau form' took place at the London Coliseum, commencing on June 23, 1913. Oswald Stoll, to mark Wagner's centenary, decided to present eight tableaux, representing the action of the opera, while Sir Henry Wood conducted the orchestra in the appropriate music. The settings and grouping were designed by Byam Shaw and the costumes by Miriam E. Garden. The cast was recruited from artists' models.

Owing to the war, *Parsifal* was not seen again at Covent Garden until the English performances in 1919 and not in German until 1927. The 'original' (1914) scenery was still in use there in 1951, though the panorama was not used after 1914. Rolling scenery was gradually abandoned in most productions in all parts of the world, the music alone being left to convey the ascent of Monsalvat. The custom of receiving the first act of the opera without applause, or curtain calls for the singers, is still encouraged.

WAGNER IN BAYREUTH

By George Bernard Shaw

Shaw, with William Archer and E. V. R. Dibdin (later Curator of the Walker Art Gallery, Liverpool) went to Bayreuth in July 1889 when the operas performed were *Parsifal, Die Meistersinger* and *Tristan und Isolde*.

He duly reported his visit in *The Star* (as 'Corno-di-Bassetto') and also wrote an article for *The English Illustrated Magazine*, which has only rarely been reprinted. It appeared in the September issue, accompanied by seven pictures.

There are many reasons for going to Bayreuth to see the Wagner Festival Plays. Curiosity, for instance, or love of music, or hero-worship of Wagner, or adept Wagnerism – a much more complicated business – or a desire to see and be seen in a vortex of culture. But a few of us go to Bayreuth because it is a capital stick to beat a dog with. He who has once been there can crush all admirers of *Die Meistersinger* at Covent Garden with – 'Ah, you should see it at Bayreuth,' or, if the occasion be the *Parsifal* prelude at a Richter concert, 'Have you heard Levi conduct it at Bayreuth?' And when the answer comes sorrowfully in the negative, the delinquent is made to feel that in that case he does not know what *Parsifal* is, and that the Bayreuth tourist does. These little triumphs are indulged in without the slightest remorse on the score of Richter's great superiority to Herr Levi as a Wagnerian conductor, and of the fact that a performance of the *Parsifal* prelude by a London orchestra under his direction is often much better worth a trip from Bayreuth to London than a performance by a German orchestra under Levi is ever worth a trip from London to Bayreuth. It is not in human nature to be honest in these matters – at least not yet.

Those who have never been in Germany, and cannot afford to go thither, will not be sorry when the inevitable revolt of English

Wagnerism against Bayreuth breaks out; and the sooner they are gratified, the better. Ever since the death of Beethoven, the champions of Music have been desperately fighting to obtain a full hearing for her in spite of professorship, pedantry, superstition, literary mens' acquiescent reports of concerts, and butcherly stage management – all trading on public ignorance and diffidence. Wagner, the greatest of these champions, did not fight for his own hand alone, but for Mozart, Beethoven, and Weber as well. All authority was opposed to him until he made his own paramount. Mendelssohn was against him at a time when to assert that Mendelssohn's opinion was of less weight than his seemed as monstrous as it would seem to-day to deny it. People do not discriminate in music as much as they do in other arts. They can see that Lord Tennyson is hardly the man to say the deepest word about Goethe, or Sir Frederick Leighton about Michael Angelo; but Mendelssohn's opinion about Beethoven was accepted as final, since the composer of *Elijah* must evidently know all about music. In England, since not only Mendelssohn, but Costa, the Philharmonic Society, the *Times*, and the *Athenæum* were satisfied when they had dried Mozart into a trivial musical box, when the overture to *Le Nozze di Figaro* was finished within three and a half minutes, when the beautiful trio of Beethoven's Eighth Symphony was made a mere practical joke on the violoncellists, when the famous theme in the *Freischütz* was played exactly in the style of the popular second subject in the *Masaniello* overture, the public could only conclude that these must be the classical ways of conducting, and that dulness was a necessary part of the classicism. Wagner did not succeed in putting dulness out of countenance until he became a classic himself. And now that he is a classic, who is to do for him what he did for his predecessors? For he is not going to escape their fate. The 'poor and pretentious pietism' which he complained of as 'shutting out every breath of fresh air from the musical atmosphere,' is closing round his own music. At Bayreuth, where the Master's widow, it is said, sits in the wing as the jealous guardian of the traditions of his own personal direction, there is already a perceptible numbness – the symptom of paralysis.

The London branch of the Wagner Society, unobservant of this danger signal, seems to have come to the conclusion that the best thing it can do for its cause is to support Bayreuth. It has not yet dawned on it that the traditional way of playing *Tristan und Isolde* will, in the common course of mortality, inevitably come to what the traditional way of playing Mozart's G minor symphony had come to when Wagner heard Lachner conduct it; or, to take instances which appeal to our own experience, what *Don Giovanni* came to be under Costa in his later days, or what the C minor symphony is to-day at a Philharmonic concert. The law of traditional performances is, 'Do what was done last time'; the law of all living and fruitful performances is, 'Obey the innermost impulse which the music gives, and obey it to the most exhaustive satisfaction.' And as that impulse is never, in a fertile artistic nature, the impulse to do what was done last time, the two laws are incompatible, being virtually laws respectively of death and life in art. Bayreuth has chosen the law of death. Its boast is that it alone knows what was done last time, and that therefore it alone has the pure and complete tradition – or, as I prefer to put it, that it alone is in a position to strangle Wagner s lyric dramas note by note, bar by bar, *nuance* by *nuance*. It is in vain for Bayreuth to contend that by faithfully doing what was done last time it arrives at an exact phonograph of what was done the first time, when Wagner was alive, present, and approving. The difference consists just in this, that Wagner is now dead, absent, and indifferent. The powerful, magnetic personality, with all the tension it maintained, is gone; and no manipulation of the dead hand on the keys can ever reproduce the living touch. Even if such reproduction were possible, who, outside Bayreuth, would be imposed on by the shallow assumption that the Bayreuth performances fulfilled Wagner's whole desire? We can well believe that in justice to those who so loyally helped him, he professed himself satisfied when the most that could be had been done – nay, that after the desperate makeshifts with which he had had to put up in his long theatrical experience, he was genuinely delighted to find that so much was possible. But the unwieldy toy dragon, emitting its puff of steam when its mouth opened, about as impressively as a mechanical doll says 'Mamma': did that realize the poet's vision of Fafner? And the trees which walk off the stage in *Parsifal*: can the poorest imagination see nothing better by the light of Wagner's stage direction in the score than that? Is the gaudy ballet and unspeakable flower garden in the second act to be the final interpretation of the visionary bowers of Klingsor? The Philistine cockney laughs at these provincial conceits, and recommends Bayreuth to send for Mr. Irving, Mr. Hare, Mr. Wilson Barrett, or Mr. Augustus Harris to set the stage to rights. It is extremely likely that when *A Midsummer Night's*

Dream was first produced, Shakspere complimented the stage manager, tipped the carpenters, patted Puck on the head, shook hands with Oberon, and wondered that the make-believe was no worse; but even if this were an established historical fact, no sane manager would therefore attempt to reproduce the Elizabethan *mise en scène* on the ground that it had fulfilled Shakspere's design. Yet if we had had a Shakspere theatre on foot since the seventeenth century, conducted on the Bayreuth plan, that is the very absurdity in which tradition would by this time have landed us.

Tradition in scenery and stage management is, however, plausible in comparison with tradition in acting, singing, and playing. If Wagner had been able to say of any scene, 'I am satisfied,' meaning, not 'I am satisfied that nothing better can be done for me; and I am heartily grateful to you – the painter – for having done more than I had hoped for,' but 'This is what I saw in my mind's eye when I wrote my poem,' then successive scene manufacturers might mechanically copy the painting from cloth to cloth with sufficient accuracy to fix at least a good copy of the original scene for posterity to look at with new eyes and altered minds. At any rate the new cloth would not rebel, since it could be woven and cut at will to the pattern of the old picture. But when it is further sought to reproduce the old figures with new persons, then comes to light the absurdity of playing Procrustes with a dramatic representation. I remember once laughing at a provincial Iago who pointed the words 'Trifles light as air,' by twitching his handkerchief into space much as street hawkers now twitch the toy parachute made fashionable by Mr. Baldwin. An experienced theatrical acquaintance rebuked me, assuring me that the actor was right, because he had been accustomed to rehearse the part for Charles Kean, and therefore had learnt every step, gesture, and inflection of that eminent tragedian's play. Unfortunately, he was not Charles Kean: consequently Charles Kean's play no more fitted him than Charles Kean's clothes. His Iago was a ridiculous misfit, even from his own shallow view of acting as a mere external affectation. In the old provincial stock companies, most of which have by this time died the death they richly deserved, there was often to be found an old lady who played Lady Macbeth when the star Shaksperean actor came his usual round. She played it exactly as Mrs. Siddons played it, with the important difference that, as she was not Mrs. Siddons, the way which was the right way for Mrs. Siddons was the wrong way for her. Thoroughly sophisticated theatre fanciers carried the fool's logic of tradition to the extremity of admiring these performances. But of those with natural appetites, the young laughed and the old yawned. Consideration of these cases suggests the question whether we are to be made laugh and yawn at Bayreuth by a line of mock Maternas and sham Maltens? If not, what can Bayreuth do that cannot be done as well elsewhere – that cannot be done much more conveniently for Englishmen in England? If Bayreuth repudiates tradition, there is no mortal reason why we should go so far to hear Wagner's lyric dramas. If it clings to it, then that is the strongest possible reason for avoiding it. Every fresh representation of *Parsifal* (for example) should be an original artistic creation, and not an imitation of the last one. The proper document to place in the hands of the artists is the complete work. Let the scene-painter paint the scenes he sees in the poem. Let the conductor express with his orchestra what the score expresses to him. Let the tenor do after the nature of that part of himself which he recognizes in Parsifal; and let the prima donna similarly realize herself as Kundry. The true Wagner Theatre is that in which this shall be done, though it stand on Primrose Hill or in California. And wherever the traditional method is substituted, there Wagner is not. The conclusion that the Bayreuth theatre cannot remain the true Wagner Theatre is obvious. The whole place reeks of tradition – boasts of it – bases its claims to fitness upon it. Frau Cosima Wagner, who has no function to perform except the illegitimate one of chief remembrancer, sits on guard there. When the veterans of 1876 retire, Wagner will be in the condition of Titurel in the third act of *Parsifal*.

It would be too much to declare that the true Wagner Theatre will arise in England; but it is certain that the true English Wagner Theatre will arise there. The sooner we devote our money and energy to making Wagner's music live in England instead of expensively embalming its corpse in Bavaria, the better for English art in all its branches. Bayreuth is supported at present partly because there is about the journey thither a certain romance of pilgrimage which may be summarily dismissed as the effect of the bad middle-class habit of cheap self-culture by novel reading; partly by a conviction that we could never do the lyric dramas at home as well as they are done at Bayreuth. This, if it were well founded, would be a conclusive reason for continuing to support Bayreuth. But *Parsifal* can be done not merely as well in London as in Bayreuth, but better. A picked London orchestra could, after half-a-dozen rehearsals under a competent conductor, put Herr Levi and the Bayreuth band in the second place. Our superiority in the art of stage presentation is not disputed, even by those who omit Mr. Herkomer and the Bushey theatre from the account. There remain the questions of the theatre and the singers.

The difference between the Wagner Theatre at Bayreuth and an ordinary cockpit and scaffolding theatre is in the auditorium, and not in the stage, which is what any large stage here would be were space as cheap in London as in the Fichtelgebirge. The top of the partition between the orchestra and the seats curves over hoodwise towards the footlights, hiding the players and conductor from the audience. The instruments are not stretched in a thin horizontal line with the trombones at the extreme right of the conductor, and the drums at his extreme left: they are grouped as at an orchestral concert: first violins to the left; seconds to the right; basses flanking on both sides; wood wind in the middle, opposite the conductor; brass and percussion behind the wood wind and under the stage. From the orchestra the auditorium widens; and the floor ascends from row to row as in a lecture theatre, the rows being curved, but so slightly that the room seems rectilinear. There are no balconies or galleries, the whole audience being seated on the cross benches in numbered stalls, with hinged cane seats of comfortable size, in plain strong wooden frames without any upholstery. The most striking architectural feature is the series of short transverse walls with pillars and lamps, apparently suggested by the old-fashioned stage side wing. Each of these wings extends from the side of the room to the edge of the stalls. Between the wings are the doors; and as each ticket is marked with the number not only of the seat, but of the nearest door to it, the holders find their places for themselves without the intervention of attendants. Playbills are bought for a penny in the town, or in the street on the way to the theatre. The wall at the back contains a row of *loggie* for royal personages and others who wish to sit apart. Above these state cabins there is a crow's nest which is the nearest thing to a gallery in the theatre; but the conditions of admission are not stated. The prevailing colour of the house is a light dun, as of cream colour a little the worse for smoke. There are no draperies, no cushions, no showy colours, no florid decoration of any kind. During the performance the room is darkened so that it is impossible to read except by the light from the stage.

The artistic success of this innovation in theatre-building is without a single drawback. The singers and the players are easily and perfectly heard, the merest whisper of a drum-roll or a tremolo travelling clearly all over the house; and the *fortissimo* of the total vocal and instrumental force comes with admirable balance of tone, without rattle, echo, excessive localization of sound, or harsh preponderance of the shriller instruments. The concentration of attention on the stage is so complete that the after-image of the lyric drama witnessed is deeply engraved in the memory, aural and visual. The ventilation is excellent; and the place is free from the peculiar odour inseparable from draped and upholstered theatres. The seats between the last doors and the back do not empty rapidly; but in case of fire the occupants could easily step over into the sections which empty at once, and so get out in time to escape suffocation or burning.

Compare this theatre with our fashionable opera-houses. In these there is for persons of average middle-class means a stifling atmosphere, a precarious and remote bird's-eye view of the crowns of the performer's hats, and an appalling risk of suffocation in case of panic. For rich people there is every circumstance that can distract the attention from the opera – blazing chandeliers, diamonds, costumes, private boxes for public chattering, fan waving and posing, fashionably late arrivals and early departures, the conductor gesticulating like an auctioneer in the middle of the footlights, and the band deafening the unfortunate people in the front rows of the stalls. Under such conditions a satisfactory representation even of *Il Barbiere* is impossible. Thus, though we have orchestras capable, under the right conductor, of playing the prelude to any Wagner lyric drama better than it is played at Bayreuth, yet we can never produce the effect that is produced there until we have a theatre on the Bayreuth model to do it in. Why should we not have such a theatre, accommodating 1,500 people, on equal terms at a uniform charge per head. The dramas performed need not always be lyric; for it must not be overlooked that the actual Wagner Theatre is also the ideal Shakspere Theatre.

In considering whether such an enterprise would pay, the practical man should bear in mind that opera at present does not pay in the commercial sense, except in Bayreuth, where the charge for admittance to each performance – £1 – is prohibitive as far as the average amateur is concerned. At Covent Garden, Mr. Augustus Harris has his subvention, not from the Government, as in Berlin or Paris, but from a committee of private patrons whose aims are at least as much fashionable as artistic. To carry a season through without losing some thousands of pounds is a considerable feat of management. Consequently no demonstration that the money taken at the doors of a Wagner Theatre here would not cover expenses of performance, plus rent, interest, and the ordinary profits of skilled management, is conclusive as against the practicability of London enjoying the artistic benefit of such an institution. The London Wagner Theatre might be an endowed institution of the type suggested by Mr. William Archer; or it might be a municipally subventioned theatre. It might be built as an ordinary commercial venture, and let for short periods to tragedians temporarily in want of a Shaksperean theatre, like Mr. Mansfield, or to impresarios like Mr. Harris, Mr. Leslie, Mr. Mapleson, or the managers of the Carl Rosa Company. Its novelty and the celebrity of its original would launch it; its comfort and its enormous artistic superiority to its rivals would probably keep it afloat until the time when its special function as a theatre for lyric drama would be in constant action throughout the year. In any case we should not waste our Wagner Theatre as the Bayreuth house is wasted, by keeping it closed against all composers save Wagner. Our desire to see a worthy and solemn performance of *Parsifal* has been gratified; but what of the great prototype of *Parsifal*, *Die Zauberflöte*, hitherto known in our opera houses as a vapid, tawdry tomfoolery for showing off a soprano with a high F and a bass with a low E? Mozart is Wagner's only peer in lyric drama: he also made the orchestra envelop the poem in a magic atmosphere of sound: he also adapted a few favourite rhythms, modulations, and harmonies, to an apparently infinite variety and subtlety of accent and purport. If we are asked whether *Die Meistersinger* is greater than this or that lyric comedy, we say yes with contemptuous impetuosity until *Le Nozze di Figaro* is mentioned; and then, brought up standing, we quote Michael Angelo's 'different, but not better.' There is no parallel between *Tristan und Isolde* and *Don Giovanni* except in respect of both being unique. At Bayreuth we have heard *Tristan und Isolde* from the first note to the last, faithfully done according to the composer's score, under the best theatrical conditions possible. But whither shall we turn to hear *Don Giovanni*? At the opera houses they occasionally try to lick the sugar off it – to sound that part of its great compass which is within the range of the shallowest voluptuary – that part within which the hero is at the level of his ancestor Punch. If the Wagnerites do not ardently desire to hear a dignified and complete representation of *Don Giovanni*, with the second *finale* restored, they are no true disciples of 'The Master.' Then there is *Fidelio*, always grimly irreconcilable with the glitter of the fashionable opera-house, and needing, more than any other lyric drama, that concentration of attention which is the cardinal peculiarity of the Wagner Theatre. Verdi, by dint of his burning earnestness about the dramas he has found music for, and of the relevance of every bar of his mature scores to the dramatic situation, has also placed his best operas beyond the reach of Covent Garden. Many persons were astonished at the power of his *Otello* as performed this year at the Lyceum by the Milan company; but an equally careful and complete performance of his *Ernani* would have been quite as unexpected a revelation after the intolerable traviatas and trovatores of ordinary 'subscription nights.' Those victims of Wagneritis (a disease not uncommon among persons who have discovered the merits of Wagner's music by reading about it, and among those disciples who know no other music than his) may feel scandalized by the suggestion of Verdi's operas at a Wagner Theatre; but they must be taught to respect the claims of the no less important people for whom Molière and Mozart are too subtle, Schopenhauer and Wagner too abstract. The simple tragedy of Victor Hugo and Verdi is what these novices have to depend on for the purification of their souls by pity and terror; and they have a right, equally with the deepest of us, to the most careful and earnest representation of any art work which appeals seriously to them. As for the composers who were chiefly musicians, or who were dramatic only by fits and starts, or whose dramatic purpose seldom rose above the production of imposing stage effects – Gounod, Rossini, Meyerbeer, and their imitators – a single Wagner Theatre would always have something better to do than to produce their works, pitiful as it would be to abandon them to the incredible slovenliness and flippancy of the fashionable houses. But perhaps the example of a Wagner Theatre might induce rival impresarios to consider the moral of the fact that Wagner himself has recorded the satisfaction he enjoyed from an uncut performance of *Il Barbiere* in which, for once, Rossini's authority was placed above that of the stage manager. Did he not point, in his practical fashion, to the superior artistic completeness gained in ballets through the necessity of giving the artistic inventor his own way on the stage?

The uses of a London Wagner Theatre would by no means be limited to the presentation of the works of Mozart, Beethoven, Verdi, Wagner, and perhaps Goetz. The spoken drama, in spite of the artistic ambition of our actor-managers, is almost as forlorn in England as the lyric. The people for whose use dramatic literature exists have lost the habit of going to the theatre, because they so seldom find anything there that interests them. Occasionally the more enterprising of them may be seen at some amateurish venture of the Browning or Shelley Society, or at the Lyceum. But there is no theatre in London which is the natural home of the plays they want to see. Shakspere's plays, Schiller's, Goethe's, Ibsen's (*Peer Gynt* and *Brand*), Browning's – what chance have we at present of knowing these in the only way in which they can be thoroughly known? for a man who has only read a play no more knows it than a musician knows a symphony when he has turned over the leaves of the score. He knows something about it: that is all. Are we then for ever to offer our children the book of the play to read, instead of bringing them to the theatre? The appetite for serious drama exists: that much has appeared whenever it has been put to the proof by a competent manager with sufficient resources to hold out whilst the lovers of serious drama were overcoming their incredulity as to any theatrical entertainment rising above the level of the commonest variety of novel. This year there was a revival of hope because Mr. Pinero, in a play produced at the Garrick Theatre, walked cautiously up to a social problem, touched it, and ran away. Shortly afterwards a much greater sensation was created by a Norwegian play, Ibsen's 'Doll's House,' in which the dramatist handled this same problem, and showed, not how it ought to be solved, but how it is about to be solved. Then came out the deplorable fact that it is possible for men to attend our ordinary theatres as professional critics constantly for years without finding occasion to employ or understand the simplest terms used in metaphysical and psychological discussions of dramatic art. Somebody, for instance, having used the word 'will' in the Schopenhauerian sense which has long been familiar to every smatterer in Wagnerism or the philosophy of art, the expression was frankly denounced by one dramatic critic as 'sickening balderdash,' whilst another adduced it as evidence that the writer could not possibly understand his own words, since they were not intelligible. The truth appears to be that the theatre of to-day, with its literature, its criticism, and its audiences, though a self-contained, consistent, and useful institution, ignores and is ignored by the class which is only interested in realities, and which enjoys thinking as others enjoy eating. The most cynical estimate of the numbers of this class in London will leave no doubt of the success of any theatre which can once make itself known as a Wagner Theatre in a larger sense than Bayreuth yet comprehends. This theatre need not oust the theatre of to-day, which will retain its place as long as it retains its use. The two can exist side by side without more friction than perhaps an occasional betrayal of the conviction of each that the literature and criticism of the other is 'sickening balderdash.'

The doubt as to the possibility of finding singers for an English Wagner Theatre might be disregarded on the ground that London is accustomed to pick and choose from the world's stock. But this plan has not hitherto answered well enough to justify us in relying upon it in the future. Fortunately, Bayreuth has shown us how to do without singers of internationally valuable genius. The singers there have not 'created' the lyric drama: it is the lyric drama that has created them. Powerful as they are, they do not sing Wagner because they are robust: they are robust because they sing Wagner. His music is like Handel's in bringing into play the full compass of the singer, and in offering the alternative of either using the voice properly or else speedily losing it. Such proper use of the voice is a magnificent physical exercise. The outcry against Wagner of the singers who were trained to scream and shout within the highest five notes of their compass until nothing else was left of their voices – and not much of that – has died away. Even that arch quack, the old-fashioned Italian singing master, finds some better excuse for his ignorance of Wagner's music and his inability to play its accompaniments, than the bold assurance that German music is bad for the voice. Plenty of English singers would set to work at the *Niblung Ring* to-morrow if they could see their way to sufficient opportunities of singing it to repay them for the very arduous task of committing one of the parts to memory. Singers of genius, great Tristans and Parsifals, Kundrys and Isoldes, will not be easily obtained here any more than in Germany; and when they are found, all Europe and America will compete for them. But Bayreuth does without singers of genius. Frau Materna and Fraulein Malten, with all their admirable earnestness and enthusiasm, are only great Kundrys according to that easy standard by which the late Madame Titiens passed as a great Semiramis and a great Lucrezia: that is, they have large voices, and have some skill in stage business and deportment; but they do nothing that any intelligent woman with their physical qualifications cannot be educated to do. Perron's Amfortas is an admirable performance; but our next Santley, falling on more serious artistic times, will equal it. Miss MacIntyre will have to be very careful and faithful in her career if she wishes to find herself, at Frau Sucher's age, as fine an Isolde; but who can say how many rivals to Miss MacIntyre we may have by that time? Theodor Reichmann must have been an excellent Sachs in his time; and he is still worthy of his place at Bayreuth; but we can produce a Hans Sachs of the same order when we make up our minds that we want him. Friedrichs, a capital comedian, and Van Dyck, who makes his mark as Parsifal by a certain naïveté and rosy physical exuberance rather than by any extraordinary endowment as a singer, exhaust the list of artists whose performances at Bayreuth this year were specially memorable. Gudehus as Walther and Vogl as Tristan proved themselves as capable as ever of carrying through two very heavy tenor parts; but though their conscientiousness and intelligence were beyond praise, they are neither young nor youthful (it is possible to be either without being the other), and their voices lack variety and charm.

Can we hope to replace the three great conductors? The chief part of the answer is that there is only one great conductor; and him we have bound to us already. Whoever has heard the *Tristan* prelude conducted by Richter on one of his fortunate evenings at St. James's Hall, or the *Parsifal* prelude as he conducted it on one memorable occasion at the Albert Hall, knows more than Bayreuth can tell him about these works. Herr Levi shows what invaluable results can be produced by unwearying care and exhaustive study. Herr Felix Mottl's strictness, refinement, and severe taste make the orchestra go with the precision and elegance of a chronometer. Discipline, rehearsal, scrupulous insistence on every *nuance* in a score which is crammed with minute indications of the gradations of tone to be produced by each player: these, and entire devotion to the composer's cause, could do no more. But they are qualities which exist everywhere, if not in every one. If Wagner's work can call them into action in Germany it can call them into action here. With Richter the case is different. He, as we know, is a conductor of genius. To make an orchestra play the prelude to *Parsifal* as Herr Levi makes them play it, is a question of taking as much pains and as much thought as he. To make them play the introduction to the third act of *Die Meistersinger* as they play it for Richter is a question of the gift of poetic creation in musical execution. The perfection attained by Herr Mottl is the perfection of photography. Richter's triumphs and imperfections are those of the artist's hand.

Before Wagner, the qualities which distinguish the Bayreuth performances were rarer in Germany than they are now in England. His work inspired them there: what is to prevent it doing so here? No more of Bayreuth then: Wagnerism, like charity, begins at home.

BAYREUTH 1976

Reflections on the Centenary Production of
Der Ring des Nibelungen
by Barry Millington

R arely can an operatic production have excited as much comment and, let it be said, prejudice as that of the *Ring* by Patrice Chéreau at the 1976 Bayreuth Festival. The prior reservations of those who regarded with suspicion the turning over of the Festival to outsiders – foreigners even – were easily outweighed by the general applause which greeted the administration at its willingness to take a calcu-lated risk in inviting a young, as yet unproven, team of producers to Bayreuth: Patrice Chéreau (producer), Richard Peduzzi (designer), Jacques Schmidt (costumes).

The conductor, Pierre Boulez, though no newcomer to Bay-reuth – he had conducted *Parsifal* there at four festivals (1966–8 and 1970) – was scarcely an established Wagnerian: his attempt to 'secularise' *Parsifal* may have stood a better chance of success had Wieland Wagner, who was in thorough agreement with the idea, lived to collaborate on the production. It was at Boulez' instigation that the French team was brought to Bayreuth and it is not beyond the realms of possibility that his reputation as an iconoclast might have helped some of the older Bayreuth loyalists to make up their minds about the production even before it reached the Festspielhaus.

It would be unfair and inaccurate, however, to dismiss the torrent of adverse criticism that descended on Chéreau and his colleagues during and after the Festival as the mindless fight for survival of old-guard reactionaries. True, there were those who were determined to disrupt not only the 1976 Festival by jeering and whistling during performances (as well as after, of course) but also the festivals of subsequent years, due to be staged by the same team; acting in the name of the 'Friends of Bayreuth', they threatened to withdraw their financial support until the administration came to reason. Such egregious blackmail was applied, in the best fascistic traditions, in the name of true art and culture.

But there were undoubtedly many who came, saw and evaluated with as little prejudice as possible in the circumstances. Many such saw things to admire and felt their horizons widened by a production which took nothing for granted. They appreciated the attempt to explore new aspects of the *Ring*, but were bewildered by the means and frustrated by the end-product. Would Wagner himself, they wondered, have countenanced a Wotan in morning-dress, a Gunther in a tuxedo, Hagen in a baggy grey business suit and coquette Rhinedaughters (nothing maidenly about *these* females in their *culs-de-Paris*)? Definitely not, according to the *New York Times*: 'he would have been shocked' ran their caption beneath a photograph of the composer. The English critic, Edward Greenfield, was convinced that Chéreau 'could never even have heard the music before putting forward his dotty ideas'. Though surely only half serious, Greenfield's allegation was of a piece with his general reception, or rather rejection, of the production. His report in the *Guardian* was one of the first to be read or heard in England and although it was admittedly backed up from several quarters the effect on the subconscious of such vitriolic criticism (even if resulting in an opposite opinion by over-compensation) should not be underestimated. The *Times* critic, William Mann, suspending judgment until he had seen the whole *Ring*, was not only more sympathetic but also provided a more balanced viewpoint, accounting for some of the idiosyncrasies yet not failing to point out what he considered miscalculations.

This type of criticism was all too rare; in the Festspielhaus itself it was non-existent. There, rationality was thrown to the winds and the audience polarised into pro-Chéreau and anti-Chéreau factions. Many of the open-minded but uncommitted found themselves compelled to support Chéreau; those already inclined to were driven to unquestioning allegiance. A regrettable state of affairs since, as so often, the answer lay not in one extreme or the other but somewhere in between. The fundamental argument, which concerned the extent of the producer's licence in interpreting the work in question, became buried beneath a morass of misleading prejudices more closely associated with such issues as nationalism and political persuasion. Few composers have left such a scar on a national conscience as Wagner. The degree to which the man himself, his ideas and his music are answerable for his identification with the pan-Germanism that became Nazism is clearly outside the scope of this account but history cannot be reversed and it is well known that the name of Wagner is still taboo in many quarters. Yet a number of the older generation of Bayreuth faithfuls would seem to be less willing to exorcise the ghost of Hitler from the Festspielhaus than might at first be expected. The importation of the French team became a ready target for barely concealed Nazi sentiments that did no credit at all to those that expressed them.

Having looked at the background to the débâcle, let us take a closer look at the production itself and attempt to put it into the context of changing styles at Bayreuth. The most striking aspect of Chéreau's approach was his theatricality. Gesture, posture, facial expression, movement were all pressed into the service of the drama and its interpretation; it was not a question of superimposition, since actions were not used primarily to emphasise points being made in the music. On the contrary, the score was treated rather like a commentary on the stage action, the latter carrying the weight of the drama. If this basic reversal of priorities is accepted (and clearly it was the major stumbling-block for many), it is but a small step to allowing the producer to invent appropriate motions for his cast as a means of interpreting the drama. Whether or not those motions might have been conceived or sanctioned by Wagner becomes irrelevant.

Two examples will serve to demonstrate the idea. In scene 2 of *Das Rheingold*, Loge is called on by Wotan to account for his wandering: has he been able to find a ransom for Freia? As Loge began the account of his search for something more appealing than 'Weibes Wonne und Wert' (women's delight and worth), Chéreau had his Loge snatch the wrap belonging to Freia, which he then continued to twirl suggestively as he waltzed around, flaunting himself like a cabaret artiste. This stroke of inspiration was not only an amusing comment on seduction but also a neat characterisation of Loge the magician, servant of the gods yet disdainful of them. The second example also involved a touch of humour more reminiscent of the theatre than the opera house: for the closing bars of *Siegfried* Act I, Mime climbed on to not a stool but the top of a ladder, where, enrobed in a purple cloak (imitating the red gown worn by Wotan), he crowned himself with a pot, brandishing as a sceptre his wooden spoon. A hilarious caricature of the dwarf who would be ruler of the world, this picture provided a welcome deflation of the super-confident music of Siegfried and only seemed out of place if one was determined to exclude humour from the *Ring* altogether.

The two foregoing examples were particularly memorable because outstanding; in other words, most of the stage business was less obtrusive. Even so, it smacked of over-emphasis for some observers: 'directorial itchiness' was one description. It is curious that the opposite extreme has for so long been taken for granted. How often have we seen a Loge or a Fricka sing a monologue as though rooted to the spot, with perhaps a few perfunctory gestures at climactic moments? In the same week as Chéreau's *Ring*, we were also able to witness in Wolfgang Wagner's *Parsifal*, a Gurnemanz delivering his heart-rending narration to four apparently disinterested apprentice Grail knights as if it were a daily ritual. A fine performance if all one wanted was to hear the music, but as drama not gripping, scarcely even thought-provoking. Could it have been Chéreau's determination to make his audience think that alienated so many?

Even those who did not care for the theatrical approach acknowledged that Chéreau made some telling dramatic points. Act II of *Die Walküre*, opening in Wotan's drawing-room instead of the specified wild rocky mountain range, had two central images. The first was a large pendulum, whose relentless motion brilliantly symbolised both the plight of Wotan and the sterility of his relationship with Fricka, described by Wagner thus: 'The rigid bond that unites them both, arising from love's involuntary mistake of perpetuating itself beyond the inescapable laws of change, of maintaining mutual dependence, this resistance to the eternal renewal and change of the objective world – lands both of them in the mutual torment of lovelessness.'[1]

When in this first scene and the subsequent one (Wotan's confiding in Brünnhilde) the course of the drama shows, as Wagner continues, 'the necessity of accepting and giving way to the changeableness, the diversity, the multiplicity, the eternal newness of reality and of life',[2] Wotan tears down the pendulum and tosses it away. He does this at 'nur Eines will ich noch, das Ende', at which point Wotan has 'reached the tragic height of willing his own downfall'.[3] The other image, a more natural appurtenance of a nineteenth-century drawing-room, was a full-length mirror. The relevance of this for the act in which Wotan comes to look into his own soul barely needs underlining; the breathtaking stillness in the Festspielhaus, as Chéreau's Wotan whispered his innermost thoughts ('Als junger Liebe Lust mir verblich') to his own reflection and hence

1. Letter to Röckel, Zurich, 25–6 January, 1854.
2. Ibid.
3. Ibid.

to Brünnhilde, had to be experienced to be believed. Donald McIntyre showed himself to be a singing actor of the first rank, while Boulez brought his orchestral forces down to the merest hush: a supreme example of musico-dramatic collaboration.

One revealing criticism levelled at Chéreau was that he cheapened the *Ring* by his dramatic portrayal of strong emotions and personal characteristics: passionate love, bitter hatred, heartfelt concern, fierce anger, childlike tenderness, inhuman callousness, all struck home with almost unprecedented force. Few who experienced it will forget the pang of compassion as Wotan embraced the son whose death he had just expedited.

If the accusation were based on the fear of histrionic excess – the exaggerated gestures of the silent movie – it would be easy to sympathise. But Chéreau received general acclaim for the conviction of his cast's acting. The objection seems to boil down to the reversal of priorities mentioned earlier, by which the musical score is relegated to an inferior role. The stock response to any attempt to highlight events in the score is that it is unnecessary: 'it's all in the music'. The time has come to question this assumption.

To begin with, if Wagner's message can adequately be conveyed by the music and by the music alone, why is it necessary to go to the opera house at all? Concert performances could be mounted far more cheaply and record playthroughs more cheaply still. Various Wagnerians have claimed at times that they prefer to listen to Wagner with their eyes closed – Bernard Shaw snuggled at the back of a box with his feet up. Blind men hear details often missed by the sighted, but it does not follow that what they apprehend is a more complete picture. Clearly the ideal, then, is a fusion of musical and dramaturgical elements. But in what proportion?

In a programme note for his first *Ring* production – *Die Walküre* at Nuremberg in 1943 – Wieland Wagner formulated the principles behind that early, rather conventional production. He believed in total fidelity to the composer's dramatic idea but suggested that as the stage action was not explicitly stipulated by the music itself, and as it could not successfully be dictated by a uniform approach, the producer was free to work out, in liaison with the singer, a convincing realisation of each musical motif. By the 1950s, Wieland had gone a stage further. He now believed that all the great composers who wrote for the theatre were inspired by what he called 'the theatrical idea'; it was this that governed the composition, the music could do no more than illuminate the psychological background and complement the drama on a higher plane. Having separated the musical and dramaturgical elements, Wieland now felt free to invent with his singer stage action that arose from an *interpretation* of the musical motif, rather than simply from the motif itself.

Wieland Wagner consequently approached operatic production essentially from the theatrical point of view, yet he expressed no interest in producing straight theatre. In this he was unlike Patrice Chéreau, whose experience and reputation had been gained in that sphere. (His only operatic ventures before the *Ring* were *Les contes d'Hoffmann* in Paris and *L'Italiana in Algeri* at the Spoleto Festival.) But Chéreau's basic premise – the priority of drama over music – was also that of Wieland Wagner, himself of course a revolutionary in his own time, though now universally recognised as an innovator of genius.

In view of Chéreau's approach, it is indeed fortunate that the conductor was Boulez and the theatre the Festspielhaus. For Boulez' intention was clearly to play down the grandiloquence and the rhetoric, and concentrate on refinement and clear textures. Aided by the famous sunken pit, the score emerged as an expressive but unobtrusive commentary on the stage action. Banished was the memory of singers ranting to make themselves heard over an orchestral flood; every word was projected with the utmost clarity, at whatever dynamic level. What would have been the outcome with a Knappertsbusch or a Goodall in the pit? The inevitable overloading scarcely bears thinking about.

In the process naturally much of the sublimity disappeared, though this would have been inappropriate in such a context. Those who found the edge taken off their favourite passages, be it the entry of the gods into Valhalla, Wotan's Farewell, or Siegfried's Funeral March, would do well to ask themselves what they expect from a performance of the *Ring*: a succession of thrilling highlights, linked by some rather lengthy and uneventful sequences of monologue, or a coherent attempt to draw attention to the shortcomings of human nature.

It is often forgotten that a large part of Wagner's original purpose in making the orchestra invisible was to focus attention on the dramatic action rather than on the musical score. As a producer, Wagner too considered the dramatic element a priority and, surprising as it may seem, went to some lengths to ensure that the music did not dominate. Only then, according to Porges,[1] did Wagner feel that the goal had been achieved. Porges quotes Wagner as saying: 'the richest orchestral language should, up to a point, not be heard, or not noticed, but should grow with the drama organically into a whole'. It should also be remembered that in his composition method, Wagner's starting-point was always the dramatic poem – 'the theatrical idea' as Wieland called it. Despite the fact that it was generally only at the composition stage that the form and meaning of the poem became apparent (even to Wagner himself[2]), and irrespective of the ultimate proportions of the musico–dramatic synthesis (consider the comparative importance of the music in *Das Rheingold* with that in *Tristan und Isolde*), there is a clear sequence of events and it was the dramaturgical dimension that preceded the musical.

After Wagner's death, Cosima perpetuated many of the principles established by him, and fossilised them into what became 'the Bayreuth style'. She also felt that there was a danger of the music becoming a distraction: 'I can't help it: a good orchestra and good choruses are all very well, but if the action on stage does not make one forget everything else, then the performance is a failure, even if they sing and play like the angels in heaven!' So intent was Cosima on observing the Master's precepts, that the individuality of the performer tended to be stifled. She prescribed a comprehensive series of gestures, for example, to express the gamut of emotions, but whereas Wagner attempted to convey to the singer an under-standing of the role he was playing in order that he might react accordingly, Cosima was prepared to take no chances and required only that her singers reproduce her ideas, which happily were in many ways enlightened and progressive.

Varying degrees of freedom were allowed the singer by subse-quent producers at Bayreuth. Wieland's method was to evolve his own interpretation and then, in hour after hour of painstaking

1. Heinrich Porges, at the request of Wagner, documented the rehearsals for the first Bayreuth Festival in *Die Bühnenproben zu den Bayreuther Festspielen des Jahres 1876* (Leipzig, 1877/R1896) in order that the com-poser's instructions might be handed down to later generations.
2. 'Curiously enough, it is only during composition that the real essence of my poem is revealed to me.' [apropos of *Siegfried*] Letter to Liszt, Zurich, 6 December, 1856.

rehearsal, help his singer to find the most natural way (for them) of expressing that interpretation. Wolfgang seems to have allowed his singer more freedom but other producers of Wagner have tended to establish their own interpretation and persuade everyone taking part 'of the rightness and necessity of what they have to do'. Götz Friedrich, whose words these are, was the producer of another *Ring* cycle staged in the centenary year, that at the Royal Opera House, Covent Garden. Though his attempt to reinterpret the *Ring* for a present-day audience was an admirable and in many ways highly successful one, Friedrich was apparently less 'persuasive' than Chéreau. It may have been, of course, that his singers had less natural acting ability than Chéreau's but, on the other hand, not nearly so much was asked of them.

One of several points of resemblance between Friedrich and Chéreau was their imaginative effort to suggest new possibilities of interpretation. Friedrich, for example, had Hagen remain on stage after the swearing of blood-brotherhood and his watchsong (*Götterdämmerung*; Act I scene 2). Though not, on a literal reading, required for the ensuing scene (in which Waltraute unsuccessfully begs Brünnhilde to give back the ring to the Rhinemaidens, and Siegfried, in the guise of Gunther, appears to Brünnhilde and forces the ring from her), Hagen's presence was a reminder that it was his scheme that was being carried out and that as Alberich's successor he was ensuring the fulfilment of the curse on the ring.

Another of Friedrich's ideas was to have the Wanderer hovering outside the cave in the latter part of the first scene of *Siegfried* Act I, unseen by Siegfried and Mime, before making his scheduled appearance. This was a subtle hint that the Wanderer was watching over the progress of the young hero-to-be; subtle because the Wanderer's face, hidden by the shadows, did not reveal whether or not he was pleased by what he saw. The liberties taken with Wagner's stage directions were thus time and again justified by Friedrich's refusal to postulate solutions; 'to open up the drama of the *Ring*, not to encapsulate it' was his intention, 'not to encircle its ideas but rather to offer them as questions'. Chéreau was less reticent: he had his Wanderer actually peering in the cave and spying it out (this was, however, in accordance with his general depiction of Wotan as an insecure, almost shifty man-god); his Wanderer also left behind a mechanical steam-hammer in Act I and, apparently, the wood-bird, in a cage (Act II), to make things easier for Siegfried. Moreover, he retained the outer pillars of Wotan's courtyard from Act II of *Die Walküre* throughout subsequent scenes of the tetralogy so as to suggest that all the events were taking place within the framework of Wotan's mind.

Both Chéreau's and Friedrich's productions were guilty of miscalculations and technical errors of a kind familiar to any opera-goer and scarcely worth cataloguing. The errors will doubtless be rectified for subsequent productions; so may the miscalculations, though there were comparatively few agreed upon by all observers. Chéreau has promised certain changes for future productions but he does not expect them to endear him to his public any more. The eagerness shown by both Chéreau and Friedrich to use their first productions simply as a base from which to evolve new ideas is a welcome sign that they will not easily fall into the traps of repetitiousness and complacency.

Both producers were also criticised heavily for inconsistencies, particularly in the area of costume. Chéreau cheerfully juxtaposed Victorian morning-dress, twentieth-century business suits, dinner jackets fit for patrons of the Bayreuth Festival itself, and costumes of no fixed period, and allowed characters spears and swords when the situation demanded. To accuse either producer of being careless is to miss the point: Friedrich mixed costumes and weapons of all periods to support his view that the *Ring* could be taking place at several different epochs in history. Chéreau too put inevitable inconsistencies to positive use. This formulation is, in a sense, the artistic realisation of Adorno's recognition that Wagner's work contains irreconcilable contradictions that should be exposed rather than covered up.

As an example might be quoted the set for the opening of *Das Rheingold*, in which the traditional flowing waters of the Rhine became, in Chéreau's hands, a hydro-electric dam. So the curtain went up not on a scene of natural beauty, but on the product of an industrialised society, which was used to make a number of points about exploitation, the rape of nature, greed, materialism – all subjects in the forefront of the composer's mind when he wrote the text of *Das Rheingold*. The swirling arpeggios in the score, however, depict the movement of the Rhine rather than the working of a hydro-electric dam, and thus this was the first example of several in which Chéreau's scenic picture was at odds with the music. But the contradiction did have a purpose: it was to make the point that nature simply cannot be represented faithfully on the stage. However closely a producer might follow the stage directions, however elaborate the stage design – with or without modern lighting technology, back projections and the rest – there will always be a gap between the portrayal of nature and the reality. Certainly the music can conjure up in our minds an ideal image of nature, but when the curtain rises at bar 126 of *Das Rheingold*, our eyes can never be met by more than an imitation of nature – extremely beautiful though it may be. This, then, is one of the irreconcilable contradictions in Wagner's work; a flaw in his conception, perhaps. Chéreau chose not to cover it up as though it did not exist, but to expose it and to put it to positive use.

When the curtain went up on Act III of *Götterdämmerung* the dam had returned, though now rusty and disused as the Rhine, deprived of its gold, had dried up. The point about the abuse of nature was well made, but one could not help wondering whether perhaps it had been made at too great expense. In the first place, the Rhine had apparently been in full flood only two days earlier – for Siegfried's journey down the river (and that was a long time after the original theft of the gold); in the second place, Chéreau was subsequently committed to a waterless Rhine for the events of the final scene, when it is supposed to overflow its banks, engulfing first Hagen and then the whole earth. It would be possible to argue that this contradiction too was foreseen and intended, but one should beware of using this as an excuse for sheer miscalculation; it will be interesting to see whether this apparently loose end is tied up in subsequent revivals.

The question of naturalism is one that has never been solved conclusively right from the first production in 1876. It is well known that Wagner himself was dissatisfied with the original realisation of his directions. How *could* it come up to his mental picture anyway? How are the rainbow bridge and the burning of Valhalla to be effected and did Wagner really want Fricka to arrive in a ram-driven chariot? Wieland Wagner's answer was that the stage directions were not the means to a perfect realisation of the composer's wishes, to be obeyed to the last comma, but an indication of his mental images: inner visions rather than practical demands. Chéreau's answer seems to be that although some of the directions can be translated on to the stage fairly literally, the audience should always be aware of the fact that the result is only an imitation of reality, a representation of life. Thus the extra height of the giants, which usually has to be taken largely on trust, was managed by sitting Fasolt and Fafner on the shoulders of two heavyweights (who took a bow at the end); the forging of the sword, which in any case has to be contrived, was here assisted to a ludicrous extent by the steam-hammer; the dragon, which is never likely to inspire fear in the audience let alone in Siegfried, became a pantomime creature rather like a giant rubber toy; the forests of Acts I and II of *Siegfried* consisted of quite realistic-looking trees, but they were shifted around in a conspicuous way by stage-hands (who did not even trouble to keep themselves hidden); the woodbird, which never perches in the lime-tree above Siegfried anyway, was here put in a cage as though to drive home the unreality of its presence at all.

So by emphasising the artificiality of his representation, Chéreau's intention was not simply to 'debunk' the *Ring* (as was generally supposed) but to involve his audience in the work as a performance, i.e. taking place at a particular time and in a particular place. For this approach there is of course ample precedent in the theatre, Brecht's 'alienation-effect' perhaps being the best-known example. Brecht was in fact strongly critical of the Wagnerian *Gesamtkunst-werk* and its tendency to hypnotise its audience into accepting illusion as reality; his own 'epic' theatre used décor and music not to seduce the audience but in such a way as to encourage it to maintain a critical awareness.

It was surely Chéreau's application of this principle to Wagner's *Ring*, more than anything else, that provoked such anger and consternation. Chéreau did not go as far as Brecht by spurning audience involvement completely, but he did take care that in the process of identification touch was not lost with reality. However, the majority of Wagnerians who go to Bayreuth year after year, go not for enlightenment or edification but simply to indulge themselves. Long before Brecht, Nietzsche spoke with mixed feelings of the narcotic effect of Wagner. It is to suffer and rejoice vicariously in the emotions of Wagner's characters, and to wallow in the uniquely powerful sensations transmitted by his music that they make the annual pilgrimage. To shatter those illusions was blasphemy enough; to direct aspects of the work against its greatest admirers as representatives of the ruling, privileged class, was to invite a reaction of cosmic proportions.

Chéreau's interpretation of the *Ring* was not essentially a Marxist one, any more than that of Friedrich at Covent Garden; neither had the coherence of, say, Bernard Shaw's account of the work as a Marxist allegory. A number of symbols identifiable with an industrialised society and the class struggle – bloated capitalists, a manipulated proletariat, formal dress, working clothes, pit-wheel, power-station, and so on – were used, but to make points of a general nature. Chéreau resisted the temptation to impose a specific interpretation on the work; instead, he simply reset the story within the nineteenth and twentieth centuries in order to stress its significance for modern times. Much of its epic quality was consequently lost, but that was precisely what he intended: a demythologising of the *Ring*.

Will the Chéreau approach survive at Bayreuth? And when it is superseded what will it be by? Only time will tell, but it is worth remembering that although Wieland Wagner's innovations were vehemently criticised when they reopened the Festspielhaus in 1951 after the war, his ideas have dominated there, with various modifications, for some twenty-five years. Perhaps the style initiated by Chéreau will be improved and developed over the next quarter-century and remain to enjoy a deluge of accolades like those bestowed belatedly on Wieland's. Perhaps then the time will be ripe for a fresh attempt at naturalism, using the resources of modern technology. One thing at least seems assured: Bayreuth will not be standing still.

BIBLIOGRAPHY

Abraham, Gerald: *A Hundred Years of Music* (London, 1938, rev. 3/1964)

Barth, Herbert, Mack, Dietrich and Voss, Egon, eds.: *Wagner: sein Leben und seine Welt in zeitgenössischen Bildern und Texten* (Vienna, 1975); Eng. trans. as *Wagner: a Documentary Study* (London, 1975)

Culshaw, John: *Reflections on Wagner's 'Ring'* (London and New York, 1976)

——: *Ring Resounding* (London, 1967)

Donington, Robert: *Wagner's 'Ring' and its Symbols: the Music and the Myth* (London, 1963, rev. and enlarged 3/1974)

Gal, Hans: *Richard Wagner: Versuch einer Würdigung* (Frankfurt am Main, 1963; Eng. trans. London, 1976)

Gutman, Robert W.: *Richard Wagner, the Man, his Mind and his Music* (New York and London, 1968)

Jacobs, Robert: *Wagner* (Master Musicians Series) (London, 1935, rev. 3/1974)

Lang, Paul Henry: *Music in Western Civilization* (New York, 1941)

Magee, Bryan: *Aspects of Wagner* (London, 1968)

Mann, Thomas: 'Leiden und Grösse Richard Wagners', *Neue Rundschau*, xliv/4 (1933), 450–501 [reprinted in *Leiden und Grösse der Meister* (Berlin, 1935); Eng. trans. as 'Sufferings and Greatness of Richard Wagner', *Essays of Three Decades* (New York and London, 1947)]

Mayer, Hans: *Richard Wagner in Bayreuth 1876–1976* (Zurich, Stuttgart and London, 1976; Eng. trans.)

Newman, Ernest: *Wagner as Man and Artist* (London, 1914, rev. 2/1924/R1963)

——: *The Life of Richard Wagner* (London, 1933–47/R1976)

——: *Wagner Nights* (London, 1949/R1977)

Shaw, George Bernard: *The Perfect Wagnerite: a Commentary on the Niblung's Ring* (London, 1898, 4/1922/R1967)

Skelton, Geoffrey: *Wagner at Bayreuth: Experiment and Tradition* (London, 1965, rev. 2/1976)

——: *Wieland Wagner: the Positive Sceptic* (London, 1971)

Stein, Jack M.: *Richard Wagner and the Synthesis of the Arts* (Detroit, 1960)

Turing, Penelope: *New Bayreuth* (London, 1969)

Wagner, Cosima: *Die Tagebücher. I: 1869–1876, II: 1877–1883*, ed. M. Gregor-Dellin and D. Mack (Munich and Zurich, 1976–7; Eng. trans. in preparation)

Wagner, Wieland, ed.: *Richard Wagner und das neue Bayreuth* (Munich, 1962)

Westernhagen, Curt von: *Wagner* (Zurich, 1968; Eng. trans. 1978)

——: *Die Entstehung des 'Ring', dargestellt an den Kompositionsskizzen Richard Wagners* (Zurich, 1973; Eng. trans. 1976)

Zeh, Gisela: *Das Bayreuther Bühnenkostüm* (Regensburg, 1974)

Zuckerman, Elliott: *The First Hundred Years of Wagner's Tristan* (New York and London, 1964)

GLOSSARY

Of Characters' Names

Ada (*soprano*) *Die Feen* Half-mortal, half-fairy; wife of Arindal of Tramond
Ada (*soprano*) *Die Hochzeit* Daughter of Hadmar; betrothed to Arindal
Admund (*tenor*) *Die Hochzeit* Companion of Cadolt
Adriano (*m-soprano*) *Rienzi* Son of Steffano Colonna; in love with Rienzi's
   sister, Irene
Alberich (*baritone*) *Das Rheingold, Siegfried, Götterdämmerung* A dwarf,
   ruler over the Nibelungs by virtue of the power invested in the Ring
Amfortas (*baritone*) *Parsifal* Son of Titurel, guardian of the Grail and ruler
   over Monsalvat
Angelo (*bass*) *Das Liebesverbot* Friend of Luzio and Claudio
Antonio (*tenor*) *Das Liebesverbot* Friend of Luzio and Claudio
Arindal (*tenor*) *Die Feen* King of Tramond; husband of Ada
Arindal (*tenor*) *Die Hochzeit* Betrothed to Hadmar's daughter, Ada

Baroncelli (*tenor*) *Rienzi* Co-leader of the Roman citizens and supporter of
   Rienzi
Beckmesser, Sixtus (*baritone*) *Die Meistersinger von Nürnberg* Mastersinger
   and town-clerk of Nuremberg; suitor to Eva's hand
Biterolf (*bass*) *Tannhäuser* Minstrel-knight; competitor in the Wartburg
   Song Contest
Brangäne (*m-soprano*) *Tristan und Isolde* Isolde's confidante
Brighella (*bass*) *Das Liebesverbot* Friedrich's unwilling chief of police
Brünnhilde (*soprano*) *Die Walküre, Siegfried, Götterdämmerung* A Valkyrie
   and favourite daughter of Wotan by his union with Erda; thereafter,
   wife of Siegfried and Gunther

Cadolt (*bass*) *Die Hochzeit* Son of Morar; in love with Ada
Cecco del Vecchio (*bass*) *Rienzi* Co-leader of the Roman citizens and
   supporter of Rienzi
Claudio (*tenor*) *Das Liebesverbot* Brother of Isabella and friend of Luzio
Cola Rienzi (*tenor*) *Rienzi* Tribune of Rome and leader of the popular
   faction
Colonna, Steffano (*bass*) *Rienzi* Member of the patrician faction in Rome
   and father of Adriano

Daland (*bass*) *Der fliegende Holländer* Sea-captain; father of Senta
Danieli (*bass*) *Das Liebesverbot* Landlord of a tavern
David (*tenor*) *Die Meistersinger von Nürnberg* Hans Sachs's apprentice; in
   love with Magdalene
Donner (*baritone*) *Das Rheingold* God of Thunder; brother of Freia and
   Froh

Dorella (*soprano*) *Das Liebesverbot* Serving-maid at Danieli's tavern; loved by Brighella

Drolla (*soprano*) *Die Feen* Lora's confidante; in love with Gernot

Eisslinger, Ulrich (*tenor*) *Die Meistersinger von Nürnberg* Mastersinger and grocer in Nuremberg

Elisabeth (*soprano*) *Tannhäuser* Daughter of Landgrave Hermann; loved by Tannhäuser and Wolfram; subsequently canonised

Elsa von Brabant (*soprano*) *Lohengrin* Duchess of Brabant in the absence of her brother Gottfried; briefly married to Lohengrin

Erda (*contralto*) *Das Rheingold, Siegfried* Earth-goddess; mother of the Norns and Valkyries

Erik (*tenor*) *Der fliegende Holländer* Huntsman; in love with Senta

Eva (*soprano*) *Die Meistersinger von Nürnberg* Daughter of Pogner; in love with Walther von Stolzing

Fafner (*bass*) *Das Rheingold, Siegfried* Giant; brother of Fasolt; co-builder of Valhalla; in *Siegfried* transformed into a dragon, in which shape he guards the Nibelung treasure

Fairy King, The (*bass*) *Die Feen* Father of Ada

Farzana (*soprano*) *Die Feen* A fairy

Fasolt (*bass*) *Das Rheingold* Giant; co-builder of Valhalla; in love with Freia; killed by his brother Fafner for the sake of the Ring

Flosshilde (*m-soprano*) *Das Rheingold, Götterdämmerung* A Rhine-Maiden

Flying Dutchman, The (*baritone*) *Der fliegende Holländer* Also known as Vanderdecken; committed by an oath to sailing the seas of the world until redeemed by a woman who remains faithful to him until death

Foltz, Hans (*bass*) *Die Meistersinger von Nürnberg* Mastersinger and copper-smith in Nuremberg

Freia (*soprano*) *Das Rheingold* Goddess of Youth and Beauty and guardian of the golden apples of youth; promised by Wotan as the price for building Valhalla

Fricka (*m-soprano*) *Das Rheingold, Die Walküre* Goddess of Wedlock; wife of Wotan

Friedrich (*bass*) *Das Liebesverbot* Puritanical viceroy of Sicily

Friedrich von Telramund (*baritone*) *Lohengrin* Former suitor to Elsa's hand; husband and henchman of Ortrud

Froh (*tenor*) *Das Rheingold* God of Light; brother of Freia and Donner

Gamuret (–) *Parsifal* Father of Parsifal

Gerhilde (*soprano*) *Die Walküre* A Valkyrie

Gernot (*bass*) *Die Feen* Huntsman in Arindal's service; in love with Drolla

Gottfried (*mute role*) *Lohengrin* Duke of Brabant and brother of Elsa; presumed dead, murdered by Elsa, until discovered by Lohengrin in the form of a swan

Grane (–) *Die Walküre, Siegfried, Götterdämmerung* Brünnhilde's horse

Grimgerde (*m-soprano*) *Die Walküre* A Valkyrie

Groma (*bass*) *Die Feen* A magician in the service of Arindal

Gunther (*baritone*) *Götterdämmerung* Historical king of Burgundy; brother of Gutrune and half-brother of Hagen; briefly married to Brünnhilde

Gunther (*tenor*) *Die Feen* A courtier at Tramond

Gurnemanz (*bass*) *Parsifal* A retainer of Amfortas

Gutrune (*soprano*) *Götterdämmerung* Sister of Gunther and half-sister of Hagen; persuaded by the latter to marry Siegfried

Hadmar (*bass*) *Die Hochzeit* Father of Ada

Hagen (*bass*) *Götterdämmerung* Son of Alberich and Grimhilde; half-brother of Gunther and Gutrune

Harald (*bass*) *Die Feen* A general in Arindal's army

Harald (*tenor*) *Die Hochzeit* Hadmar's retainer

Heinrich der Schreiber (*tenor*) *Tannhäuser* Minstrel-knight; entrant in the Wartburg Song Contest

Heinrich der Vogler (*bass*) *Lohengrin* Henry I of Germany (the Fowler); in search of allies for his campaign against the Hungarians

Helmsman (*baritone*) *Tristan und Isolde* Helmsman of the ship which brings Isolde to the dying Tristan

Helmwige (*soprano*) A Valkyrie

Henry the Fowler (*bass*) *Lohengrin* see Heinrich der Vogler

Herald (*bass*) *Lohengrin* In the service of the Brabantine court

Hermann of Thuringia (*bass*) *Tannhäuser* Landgrave of Thuringia; father of Elisabeth

Herzeleide (–) *Parsifal* Mother of Parsifal

Hunding (*bass*) *Die Walküre* Husband of Sieglinde

Irene (*soprano*) *Rienzi* Sister of Rienzi; in love with Adriano

Isabella (*soprano*) *Das Liebesverbot* Sister of Claudio; a novice in the Convent of the Order of St. Elizabeth

Isolde (*soprano*) *Tristan und Isolde* Princess of Ireland; betrothed to Morold; wooed by Tristan on Marke's behalf

Klingsor (*bass*) *Parsifal* A magician; envious of the Grail

Kothner, Fritz (*bass*) *Die Meistersinger von Nürnberg* Mastersinger and baker in Nuremberg

Kundry (*soprano*) *Parsifal* Would-be penitent in Klingsor's power

Kurwenal (*baritone*) *Tristan und Isolde* Tristan's retainer

Loge (*tenor*) *Das Rheingold* God of Fire; renowned for his cunning

Lohengrin (*tenor*) *Lohengrin* Son of Parsifal; sent by the company of the Grail to support Elsa in her litigations with Friedrich von Telramund

Lora (*contralto*) *Die Hochzeit* In love with Arindal

Lora (*soprano*) *Die Feen* Sister of Arindal; wooed by Morald

Luzio (*tenor*) *Das Liebesverbot* Sicilian nobleman; in love with Isabella

Magdalene (*m-soprano*) *Die Meistersinger von Nürnberg* Eva's former nurse and confidante; in love with David

Mariana (*soprano*) *Das Liebesverbot* Wife of Friedrich; novice in the Convent of the Order of St. Elizabeth

Marke, King (*bass*) *Tristan und Isolde* Widowed king of Cornwall; uncle of Tristan; persuaded to marry Isolde

Mary (*m-soprano*) *Der fliegende Holländer* Senta's former nurse

Melot (*tenor*) *Tristan und Isolde* Courtier at Tintagel; Tristan's false friend; in love with Isolde

Messenger of Peace (*soprano*) *Rienzi* Patrician youth entrusted by Rienzi with bearing a message of peace throughout Italy

Messenger (*tenor*) *Die Feen* Responsible for informing the court of Tramond that Arindal has returned

Mime (*tenor*) *Das Rheingold, Siegfried* A Nibelung dwarf; Siegfried's foster-father

Morald (*baritone*) *Die Feen* Courtier at Tramond; in love with Lora

Morold (–) *Tristan und Isolde* Irish prince; betrothed to Isolde

Moser, Augustin (*tenor*) *Die Meistersinger von Nürnberg* Mastersinger and tailor in Nuremberg

Nachtigall, Konrad (*bass*) *Die Meistersinger von Nürnberg* Mastersinger and tinsmith in Nuremberg

Night-Watchman (*bass*) *Die Meistersinger von Nürnberg* Employed to keep order in Nuremberg

Norns (*contralto, m-soprano, soprano*) *Götterdämmerung* The Norse Fates; daughters of Erda; they spin men's destinies into the rope of fate; their function in *Götterdämmerung* is recapitulatory

Orsini, Paolo (*bass*) *Rienzi* Roman patrician

Ortel, Hermann (*bass*) *Die Meistersinger von Nürnberg* Mastersinger and soap boiler in Nuremberg

Ortlinde (*soprano*) *Die Walküre* A Valkyrie

Ortrud (*m-soprano*) *Lohengrin* Descendant of Radbod of Friesland and wife of Friedrich of Telramund; an aspirant to the throne of Brabant

Parsifal (*tenor*) *Parsifal* Son of Gamuret and Herzeleide; father of Lohengrin; the pure fool required to reinvigorate the order of the Grail

Pogner, Veit (*bass*) *Die Meistersinger von Nürnberg* Mastersinger and goldsmith in Nuremberg; father of Eva

Pontio Pilato (*tenor*) *Das Liebesverbot* Employed by Danieli

Radbod (–) *Lohengrin* King of Friesland and ancestor of Ortrud

Raimondo (*bass*) *Rienzi* Papal legate in Rome

Reinmar von Zweter (*bass*) *Tannhäuser* Minstrel-knight and entrant in the Wartburg Song Contest

Rossweisse (*m-soprano*) *Die Walküre* A Valkyrie

Sachs, Hans (*bass-baritone*) *Die Meistersinger von Nürnberg* Mastersinger and cobbler in Nuremberg

Schwarz, Hans (*bass*) *Die Meistersinger von Nürnberg* Mastersinger and stocking-maker in Nuremberg

Schwertleite (*m-soprano*) *Die Walküre* A Valkyrie

Senta (*soprano*) *Der fliegende Holländer* Daughter of Daland; loved by Erik; in love with The Flying Dutchman

Shepherd (*tenor*) *Tristan und Isolde* In charge of the flocks on Tristan's estates; given to playing the cor anglais

Siegfried (*tenor*) *Siegfried, Götterdämmerung* Son of the incestuous union between Siegmund and Sieglinde; forges the sword Nothung and marries his step-aunt Brünnhilde

Sieglinde (*soprano*) *Die Walküre* A Volsung; twin sister of Siegmund; daughter of Wotan; wife of Hunding; mother of Siegfried

Siegmund (*tenor*) *Die Walküre* A Volsung; twin brother of Sieglinde; son of Wotan; father of Siegfried; also known as Wehwalt

Siegrune (*m-soprano*) *Die Walküre* A Valkyrie

Steersman (*tenor*) *Der fliegende Holländer* Helmsman of Daland's vessel

Tannhäuser (*tenor*) *Tannhäuser* Minstrel-knight; lover of Venus; in love with Elisabeth; generally apostrophised as Heinrich

Titurel (*bass*) *Parsifal* Father of Amfortas; erstwhile guardian of the Grail and ruler over Monsalvat

Tristan (*tenor*) *Tristan und Isolde* Nephew of Marke; slays Morold; healed by Isolde, whom he woos on his uncle's behalf

Valkyries (*soprano, m-soprano*) *Die Walküre* Nine daughters of Wotan and Erda, conceived to bring back fallen warriors to Valhalla, which they are to defend against Alberich's assaults

Vanderdecken (*baritone*) *Der fliegende Holländer* see The Flying Dutchman

Venus (*soprano*) *Tannhäuser* Goddess of Love whose home is the Venusberg

Vogelgesang, Kunz (*tenor*) *Die Meistersinger von Nürnberg* Mastersinger and furrier in Nuremberg

Walther von der Vogelweide (*tenor*) *Tannhäuser* Minstrel-knight; competitor in the Wartburg Song Contest

Walther von Stolzing (*tenor*) *Die Meistersinger von Nürnberg* A Franconian knight in love with Eva

Waltraute (*m-soprano*) *Die Walküre, Götterdämmerung* A Valkyrie

Wanderer, The (*bass-baritone*) *Siegfried* see Wotan

Wehwalt (*tenor*) *Die Walküre* see Siegmund

Wellgunde (*soprano*) *Das Rheingold, Götterdämmerung* A Rhine-Maiden

Woglinde (*soprano*) *Das Rheingold, Götterdämmerung* A Rhine-Maiden

Wolfe (*bass-baritone*) *Die Walküre* see Wotan

Wolfram von Eschenbach (*baritone*) *Tannhäuser* Minstrel-knight; in love with Elisabeth; competitor in the Wartburg Song Contest

Woodbird (*soprano*) *Siegfried* Required to encourage Siegfried to take possession of the Ring and Tarnhelm and to direct him to Brünnhilde's rock

Wotan (*bass-baritone*) *Das Rheingold, Die Walküre, Siegfried* Chief of the Gods; Fricka's consort; father of the Valkyries and (in the form of Wolfe) of the Volsungs, Siegmund and Sieglinde; appears in *Siegfried* in the passive role of the Wanderer

Young Shepherd (*soprano/treble*) *Tannhäuser* In charge of the flocks in the valley at the foot of the Wartburg on Hermann's estates

Zemina (*soprano*) *Die Feen* A fairy

Zorn, Balthasar (*tenor*) *Die Meistersinger von Nürnberg* Mastersinger and pewterer in Nuremberg

INDEX

Of names and works mentioned
in the text

English translations of Wagner's works have only been included where the entry is separated from the original. The order is strictly alphabetical, ignoring commas (i.e. *Bellini, Vincenzo* precedes *Bell, John*). In cases where it has not been possible to trace an entry's first names, an indication has been given of his/her profession or vocal register. Mutated vowels are treated as diphthongs (ä= ae, etc.; *Döll* precedes *Doepler*).